COVERT GESTURES

Crypto-Islamic Literature as Cultural Practice in Early Modern Spain

VINCENT BARLETTA

University of Minnesota Press

Minneapolis

London

The University of Minnesota Press gratefully acknowledges financial assistance provided for the publication of this book by the Program for Cultural Cooperation between Spain's Ministry of Culture and United States Universities.

Published by the University of Minnesota Press
111 Third Avenue South, Suite 290
Minneapolis, MN 55401-2520
http://www.upress.umn.edu

Library of Congress Cataloging-in-Publication Data

Barletta, Vincent.
  Covert gestures: crypto-Islamic literature as cultural practice in early modern Spain / Vincent Barletta.
    p. cm.
  Includes bibliographical references and index.
  ISBN 0-8166-4475-6 (alk. paper) – ISBN 0-8166-4476-4 (pbk. : alk. paper)
  1. Mozarabic literature–History and criticism. 2. Islamic literature–Spain–History and criticism. 3. Spanish literature–Arab influences. I. Title.
  PQ6056.B37 2005
  860.9'921297'09031–dc22

                                                             2004029218

Printed in the United States of America on acid-free paper

The University of Minnesota is an equal-opportunity educator and employer.

12 11 10 09 08 07 06 05   10 9 8 7 6 5 4 3 2 1

COVERT
GESTURES

Like Robinson Crusoe on the shore of his island, before the "vestige of a naked foot imprinted upon the sand," the historian travels along the borders of his present; he visits those beaches where the other only appears as a trace of what has passed. Here he sets up his industry. On the basis of imprints that are now definitely mute (that which has passed will return no more, and its voice is lost forever), a literature is fabricated.

— Michel de Certeau, *L'Absent de l'histoire*

They might substitute for public ritual prayer some covert gesture.

— Ahmad ibn Bu Jum'a al-Maghrawi (1503)

Contents

Introduction

The Fabric of Time

Oh, were not all sufferings time?
— Herman Hesse, *Siddhartha*

The Castilian Muslims who accepted Christian baptism in 1502 in exchange for the right to remain in the Iberian peninsula could not have known that a century later their grandchildren would be expelled from Spain. In Aragon these Christian conversions happened twenty-three years later, though even then there would have been little reason to suspect that a Spanish king would ever order the expulsion of several hundred thousand Christian converts. That Felipe III ordered this expulsion in 1609 stands as one of the larger errors of Spanish domestic policy during the early modern period and, from the perspective of those who were expelled, a callous and unjust act of inhumanity against a population that had an eight-century history in the peninsula.

Between the time of their conversion to Christianity and their expulsion, the Muslims of Spain were commonly (though not exclusively) referred to as *moriscos*. This term is derived from *moro*, the most common Castilian term for a Muslim during the medieval and early modern periods, and *-isco*, a suffix that suggests the origin of the term it modifies, as in Juan Ruiz's example of the *guitarra morisca* (Moorish guitar) in his fourteenth-century *Libro de buen amor* (Book of good love). The Moriscos formed a large minority population that for the most part lived in a string of communities throughout Castile, Aragon, and Valencia. Given the largely coercive nature of the Moriscos' conversion to Christianity (a deal they could not have refused) and the fact that most communities were located in rural, relatively isolated parts of the country, the vast majority of these converts from Islam, and their descendents, led a complex and largely hidden life as secret or crypto-Muslims throughout the sixteenth and into the seventeenth centuries.

One of the principal ways in which the Moriscos held on to their Muslim faith and practice was through the steady copying, circulation, and use of traditional narratives about Islamic themes and figures from the Qur'an. Such practice has traditionally been seen as part of a collective effort to facilitate the process of cultural resistance in the face of persistent Christian pressure (which in many cases took violent and direct form) to abandon Islam and everything associated with it (Galmés de Fuentes 1986; Hegyi 1978). Official censure of Islamic culture in sixteenth-century Spain did in fact focus on a wide range of issues, some only tangentially associated with religion. These could include styles of dress, popular celebrations, marriage, baptismal, and funerary customs, the use of public baths, the Arabic language, and the possession of books in Arabic script (Garrad 1954).

Evidence of a direct link between written texts and more common tools of resistance in Morisco communities is certainly not hard to find. We may take as a not so singular case the fact that in the nineteenth century a small collection of Morisco books — including a copy of one of the most popular of their narrative works, the *Hadith de Yuçuf* (Story of Joseph) — was found in a cave in Aragon, hidden alongside a small cache of rusted weapons. Also important for Morisco resistance, at least from a symbolic perspective, is the relatively large corpus of polemical texts inherited from the medieval period, in which Moriscos directly attack Christian and Jewish beliefs (Cardaillac 1979).

There is, however, another very important aspect of the traditional narratives of the Moriscos, namely, the question of how these narratives facilitated and helped to give shape to social processes at a much more local, even personal level in Morisco communities themselves. As a growing corpus of ethnographic work in minority communities has shown, it is a fundamental analytical mistake to frame their cultural practice in terms solely of their resistance to the social and cultural pressures of the dominant group. Such a perspective runs the risk of presenting minority communities as homogeneous to the point of blurring any sense of the internal diversity that exists within them; it also defines these communities negatively, by showing them through the lens of what they are not, namely, the dominant majority. In fact, it is frequently the case that local, even face-to-face, interactional factors shape social organization and practice in minority communities to a much larger degree than the more large-scale project of cultural resistance. And while the difficult situation that the Moriscos faced with respect to Spanish Christians is certainly an integral part of any full consideration of Morisco literature (as a long, painful history of slavery is also a crucial part of any comprehensive view of African American literature), it is necessary to be careful not to exaggerate its importance and to take into full account issues that are specific to cultural life within the Morisco communities themselves.

The specific argument of this book is that the traditional Islamic handwritten narratives of the Moriscos helped this minority community to survive for more than a century in early modern Spain largely by giving them powerful cultural tools to deal with time. By time I do not mean its seemingly objective organization into days, weeks, and years, but rather the more phenomenological issue of our experience of, or, as Martin Heidegger has put it, our "reckoning with" time in socially embedded settings characterized by emotional engagement and agentive action, as well as complex and dynamic relations of power. In the case of the Moriscos, traditional Islamic narratives aided in the social construction of theories regarding inherently time-related issues such as their very uncertain present, an increasingly murky Islamic past, and the inescapable question of their individual and communal mortality. Such theories of time, experience, and action permeate the literature of the Moriscos. This fact places their handwritten narrative texts upon a unique, inherently vital plane. Much more than a mere epiphenomenon or ornament of aesthetic pleasure, the literature of the Moriscos needs to be understood in the light of its power to mediate a range of social processes, all of which revolved in differing ways around issues of time and temporality that in a general sense form the very fabric of human life.

Narrative and the Fabric of Time

Like Herman Hesse's pilgrim, Siddhartha, we often speak of time as we might speak of a river, "the water running and running, constantly running, and yet...always there,...always and forever the same, and yet new every instant" (1999, 89). Standing beside this metaphorical river, dry on the riverbank, we point at a fixed spot, one directly in front of us, and call it *now*. From time to time we divert our gaze and watch the current carry our accumulated nows downstream, into a continuously growing section of the river that we call our past. We may also look in the opposite direction and wonder about the nows that await us. What remains constant is our resolute sense that the past and future are in some meaningful way separate and distinct from the spot directly in front of us — the present — even if there is a certain continuity to the flow of these moments, one into the next. Standing on the riverbank, we divide the running water before us into that which will come, that which is here (for a fleeting instant), and that which has passed, never to return.

Time, we say, passes in an autonomous and unswerving way, whether we like it or not. As humans we dream, hope, act, remember, and weep for our dead and dying, while time and the physical world around us merely move along (to use an Aristotelian image), impassive to our sufferings. If thousands of people die in a famine, this is of no concern to time. If lovers are separated, time moves on as it did before they met. If an entire people is denied a future in its homeland (an example of central concern to the present study), that future of painful exile will come as soon as if it brought joy and peace. At a conscious, discursive level, we seem to accept that we cannot alter or slow down the implacable unfolding of time, although we go to great pains to measure and mark it, marking our own passage through the world in the process. Through the use of calendars, clocks, books, registers, digital media, and an extensive list of other cultural tools, we keep track of time, counting the days as they pass and folding them into the culturally embedded forms of knowledge and practice by which we live and interact. Standing again on the riverbank, we plot points in the water, giving them names: *date of birth, wedding day, projected date of retirement, conquest of Granada.*

But is it possible to find a deeper expression of our relation to time than the mere marking and measuring of it? Are we able — at either the individual or communal level — to understand and articulate our passage through the world and that of our ancestors and children as something more than sequences of events that occur within and across specific slots of time? Can we do more than approach time as a sort of contextual backdrop for our actions and interactions in the world?

The argument that underlies this book is that in all cultures there exist activities by which participants negotiate and give form to their continuous encounter with time. This is not necessarily a philosophical or even conscious process, and I am not seeking to argue against commonsense or folk notions of time's unswerving course. I am aware that in a host of meaningful ways my world is not what it was twenty years ago, and that in another twenty years it may seem unrecognizable to me, or I may no longer be alive. I am diverging, however, from the conventional line of reasoning that focuses upon time (understood to be an autonomous, unfeeling, or disconnected phenomenon) as a mere backdrop to these profound alterations. Rather, my point is that in our analysis of human culture — specifically where this intersects with various forms of language use — it is necessary to address the fact that we continually negotiate the temporal character of our being through our contact with the world and with each other.

In our lived experience we do not witness time so much as it permeates our actions and words. What I mean by this is that no human being encounters the river suggested by Hesse as a dry bystander: we see and feel the water passing above, through, and all around us, filling our lungs; we are submerged in it, we are literally soaked through and through by time. As Heidegger and an entire tradition of continental philosophy have argued, we are everywhere *in* time, and our lives are in every way conditioned by it.

Reflecting on the human experience of time, American pragmatist philosopher William James wrote near the turn of the twentieth century that "the practically cognized present is no knife-edge, but a saddleback, with a certain breadth of its own on which we sit perched, and from which we can look in two directions into time" (1890, 609). According to James, the present — a *duration* with a "rearward- and a forward-looking end" — is compound in nature, composed of elements of the past as well as of the future. Within this temporal framework we experience, on one hand, every present moment as a duration that retains portions of the past within it. This process of retention, as Edmund Husserl would later term it, is complemented, on the other hand, by a process of protention by which we also anticipate the range of possible futures that extend before us. In a very literal sense, we move through each present moment gazing, Janus-like, at what we have known as well as at what we cannot predict.

James's approach to time and perception is a key subtext for the ideas developed in this book about written narrative, culture, and time in two ways. First, James speaks of a "practically cognized present." Such an idea of the present situates time not only within the perception of human individuals but also, more importantly, it relates time to the innumerable practical activities carried out by these individuals in social settings. In this, James intersects with ideas regarding the social roots of linguistic form and meaning developed by V. N. Voloshinov (1986) and other researchers in the Soviet Union (e.g., psychologists such as Lev Vygotsky, A. N. Leont'ev, and Alexander Luria) primarily working during the first half of the twentieth century. Central to the ideas of these researchers — whose work has enjoyed a serious resurgence in American departments of psychology, education, linguistics, sociology, and anthropology — is the notion that the social world plays a significant role in the construction of perception, action, and cognition. According to Vygotsky:

> A special feature of human perception — which arises at a very young age — is the *perception of real objects*. This is something for which there is no analogy in animal perception. By this term I mean that I do not see the world simply in color and shape but also as a world with sense and meaning. I do not merely see something round and black with two hands; I see a clock and can distinguish one hand from the other. Some brain-injured patients say, when they see a clock, that they are seeing something round and white with two thin steel strips, but they do not know it is a clock; such people have lost their real relationship with objects. These observations suggest that all human perception consists of categorized rather than isolated perceptions.
>
> The developmental transition to qualitatively new forms of behavior is not confined to changes in perception alone. Perception is part of a dynamic system of behavior; hence, the relation between transformations of perceptual processes and transformations in other intellectual activities is of primary importance. (1978, 33)

The "categorized perception" to which Vygotsky refers, as well as the processes by which "transformations of perceptual processes" take place throughout the human lifespan, depends on a rootedness of human thought in social activity (Cole 1996; Hanks 1996; Wertsch 1981). Speaking of the active, situated relation among human thought, inner or egocentric speech, and reality, Vygotsky goes on to argue:

> Activity and practice: these are the new concepts that have allowed us to consider the function of egocentric speech from a new perspective, to consider it in its completeness.... But we have seen that where the child's egocentric speech is linked to his practical activity, where it is linked to his thinking, things really do operate on his mind and influence it. By the word *things*, we mean reality. However, what we have in mind is not reality as it is passively reflected in perception or abstractly cognized. We mean reality as it is encountered in practice. (1987, 78–79)

The notion of "reality encountered in practice," which also implies the very social construction of reality through the continuous stream of activity that takes place within a person's lifetime, presents as the axis of human thought, perception, language use — and thus narrative — the network of social interaction within which such activity is carried out. The unit of analysis for psychological as well as anthropological and linguistic research becomes situated activities and the human agents who routinely engage in them (Duranti 1994; Goffman 1959; C. Goodwin 1997; C. Goodwin and M. H. Goodwin 2000; Wertsch 1998).

What these socio-cognitive ideas mean for the present study has to do with the question of where to situate the locus of textual meaning with respect to the written narrative texts under consideration in this book. I have characterized my own approach to the question of textuality and time as an *activity-centered* approach, due to its commitment to: (1) the analysis of how members of human communities make use of written texts in socially and temporally embedded (or *situated*) activities; (2) how such socially embedded use operates to give shape to both the meaning and subsequent form (especially in the case of hand-copied manuscripts) of these texts; and (3) how such use is indexically encoded in the texts themselves. This approach takes as its starting point the social and temporal embeddedness of all narratives, including those found in written form. I will be elaborating on these points throughout the first three chapters of this study; however, it is useful to mention here that the thread that runs through all of these analytical issues is the question of time and the implementation of narrative as a tool by which we — as members of communities — reckon with it.

The second important point within James's comments on time and human perception is the idea of the link that exists between past and future within a "thick present" (Husserl 1991). As James puts it, any present moment is "no knife-edge, but a saddle-back," meaning that even in our efforts to isolate a discrete *now*, we are inevitably dealing with shades of the past and future (a complex phenomenon that Husserl, as I have already mentioned, refers to as *retention* and *protention*). And if we are right to frame any present moment as temporally thick in James's terms (a "saddle-back"), then our analyses of text, processes of textual interpretation, and performance must take into consideration the means by which the use of texts by human agents mediates the phenomenological experience and culturally structured implementation of temporality.

What is of most concern to me in the present book, in fact, are the ways in which written narratives — even those traditional texts explicitly concerned with seemingly timeless values and events — are used by communities to shape and alter their future.

Traditional *Aljamiado-Morisco* Narrative Texts

The narrative texts that serve as the specific analytical focus of the present book are the handwritten, traditional Islamic narratives produced and used by members of Morisco communities (referred to also as *crypto-Muslims* due to their continued secret practice of Islam) living in Castile and Aragon during the sixteenth and early seventeenth centuries.[1] Focusing my analysis on three of these narratives — the portion of the *Libro de las luces* that deals with the miraculous birth of the Prophet Muhammad, the *Alhadith del xakrifixi'o de Isma'il* (Story of the sacrifice of Ishmael), and the poetic version of the *Hadith de Yuçuf* (Story of Joseph) — my goal is to provide a contextualized account of the complex relations in force between these narratives, the temporalities they encode, and the cultural practice of the Morisco communities within which they were engaged.

I have chosen these three texts in particular for three principal reasons. First, various orders of time are all explicitly framed and developed within each of them. Biblical/Qur'anic time, historical time, the scripted and cyclical time of religious holidays and daily practice, prophetic time (a past that steps into the future through the speech-act of prophecy), narrative time, and a highly contingent present and future all take center stage within these narratives, providing valuable information about their contextualized meaning for members of the Morisco communities that secretly copied, read, and recopied them. The text of the *Alhadith del xakrifixi'o de Isma'il,* for example, significantly begins with a combined indexical reference to its listening public as well as to its performed temporal setting, the yearly *'Eid al-Adha* (Feast of the sacrifice). Addressing those present directly, the text begins:

> Servants of God, God has purified this your day, and has made it a Holy Day and an obligation for Muslims, and a path to your religion. It is a day in which you give alms, and a day in which all of your good works are multiplied and your sins lessened. . . . (Madrid, Junta ms. 25 ff. 124^v–125^v)[2]

This double reference (to the listening public/participants of a specific narrative performance and to the *'Eid al-Adha* itself) functions powerfully to situate the text and its performance within a particular time during the Islamic year — a time linked to the traditional past through the events of the story and to a potential future through the theme of divine providence expressed through it.[3] In the other texts that I have selected as well, time and various orders of temporality are at the very forefront of what is negotiated through the recontextualization of events from the traditional Islamic past.

The second reason that I have chosen these particular texts stems from my interest in a number of intriguing features contained within the manuscript copies of these works. Beyond the fact that each of these texts was written in *aljamiado* (pronounced *al-ham-ee-AH-do*) — a system of handwritten textual production that made use of an idiosyncratic form of Arabic script to copy out Castilian and Aragonese texts — they also present the reader with significant features with regard to their *mise-en-page,* the marginal annotations that surround them, and the quantity and kind of texts with which they were bound.

The extant manuscript copies of the verse *Hadith de Yuçuf* provide a good example of the sort of variability to which I am referring. There are three known copies of this work, two of which are contained in the Biblioteca Nacional in Madrid and the other in the library of the Real Academia de la Historia, also in Madrid. Of these copies, two present the text in verse (specifically in *cuaderna vía,* a poetic form made popular in the thirteenth century by Christian clerical poets) while the remaining copy contains a prose version of the narrative, written in a one-column format. As William Weisiger Johnson has shown in his edition of the work (1974), there are significant differences between the texts of the two *cuaderna vía* versions of the *Hadith de Yuçuf* (Madrid, BN ms. Res. 247, and Madrid, BRAH ms. 11/9409 *olim* T-12 respectively), while both of these obviously differ considerably from the prose version (Madrid, BN ms. 5292).

The textual variations that exist between the extant manuscript copies of the *Hadith de Yuçuf* are compounded by the differences that exist with respect to the physical manuscript context of each copy. For example, while Madrid, BN ms. 5292 (the prose *Yuçuf*) is bound alone, the copy held in the library of the Real Academia de la Historia is followed by seventeen other texts, including other religious narratives (*Alhadith del xakrifixi'o de Isma'il* [Story of the sacrifice of Ishmael], *Alhadith de la muerte de Muhammad* [Story of the death of Muhammad], *Dixputa kon lox k'risti'anos* [Dispute with the Christians], and *Asala de la despedida del mes de ramadan* [Prayer for the end of the month of Ramadan]). The presence of these other texts, as well as their absence from Madrid, BN ms. 5292 and Madrid, BN ms. Res. 247, provides important information about the specific ways in which the *Hadith de Yuçuf* may have been used and understood by Morisco readers and scribes (the latter normally being local and itinerant *alfakíes,* or Qur'anic scholars charged with various forms of religious instruction within Morisco communities) over time.

Finally, I am focusing on these three particular texts because of issues related to genre and communicative practice. In his presentation on the "literary interest" in Morisco literature before the 1972 International Congress of Morisco Studies in Oviedo, Alvaro Galmés de Fuentes offers a generic taxonomy of this literature, separating narratives according to their structure and thematic content. He divides up Morisco narratives between *novelas, cuentos,* and *leyendas* (novels, stories, and legends), later placing texts such as the *Alhadith del xakrifixi'o de Isma'il* within a smaller category of "narraciones que se refieren a personajes bíblicos" (narratives that refer to biblical characters) (1978, 190–94). While these categories, which are based on Galmés de Fuentes's careful and extensive research on these texts, certainly make a great deal of sense to modern scholars, we must ask how texts such as the *Alhadith del xakrifixi'o de Isma'il* were generically framed by the Castilian and Aragonese Moriscos who produced and engaged them. I am not contesting Galmés de Fuentes's editorial decisions; rather I am suggesting that we expand our inquiries regarding genre to include a consideration of how genre, written narratives, and communicative practice interrelate, especially in the case of marginalized minority communities such as the Moriscos.

There are generic elements in the manuscript copies of the texts that serve as the focus of the present book that suggest a more expansive, contextualized, and dialogic approach. The juxtaposition of, for example, "narraciones que se refieren a personajes bíblicos" to various other sorts of texts within manuscript codices, as in the case of Madrid, BRAH ms. 11/9409 *olim* T-12, seems to suggest the existence and implementation of a more complex set of generic principles based on practical utility (at specific moments during the Islamic year) rather than strictly thematic criteria. John Dagenais has discussed the general importance of considering such contextual issues in his study of the Toledo manuscript of the fourteenth-century *Libro de buen amor* (Book of good love) (Madrid, BN ms. V^a 6–1), which contains, along with the text of the *Libro de buen amor*, a copy of the *Visión de Filoberto* (Vision of Filoberto):

> What is the significance of the medieval person's inclusion of the *Visión* at the close of the *Libro?* Thematically, the *Visión*'s inclusion supports the arguments of several scholars...who find an increasing preoccupation with death to be the organizing structure of Juan Ruiz's book.... Even if we deny thematic links or argue that the combination of the *Libro* and the *Visión* is merely casual, in the end there is one unity we cannot escape: the medieval individual who had in his possession at approximately the same time copies of both texts. (1994, 126)

These contextual considerations are supported and expanded by recent reconsiderations of the notion of "genre" itself in the humanities and social sciences. In a seminal analysis of recent anthropological and folkloric approaches to genre, Charles L. Briggs and Richard Bauman make the following claims:

> Like reported speech, genre is quintessentially intertextual. When discourse is linked to a particular genre, the process by which it is produced and received is mediated through its relationship with prior discourse. Unlike most examples of reported speech, however, the link is not made to isolated utterances, but to generalized or abstracted models of discourse production and reception. When genre is viewed in intertextual terms, its complex and contradictory relationship to discourse becomes evident. We suggest that the creation of intertextual relationships through genre simultaneously renders texts ordered, unified, and bounded, on the one hand, and fragmented, heterogeneous, and open-ended on the other. (1992, 147)

The intertextual relations that shape and give power to genre are especially significant for a generic account of the traditional written narratives of Castilian and Aragonese Moriscos, in that nearly all of these narratives are explicitly intertextual. Each of the narratives analyzed in the present book is a conscious copy of previous works in Arabic, translated into Romance, and recontextualized within locally produced manuscripts designed to mediate Morisco communicative practice. As such, these narratives have a much more complex generic character than an initial thematic analysis might indicate.

According to Briggs and Bauman's reframing of genre within social contexts and activities, genre operates as a dynamic and shifting resource for communicative practice and the accumulation of social power rather than just as a discursive constraint or principle of discursive classification:

> Genre thus pertains crucially to negotiations of identity and power — by invoking a particular genre, producers of discourse assert (tacitly or explicitly) that they possess the authority needed to decontextualize discourse that bears these historical and social connections and to recontextualize it in the current discursive setting. (1992, 148)

This notion of genre draws a great deal from Mikhail Bakhtin's reflections on the operation and use of speech genres in written and verbal communication (1986) as well as Pierre Bourdieu's theories regarding the hierarchical ordering of genre (1991). I will be discussing these and other considerations of genre that inform my own approach to traditional *aljamiado-morisco* narrative texts in my analysis of the verse (specifically, *cuaderna vía*) version of the *Hadith de Yuçuf*. For the moment, it is my intention simply to introduce the idea that generic considerations of *aljamiado-morisco* narratives should seek not only to understand the organization of various types of textual discourse but should also consider genre as a resource for the generation and negotiation of this discourse within socially and temporally situated activities such as storytelling and religious instruction.

Approaching *Aljamiado-Morisco* Narrative: Origins in Discourse

As this is a book about discourse, written narrative, and interaction, it is perhaps fitting that it began as an e-mail exchange between a graduate student and myself. While discussing various ways of approaching the traditional written narratives produced by Castilian and Aragonese crypto-Muslims, this student and I began to speak in general terms of the complex relation between text and context. In the seminar that I was then teaching, we had been reading Richard Bauman and Charles L. Briggs's study of poetics and performance (1990), as well as Charles Goodwin and Alessandro Duranti's introduction to their edited book on context, language, and interaction (1992). As a result of these and other readings (most notably Steven C. Caton's groundbreaking ethnography of tribal poetry and performance in Northern Yemen [1990] and selected chapters of Julian Weiss's 1990 study of courtly poetics in early fifteenth-century Castile), notions of context as a co-constructed and emergent process — as well as the common use of written texts to mediate its generation — were fresh in our minds.

Also, while I had written previously on the mediational role of manuscript texts in the processes by which medieval Christian readers and scribes collaboratively generated context and textual meaning (Barletta 1999, 2001), I had not given sufficient thought to the unique case of crypto-Muslim traditional narratives at the time that I began the e-mail dialogue with my student. My intuition before the course began (hence its eclectic reading list) was that as manuscript discourse, these crypto-Muslim narrative texts would present many of the same discursive features found in earlier Castilian and Aragonese works produced in a Christian milieu: marginal glosses and annotations, varied recontextualizations of preexisting textual discourse within new settings, a strong link to verbal discourse and performance, and a good amount of indexical reference. Given these intuitions, the instructions that I gave to my students at the beginning of the course were simply to be aware of these sorts of features and to be prepared to discuss them in relation to the Morisco narratives that we would be studying in class.

As it turns out, however, the traditional handwritten narratives of the Moriscos — understood as part of the cultural expression and practice of a loosely connected archipelago of marginalized communities — present complexities that I could not have foreseen based upon my experience working with manuscripts produced and engaged by Christian readers in medieval Spain. Foremost among these complexities are the specific ways in which handwritten texts functioned to mediate the social processes by which context and meaning were achieved within, between, and beyond the crypto-Muslim communities of Castile and Aragon. Luckily for me, many of the formal features that shape this mediating function have already been thoroughly studied, especially by Romance philologists working to situate Morisco narratives in the larger stream of language produced in the Iberian peninsula during the early modern period. Excellent examples of this sort of research are Alvaro Galmés de Fuentes's analyses of language use within a wide variety of Morisco texts of various genres (1965, 1978, 1981, 1986, 1989), Luce López Baralt's extensive work on the literary themes and intertextual relations present in Morisco narratives (1980, 1985, 1995, 2000), Consuelo

López-Morillas's painstaking work on translations of and commentaries on the Qur'an as well as other religious narratives (1975, 1978, 1981, 1995), and Alberto Montaner Frutos's thorough philological analyses of *aljamiado-morisco* texts (1988a, 1988b, 1989, 1993). What remains to be established is precisely how the discursive and linguistic features of these texts — as well as the codices and loose folia that contain them — intersected with context and practice within the Morisco communities of Castile and Aragon. To fill this critical gap, or at least to learn more about the working of narrative from a more dialogical perspective, was my original intention in setting out to write the present book.

To develop a concrete idea of the mechanics by which the texts produced and used by crypto-Muslims in Castile and Aragon intersected with the life world of the Moriscos themselves is of the utmost importance. For if the traditional narratives that serve as the focus for the present book played a mediational role in the social processes by which members of Morisco communities in Castile and Aragon negotiated their conceptions of reality, they were also crucial discursive tools that Moriscos actively employed in order to survive as long as they did as a marginalized ethnic-religious community in early modern Spain. Struggling to be at once fully Spanish and Muslim in a nation that was steadily growing to see these social categories as mutually exclusive, the Moriscos of Castile and Aragon who produced and engaged the traditional material studied in this book were — especially after the second half of the sixteenth century — fighting for their very existence. And the traditional narratives that recounted the adventures, actions, and adversities of Muslim prophets and heroes served as powerful weapons in this fight, both at the semantico-referential and pragmatic levels of signification. Indeed, a heightened understanding of the dynamic role of traditional Islamic narratives within processes of cultural negotiation, resistance, and survival among the Moriscos has served to alter not only my understanding of the thematic connection between texts and social contexts but also my sense of the powerful mediational force that manuscript narratives can possess.

But these realizations came only later, long after my e-mail exchange with the graduate student mentioned above. At the time of our dialogue, I simply suggested to him that he find a way to speak of how these handwritten texts were used, commented on, and recopied in crypto-Muslim communities, my thinking being that the *meaning* of these texts would, from an emic perspective, be predicated in part by the local activities within which they were used. This seemed to me to be sound advice, even if I was to some extent simply stating the obvious. However, a couple of days after suggesting this course of analysis to my student, he responded with a long message, containing several specific points and difficult questions. The question that jumped out at me and has stuck in my mind ever since was the following, placed at the very end of his message: "How are we to pick up a conversation that was dropped over four hundred years ago?"

A conversation. Or more specifically, many conversations at many different times. In a very real sense, the present study can be read as a lengthy response to this graduate student's difficult question. How are we to speak of communicative practice, as well as its back-and-forth relation to textual meaning, centuries after the people about whom we are concerned have ceased to exist? To approach the traditional *aljamiado* narratives (i.e., Castilian-Aragonese texts written in Arabic script) produced and used by crypto-Muslims in Castile and Aragon throughout the sixteenth century until their expulsion from Spain in 1609–14 in this radically contextualized way requires above all a very flexible handling of the only body of data at our disposal—the manuscripts themselves. I will speak at length throughout this book of the information regarding practice and interaction encoded within the manuscripts containing *aljamiado* narratives. Before discussing this material I think it most useful to present a brief review of the general historical frame within which these "conversations" that I am attempting to elicit were carried out. This review — my own third-person narrative summary of my earlier readings of several other such narratives — is necessarily provisional and incomplete. Nonetheless, it will give the reader unfamiliar with the events important to the study of sixteenth-century Spanish Islam a general sense of the larger socio-political setting within which the corpus of *aljamiado* narratives under consideration in this study were produced and used.

Spanish Islam after the Fall of Granada

As with many narratives set in Spain, this one begins in 1492. In early January of that year, the Catholic Monarchs decisively ended more than eight centuries of sporadic Christian reconquest by finally taking the isolated and very vulnerable Nasrid kingdom of Granada. This victory, the ground for which had been set up by the earlier campaigns of Castilian Queen Isabel's half-brother Enrique IV, came as little surprise. Like a chess king that had sat in check for several turns, Granada was in effect a conquered city long before the entrance of Christian forces, though it had managed to maintain its precarious and mostly nominal autonomy through a complex system of tributes and treaties with Christian monarchs. That this autonomy ended precisely when the consolidation of political will in Castile and the development of an efficient military strategy took shape is anything but coincidental.

Despite the near inevitability of this final victory over Granada, its culmination was a significant symbolic breakthrough for Christian Spain. It signaled nothing less than the definitive end of Muslim rule in the Iberian peninsula, a rule that had begun dynamically with the fall of the Visigothic empire to invading Muslim forces during the first quarter of the eighth century and had reached its apogee during the period of the Umayyad Caliphate of Córdoba from 912 to 1031 CE. With the disintegration of the Caliphate of Córdoba (due to extreme internal tensions), Muslim power in Spain began its slow decline. This decline was punctuated by temporary stays that often came at a very high cost, such as the early victories of fundamentalist Almoravid and Almohad troops from Morocco and the labyrinthine series of treaties and tributes set up between Muslim and Christian rulers. Still, as early as the years following the Christian victory at Las Navas de Tolosa in 1212 — years that saw the fall of important cities such as Córdoba, Sevilla, Murcia, and Jaén — the Christian reconquest of the Iberian peninsula as a whole began to look more and more like an inevitability.

Despite this steady trend of declining political power and the overall importance of Granada's fall in 1492, it is crucial to remember that the end of Muslim rule in Spain did not mean the end of Muslim life and culture there. At the beginning of the sixteenth century — eight years after Granada's fall — roughly half a million Spanish Muslims were still living under Christian rule (out of a total Spanish population of just under eight million). These *mudejar* (i.e., Muslims living under Christian rule) communities were centered mostly in and around Granada and Valencia, though there were also sizeable communities in Aragon and smaller, more assimilated groups scattered throughout Castile.

Dragged under the Christian umbrella by force, the Granadan Muslims were hardly the sort of citizens that the Catholic Monarchs sought for their burgeoning nation-state: most were monolingual Arabic speakers, and there were numerous cases of Granadans expressing a common cause with other Muslim communities around the Mediterranean, including the ascendant Ottoman Turks. Yet, as evidenced by the surrender terms offered to the Granadans in 1492, there seemed to be little official desire on the part of Christian authorities to change the practices or allegiances of their new subjects. As had been the custom throughout most of the long period of Christian reconquest, these conquered Muslims, new subjects of the Spanish crown, were allowed, de jure, a significant amount of political, cultural, and religious autonomy.

Shortly after the start of the sixteenth century, however, the fortunes of Spanish Muslims began to change. Pressured by the Granadan Archbishop Francisco Jiménez de Cisneros to take measures to bring the Muslims of that region into the Christian faith, and aware that alleged Christian abuses had provoked an uprising in the Alpujarras, King Ferdinand issued an order in 1502 requiring all Muslims in Castile to convert to Christianity or leave. The same law would reach Navarre in 1515 and Aragon in 1525. The king's order was widely enforced (executed in large part by mass baptisms and coercive tactics), and by the end of the first quarter of the sixteenth century, the Muslim population of Spain had been reduced from half a million to nearly zero.

Of course the speedy, mostly nominal conversion of Spanish Muslims to Christianity does not tell the whole story. Because the overwhelming majority of these conversions were performed by coercion and under duress, whole communities of Muslims (now nominally Christians) continued to practice Islam as they had before, some even doing so openly. As L. P. Harvey has put it:

> What happened to Spain's Muslims after they had all been forcibly converted is, surprisingly: nothing very much. No energetic campaign of mass evangelization, no wave of repression or persecution followed. And nothing very much continued to occur for the next quarter century or so. (1993, 222)

Oddly enough, even as members of the Spanish clergy were actively (and in many cases, brutally) seeking the conversion and religious instruction of indigenous populations in the Americas, there seems to have been only sporadic and largely unsuccessful efforts to catechize Spain's newly converted Muslim population. Whether such efforts could ever have been successful in the first place is, of course, open to debate. In any case, as late as 1565 Spanish Muslims continued to practice their religion and maintain their cultural characteristics in areas where their population was most concentrated, such as Granada, Aragon, and Valencia. All this, one should keep in mind, in spite of the best efforts of the Inquisition.

Violent and abrupt change came with the 1566 decrees, issued by King Felipe II. Through these laws, the Spanish crown went much further than it had ever gone in the past with respect to its Muslim — or crypto-Muslim — population. In a series of specific points, these decrees called for the fundamental cultural, linguistic, and religious assimilation not only of crypto-Muslims but of sincerely converted Christians as well. Besides other troubling points, the decrees called for Spain's former Muslims — now referred to as *moriscos* — to cease dressing in a style different from the Christian population, to cease speaking Arabic, to destroy all books written in Arabic, to leave the doors to their homes open for inspection on Muslim holy days, and to marry only according to the rules and customs of the Catholic Church. The impact of these new laws was tremendous in largely assimilated Castilian as well as Granadan, Aragonese, and Valencian Morisco communities, as it mandated not only orthodox Catholic religious faith and practice but also a wholesale adoption of Christian language and culture as well. Granadan Morisco Francisco Muley Núñez highlights the important difference between these two orders of practice in his address to royal authorities in 1566:

> The Morisco traits that you wish to have repressed do not belong in any way to the religious sphere, but rather to that of local customs. They are outward manifestations that do not touch the subject of faith, but rather the respected inheritance received from ancestors. (Bernabé Pons 1998, 100)[4]

Elsewhere in his address, Muley Núñez brings up the issue of Christians living in Palestine who manage to practice the Christian faith perfectly well while maintaining their distinctive cultural traditions, and even the Arabic language. Spanish authorities seem not to have been convinced by even these compelling arguments. Perhaps unsurprisingly (and due largely to Christian inflexibility) the laws of 1566 — along with new royal policies that actively sought to rob agricultural land from Moriscos — also met with more combative, violent resistance. This was especially true within Granada and Valencia, where Arabic speech and Muslim customs had been most widely preserved.[5]

Combative resistance in fact led to open rebellion in Granada, where an army of roughly ten thousand Moriscos took to the hills of the Alpujarras in 1568, gamely resisting Spanish military forces for nearly three years. The rebellion was violently put down by a seasoned army under the direction of Don Juan de Austria in 1570, and in its aftermath the Moriscos of Granada — not just the surviving combatants but the whole population — were forced to leave Granada and relocate to other regions of Spain, principally Castile.

This mass relocation constituted a significant socio-cultural change for both the transported Granadans and the largely assimilated Castilian Moriscos, who in fact had very little in common with their new neighbors. Luis F. Bernabé Pons makes this point quite strongly in his study of the Moriscos of Granada before and after the Alpujarras rebellion:

> When the recently defeated Granadan Moriscos arrive in Castile, their differences from the local population are immediately noted, and not only by the Christian population, but also, and with great emphasis, by the Castilian Morisco population that resides there.... These Granadan Moriscos, who travel with different cultural baggage, are seen as strange — at times dangerously strange — by the Moriscos who have spent generations living peacefully in the same place, and it is possible that they themselves were conscious of their own "otherness." (1998, 92)[6]

This massive internal population shift had less of an impact on Morisco communities in Aragon, though it is safe to say that the decrees of 1566 themselves, as well as the unsuccessful rebellion in the Alpujarras, made things difficult for Moriscos everywhere in the Iberian peninsula.

By the turn of the seventeenth century there was a wide debate in Spain about what should be done in response to the *cuestión morisca*. A number of Christian clerics advocated renewed efforts to give the Moriscos the religious instruction necessary for their full assimilation into Spanish society. Aragonese and Valencian nobles, whose large tracts of agricultural land depended extensively on Morisco labor, were often outspoken advocates for patience and tolerance with respect to the Moriscos. On the other side there were much louder and more powerful voices calling for the immediate expulsion of the Moriscos from Spain.

In one of the more unfortunate political coincidences of Spanish history, the public debate regarding the Moriscos heated up during the reign of the exceptionally weak King Felipe III, who reigned from 1598 to 1621. King Felipe's government was run by the ambitious Francisco Gómez de Sandoval y Rojas, duke of Lerma (1533–1625), who personally saw to it that the policies of the Spanish state reflected his will during his tenure as the king's right hand. One of a group of strong proponents of Morisco expulsion, the duke of Lerma convinced Felipe to sign into law the forced expulsion of all Moriscos from Castile in 1609 and from the rest of Spain by 1614.

It is estimated that by 1609 there were slightly less than four hundred thousand Moriscos in Spain, making up almost 5 percent of the total Spanish population. This percentage increases significantly in areas such as Aragon and Valencia, where Moriscos made up a much higher portion of the regional population. Especially in Aragon, the expulsion of the Moriscos left whole villages empty, large quantities of crops ruined, and the local economy devastated. Beyond its economic cost, the expulsion exacted a high human cost as well: having to leave Spain by sea, many people, including the elderly and children, died in the rough waters of the Mediterranean or found themselves under attack by thieves, brigands, and even regional authorities upon landing in North Africa.

As with its expulsion of the Jews in 1492 and its policies and practices in the Americas during the same period, Spain's treatment of the Moriscos stands as a tremendous scar on its national history. As early as the first decades after the fall of Granada, Spanish authorities began to single out this minority population of several thousand people, harassing them to varying degrees for more than a century before expelling them by force: a cruel and narrow-minded solution to a difficult but workable — and hardly novel — question of coexistence. But, as Francisco Márquez Villanueva has argued, the Morisco expulsion was but part of a series of policies that allowed a powerful minority to chart a future for Spain that would transform it into the nation they desired it to be: homogeneous, resolutely Catholic, and secure from unwanted outside influences (1991).

During this entire century-long period of conversion, adaptation, negotiation, and flux, Spanish crypto-Muslims did a number of things to continue practicing Islam and hold themselves together as communities. One of these was the practice of *taqiyya*, a religious dispensation by which Muslims under compulsion or threat of injury were relieved of their religious requirements, including the observance of Ramadan, daily prayers, and dietary restrictions (Harvey 1993, 211). This flexibility built into Islamic religious practice allowed crypto-Muslims to adapt their faith and religious practice to their difficult situation and thus continue on as Muslims in a real sense despite serious limitations and even danger. The concrete form of *taqiyya* practiced by crypto-Muslims in Spain throughout the sixteenth century varied from community to community, from person to person. However, a general framework for how the Moriscos were to maintain Islam in the wake of their forced conversion to Christianity can be found in a document written in 1503 by an Islamic jurist from Oran, Ahmad ibn Bu Jum'a al-Maghrawi. In this document, al-Maghrawi addresses the specific practical problems of the recently converted Moriscos, presenting in clear terms that:

> They might bow down to idols [i.e., images in Christian churches];
> They might substitute for public ritual prayer some covert gesture; The
> code of ritual purity could be suspended: in case of need a gesture in the
> direction of a ritually pure object would suffice as a substitute; Wine
> might be drunk, so long as the believer had no intention of making use
> of it; Pork and other forbidden foods might be eaten if they could not
> be avoided, so long as they were still considered unclean; Usury might
> be taken, but subsequently the profit should be given away to the poor;
> If forced to do so, Muslims might in the last resort even deny their faith:
> what they were forced to say openly they should deny in their hearts.
> (Harvey 1993, 210)

Undoubtedly, these precepts allow for a tremendous amount of latitude in the daily practice of Spanish crypto-Muslims. Nonetheless, even this much religious flexibility could not protect the Moriscos from the force of the 1566 decrees, which went far beyond merely restricting religious aspects of their daily life.

Another important and effective means by which the Moriscos were able to maintain their religion and culture was the production and use of traditional narratives handwritten and actively recopied despite their illegality after 1566. These narratives were copied down in Castilian and Aragonese (with varying amounts of intercalated Arabic) using an adapted form of Arabic script known to modern scholars as *aljamiado*. This term comes from the Arabic adjective *'ajamiyya,* which means, in different though related contexts, "barbarian," "non-Arabic," or "foreign" and serves to mark the liminal status of Morisco written discourse. Defined in negative terms (as neither fully Castilian nor in any real sense Arabic), the written narratives of the Moriscos have been framed by

Christian Spaniards and Arabs alike as the discourse of an intellectu-
ally, culturally, and spiritually impoverished "Other." Yet these narrative
texts played a number of very complex and important roles within
Morisco communities, roles that were neither negatively defined nor in-
stantiated without a keen first-hand sense of the dire situation in which
these texts' readers and scribes found themselves.

Time, Written Narrative, and
the Social Life of the Moriscos

Throughout this book I make the argument that there is a very
direct though fluid relation between traditional *aljamiado-morisco* narratives and the cultural practice of crypto-Muslims in sixteenth- and
seventeenth-century Castile and Aragon. It is for this reason that I also
approach written narrative in general not as an epiphenomenal or even
peripheral element of human activity, but as an integral feature of social
life in settings where it is produced and used.

In the interest of clearly defining the approach to time, narrative, and
manuscript texts implemented throughout the course of this book before
moving on to a detailed analysis of specific *aljamiado-morisco* narratives,
I have divided this book into two parts. The first part is devoted to a
theoretical framing of topics related to time, narrative, cultural practice,
and manuscript discourse, while the second deals with issues specific to
the three individual *aljamiado-morisco* texts that serve as the focus of
this book.

The first part of the book is itself divided into three separate chapters. The first of these chapters deals exclusively with a presentation and
discussion of the critical and philosophical approaches to time and narrative that directly inform this book. Specifically, I offer an explanation
for the interdisciplinary approach that I have adopted in this study —
a blend of linguistic anthropology, phenomenological philosophy, and
literary analysis. My main point in this chapter is that the existing tools
of literary analysis are of only limited utility with respect to manuscript
discourse on one hand, and that issues of temporality and textual meaning within Castilian and Aragonese crypto-Muslim communities simply
require a broader, extraliterary approach on the other. Stressing both
the *handwritten* and folkloric character of traditional *aljamiado-morisco*
narrative texts, I map out the need for a mode of textual analysis that

can more precisely deal with the complex intersections of language use and culture.

The second chapter, an elaboration of the activity-centered approach to narrative that I allude to in the first, has three complementary and equally important theoretical foundations. It draws in part from a long tradition of phenomenological approaches to human experience, knowledge, and meaning. Taking as its starting point Husserlian notions of the "thick present," as well as similar notions of temporality central to William James's psychology of human experience, this chapter goes on to speak of what David Carr has described as the "narrative structure of temporality" in force for both individuals and social groups.

Carr's ideas about temporality and narrative enter into provocative dialogue with Hayden White's earlier problematization of traditional accounts of history, reality, and narrative. In his most influential work, *The Content of the Form* (1987), White has offered a probing analysis of what he considers to be the distance that always exists between ordered historical narratives and chaotic reality. White's arguments, aimed at making sense of a long debate among historical scholars about the truth value of their accounts of past reality, offer a radically situated account of historical analysis as the imposition of narrative order on essentially unordered reality.

In his philosophical analysis of history, narrative, and truth, Carr shifts the focus of this historiographical debate by using as his starting point the phenomenological (specifically Husserlian) maxim that all we can mean by "reality" — especially when we are addressing its discursive negotiation — is the human experience of it. What this means is that while there is without a doubt a spatio-physical world that exists independently of human experience, action, and discourse, the "reality" that concerns us in any historical (as well as literary or ethnographic) analysis does not. Carr goes on to make the argument that reality itself is for humans always temporal and imbued with an inherently narrative "beginning-middle-end" structure. According to this view of reality-as-phenomenon, historiography is inherently no more divorced from what is "real" or "true" than any other possible account of it: what we say, do, and experience in the world is always in any case structured by a practical beginning-middle-end frame that exists prior to our conscious theorization and framing of phenomena. So while Carr agrees with White's claim that historical accounts of the past are essentially narrative in character, he disagrees with his claim that this fact necessarily renders them "fictional" or in some meaningful way divorced from the way that humans actually act in and experience the world around them.

Carr's ideas regarding the "narrative structure" of temporality constitute an integral part of the present book's theoretical framework. Following his theories of narrative and reality, I will be arguing against approaches that posit a discontinuity between the two. I do not see narrative as temporally ordered representations placed over human experiences and actions ex post facto — as a way of merely dressing up reality in line with the interests of power (Barthes 1970; White 1987) — but rather as the very principle by which experiences and actions exist as such. As Carr argues:

> [M]y account will not take the form of claims about how literary and historical narratives "represent." Instead I shall begin by uncovering narrative features of everyday experience and action. If I succeed in showing a certain community of form between "life" and written narratives, my account may have some implications for the problem of representation. But that is not my initial concern. To the extent that I discuss narrative at all in its literary guise, I shall be stressing the fact that it arises out of and is prefigured in certain features of life, action, and communication. Historical and fictional narratives will reveal themselves to be not distortions of, denials of, or escapes from reality, but extensions and configurations of its primary features. (1986, 16)

These ideas are of particular importance insofar as they intersect with aspects of Martin Heidegger's philosophical considerations of being and time (1996), as well as with Maurice Merleau-Ponty's writings on time, language, and the body (1996). Looking at being not from the standpoint of a "continuous present" somehow outside of time (what Heidegger criticizes as the fallacious *nunc stans* of Western metaphysics), but rather from the position of situated being-in-the-world (*In-die-Welt-Sein*), Heidegger and Merleau-Ponty underscore the fact that human agents are not only engaged in a constant negotiation of their past and present, but also of their future. Merleau-Ponty emphasizes the fundamental role of time in any consideration of human perception and interaction, writing that "time is ... not a real process, not an actual succession of what I am content to record. It arises from *my* relation to things" (1996, 412).

Conscious of these philosophical ideas, Carr underscores the importance of practical future-consciousness within his own project of addressing the temporal underpinnings of human experience and action. What emerges through Carr's study is a view of both narrative and time that positions them as primary features of human activity and experience. And by making use of these philosophical approaches to temporality, narrative, as well as human experience and action in the present book, I am able to conceptualize narrative — specifically the traditional handwritten narratives of Castilian and Aragonese crypto-Muslims — as a mode of cultural practice intricately linked to the ordering of the past within an emergent present as well as to the negotiation of theories regarding an uncertain, and in the case of the Moriscos, desperate, future.

Philosophical ideas on narrative and temporality — especially when they intersect with analyses of the other activities by which human agents negotiate the shaping of their individual and collective identities and practice — have been fundamental for analyses of narrative and human experience in the social sciences, particularly within anthropology. This branch of inquiry forms the second important foundation of the ideas regarding narrative and time developed in this book. We may take as an example of this work Linda C. Garro and Cheryl Mattingly's introductory comments to their *Narrative and the Cultural Construction of Illness and Healing*:

> Within anthropology (though this is not exclusive to anthropology), what binds together the diversity of analytic approaches to narrative is an appreciation of the intertwining of the personal and the cultural. Thus, concern for narrative reflects an interest in representing those the anthropologist studies, not just as members of a cultural group but as individuals with their own personal histories. Narrative becomes a vehicle for the problematic issue of representing experiences and events as seen from the perspective of particular actors and as elements of a cultural account that can tell us something about a social world, however local that world. (2000, 24)

For anthropologists working over the past decade, narrative has increasingly become a tool by which one might gain insight into very local theories of temporality, experience, and identity. By no means without its problems as a locus of research, narrative — as it has been framed and used within anthropology over the past twenty years — informs my analyses of Morisco narrative at the theoretical as well as methodological levels.

The third branch of this book's consideration of time, human experience, and narrative comes from research trends within literary studies. Fundamental for this form of critical inquiry are the ideas of the Bakhtin Circle as well as those contemporary critics, such as Gary Saul Morson, who work within the frame of the "social poetics" mapped out by Mikhail Bakhtin. The importance that these ideas have for my analysis of traditional *aljamiado-morisco* narratives stems principally from their clear theorization of literary discourse as socially embedded language use intricately and ineluctably linked to frameworks of time, human experience, and cultural practice.

Perhaps the most useful aspect of Bakhtin's work for the present study is his notion of the "chronotope" (literally, "time-space"). Defined by Bakhtin as "the intrinsic connectedness of temporal and spatial relationships that are artistically expressed in literature" (1981, 84), the chronotope serves as solid link between issues of temporality and genre that operate within written narratives, while exhibiting strong bonds with parallel issues beyond the boundaries of these texts. As Bakhtin argues:

> The chronotope in literature has an intrinsic *generic* significance. It can even be said that it is precisely the chronotope that defines genre and generic distinctions, for in literature the primary category in the chronotope is time. The chronotope as a formally constitutive category determines to a significant degree the image of man in literature as well. The image of man is always intrinsically chronotopic. (1981, 85)

Bakhtin's ideas about "time-space" are picked up and developed by Morson, who makes use of the concept of chronotope to argue for a temporal openness in the novels of Leo Tolstoy and Fyodor Dostoyevsky. These arguments, which link the lack of determinism in the novels of these Russian novelists to the inherently unscripted and contingent "human dimension of time" about which Morson is concerned, serve to draw written narrative into even tighter alignment with human experience and action in the world. What Morson, working in line with Bakhtinian notions of time and genre, develops is a social poetics that intersects almost seamlessly with the life world of human agents who engage written narratives. Instead of a rare, separated literary world, Morson explores the complex intersections that exist (consciously in the case of the novels of Dostoyevsky and Tolstoy) between the "world of the text" and the "world of the reader" (Ricoeur 1988, 3:101).

The third chapter of this book will serve as a preliminary catalogue of the uses to which both Castilian and Aragonese crypto-Muslims and modern critics have put traditional *aljamiado-morisco* texts. Beginning in the nineteenth century, when Arabic literary studies took root in Spanish cultural and educational institutions, the literature of the Moriscos has been used in a variety of ways by historiographers, literary critics, and cultural figures within and beyond the peninsula. From Serafín Estébanez Calderón's creative reframing of Morisco literary themes within a nineteenth-century *costumbrista* aesthetic to Alvaro Galmés de Fuentes's modern philological approach, the traditional narrative texts of Castilian and Aragonese Moriscos have served as the raw matter for a number of analytical confections, all of which are no less ideologically shaped or less temporally situated than those generated by Morisco readers and scribes themselves. Reflecting in a variety of ways the cultural values and practices of our own widespread, perhaps imagined, speech community of students and scholars (Anderson 1983), the uses to which we have put traditional *aljamiado-morisco* narrative texts over the past two centuries represent one side of the dialectic by which we attempt to understand the contextualized — rather than merely formal or thematic — meaning of these texts. For this reason, I have dedicated a chapter to tracing out, in admittedly rough form, the events surrounding the accidental rediscovery of many of these texts and the subsequent uses to which we have put them.

The second part of this book also consists of three chapters. These chapters contain analyses of the three *aljamiado-morisco* texts upon which I have chosen to focus. These texts present different thematic as well as structural features, and I will be studying each in turn. By focusing upon these texts in this detailed, individual way, I hope to bring sufficient analytical specificity to my larger theoretical claims. A representative example of my approach to these texts is the fourth chapter, "The Prophet Is Born, Muslims Are Made." In this chapter I will examine extant manuscript copies of the *Libro de las luces* (Book of lights) as well as the Arabic text from which it was translated (*Kitab al-anwar*) in order to speak of the role of the *Libro de las luces* in various socializing and performative activities within Castilian and Aragonese crypto-Muslim communities. For example, as a tool used in the religious instruction of Morisco youths, the *Libro de las luces* served as a means of transmitting and negotiating many other cultural beliefs and practices. The marginal commentaries within these manuscripts, as well as key differences between the texts of the different manuscript copies of the *Libro de las luces,* provide concrete information regarding the uses to which this work was put during the sixteenth and early seventeenth centuries.

As the present book is an analysis of the dynamic intersections between time, human experience, and narrative within crypto-Muslim communities in Castile and Aragon, I have adopted a thoroughly interdisciplinary approach. My decision to adopt such an approach is due primarily to the complexity of the narratives under analysis, which often move fluidly between religious prophecy, historical narration, Qur'anic exegesis, and anti-Christian polemic. In my efforts to address the many "conversations" encoded within these narratives, I have had to resort to a range of theoretical and methodological frameworks developed outside the disciplinary boundaries of literary studies. My hope is that my use of these frameworks will help to bring a higher level of depth and precision to my analyses while not compromising their clear presentation.

If the Moriscos ceased to exist as a loosely connected group of communities centuries ago, and their literature reflects, from our temporal perspective, the "distant pastness" of their culture, does this mean that we should not try to engage in some sort of dialogue with them through this literature? This is not the same process as summoning the deceased through some form of intellectual divination, nor is it a matter of "thinking like a Morisco." Clearly none of us, Muslim or Christian (or whatever else), will be able to accomplish any such miracle. It is, however, a matter of coming to some contextualized understanding of *aljamiado-morisco* literature as part of a larger system of cultural practice carried out and experienced by Morisco scribes, readers, and the larger public. In a very real sense, to understand what the *aljamiado-morisco* texts that we study meant to members of crypto-Muslim communities in sixteenth- and seventeenth-century Castile and Aragon (and could mean to us), we must deal with how they were employed in activities that took place within social, and thus temporal, settings.

I

Toward an Activity-Centered Approach to *Aljamiado-Morisco* Narrative

And whereas historiography recounts in the past tense, the strategies of instituted powers, these "fabulous stories" offer their audience a repertory of tactics for future use.
— Michel de Certeau, *The Practice of Everyday Life*

Literary critic Frank Kermode has argued, in an essay dealing with the relation between time and narrative, that "it is not expected of critics as it is of poets that they should help us to make sense of our lives; they are bound only to attempt the lesser feat of making sense of the ways we try to make sense of our lives" (2000, 3). The present book, a work of literary criticism, investigates the ways in which members of Morisco communities in sixteenth- and early seventeenth-century Castile and Aragon made use of handwritten traditional narratives to make sense of and give shape to their social lives. These narratives — the locally produced, handwritten texts of crypto-Muslim communities that survived in Spain for roughly a century before their forced expulsion over the five years between 1609 and 1614 — reveal a serious interest in preserving Islamic knowledge, practices, and faith, as well as a pronounced collective sense of anxiety regarding a future that seemed with each passing year more and more uncertain.

In light of the temporally situated ethico-religious concerns that give shape to *aljamiado-morisco* narratives, my focus in this book is the various ways in which time (understood both as a culturally structured value and as the horizon against which Castilian and Aragonese crypto-Muslims, like all humans, necessarily reckoned with their personal and collective existence) serves as an axis about which the socially contextualized meaning of these handwritten narratives revolve. My larger argument, which I will be discussing in detail in this and the following two chapters, is essentially that in our continued attempts to understand what traditional *aljamiado-morisco* narratives might have meant to the people that first produced, copied, and engaged them (a necessary aspect of what these texts might in turn mean to us as scholars of medieval and early modern literature and culture), it is of absolute importance to keep in mind that time, as Gary Saul Morson has cleverly put it in his study of Bakhtinian thought and the nineteenth-century Russian novel, is "of the essence" (1994, 4).

To connect time as a socially embedded phenomenon and written narrative to ongoing processes of sense-making carried out within crypto-Muslim communities in early modern Spain implies a certain departure from traditional forms of literary criticism. Equal parts anthropology and literary analysis, such an inquiry into the social foundations of textual meaning necessarily takes place in between academic disciplines, and for this reason it runs the risk of appearing incommensurate — for different reasons — with the sort of argumentation familiar to readers from both areas. For example, discussions of socially embedded language use, speech genres, and cultural practice may sound foreign or even suspiciously scientistic to literary scholars, even as the particulars of close textual analysis — especially when dealing with manuscript texts produced over four centuries ago — are likely to frustrate social scientists unaccustomed to working with texts in the absence of more thoroughly contextualized, moment-to-moment ethnographic data. Indeed, even though there has been a great deal of crossover between ethnography and literary studies over the past five or so decades (especially in the wake of Claude Lévi-Strauss's structuralist analyses of myth and the development of Clifford Geertz's quasi-Weberian interpretive paradigm), as well as a renewed sense of the literary underpinnings of ethnographic analysis itself (Clifford and Marcus 1986; Daniel and Peck 1996), the threat of incommensurability always looms in projects that proceed along an interdisciplinary path.

In order to avoid the appearance of speaking in tongues to readers from different intellectual traditions and academic disciplines, I will be taking special care throughout this book when developing arguments based to any significant degree on concepts specific to one or the other discipline. My hope is that such elaboration, though somewhat self-evident for specialists in the fields from which such arguments stem, will allow nonspecialists to get the most of the presentation and analysis of traditional *aljamiado-morisco* narratives within this book. All of this begs the important question: Why have I chosen such an interdisciplinary approach in the first place, especially given the risks inherent in such an undertaking? Why, in other words, have I decided to produce such an unliterary work of literary criticism?

The Folkloric Character of *Aljamiado-Morisco* Texts

To begin, the texts in question have little in common with the material with which Western literary scholarship tends to occupy itself. Anonymously written and recopied in secret for a very small readership, the handwritten narrative texts of Castilian and Aragonese Moriscos for the most part do not respond to any "literary" pretensions. With respect to the narrative works at the center of the present analysis, it is necessary to keep in mind that they represent the traditional Islamic writings of a large minority community (making up slightly less than 5 percent of the Spanish population by 1600, and a much higher percentage in the regions of Aragon and Valencia) that ceased to exist only decades after the manuscript texts to which we have access were copied. A short passage from one of the texts studied in this book, the *Libro de las luces,* helps to demonstrate what I mean:

> The recounting of the transfer of the Prophet Muhammad (the blessings of God be upon him and peace). And of his grandfather 'Abd al-Muttalib [the recounter] said: At that time 'Abd al-Muttalib took out his sword and said: "Bring [the boy] out or let me know how he is or I'll kill you!" And when Amina saw this, she said: "Go see him then, there you'll find him." He said: "Where is he?" She said: "He's in that house, wrapped in a cloth of white wool." 'Abd al-Muttalib said: And he [sic] went to the house and he [sic] tried to enter it, and a man came from within the house whose looks were more frightening than any other, and with a sword in his hand. And he gave a call that made all of my limbs tremble and my heart faint, and he said to me: "Where are you going?" And I said to him: "To see my son." He said: "Neither you nor anyone else can see him now." I said to him: "I have more right to see him than anyone, as he is my son." He said to me: "He will be kept from all the nations here until the visitation of the angels is finished, and now the angels of heaven are ascending and descending, and the visitation won't be finished for three days." And when 'Abd al-Muttalib saw that, he turned away frightened from what he saw and

heard, and said: "This is a great miracle." (BRAH ms. 11/9414 *olim* T-18 ff. 103ᵛ–104)[1]

The brusque, conversational style of this text, as well as its movement back and forth between speakers whose turns of talk are signaled and swapped in a perfunctory way by the repetition of "he/she said" (*dixo*) — a calque of the Arabic *qala* — are consistent with the uses to which this text was put as a didactic narrative that facilitated the religious education of young boys and as a ritual text to be performed during specific religious celebrations.

From the point of view of religious instruction, this text worked powerfully to link its readers to a centuries-long genealogy of devout Muslims. The Prophet's mother Amina, and his grandfather, 'Abd al-Muttalib, represent the very first witnesses of the miraculous nature of the newborn Muhammad and serve as the first links in a long chain of witnesses to the miracle of Islam. In a very real sense, these first late sixth-century witnesses to Muhammad's special relationship with God prefigure all followers of the divine revelation received by the Prophet several years after his birth. That the actual details of Muhammad's birth had little to do with the folkloric representation of this historical event found in the text above goes without saying; however, we should not assume from this that the folkloric account lacked the power to shape reality for its readers. Marginal notes found in the manuscript copy just cited reinforce the hypothesis that this text was used to mediate the religious and lectoral instruction of young Moriscos, a process that also entailed the socialization of these youths into their respective communities as well as the larger Muslim *umma* (Heath 1983; Ochs 1999). These notes, as well as what they reveal to us about the literacy practices of the Moriscos, will be taken up in chapter 4; for the moment it is important only to point out that there various orders of textual data support the notion that texts such as the *Libro de las luces* were *made use of* within a range of socially embedded activities within Morisco communities.

With regard to the ritual practice of Castilian and Aragonese Moriscos, it is known that portions of the *Libro de las luces* that deal with the birth of the Prophet were read in communal settings during Muslim holidays (*paxkuʷax*) like the Celebration of the Birth of the Prophet (*Mawlid al-Nabi*) (Guillén Robles 1889, 39). This simple fact, that passages from manuscript copies of the *Libro de las luces* formed an integral part of the celebration of Islamic holidays and prayer, offers contemporary scholars a unique opportunity to solidify and refine theories about Morisco narrative and culture that situate both within specific temporal, physical, and social settings. In addition, knowledge of the socially embedded, inherently pragmatic nature of narratives such as the *Libro de las luces* also forces us to question the extent to which notions of textual discourse and meaning that see the latter as a value predominately shaped by the former (a sort of tautology in any case) are in any real sense productive when analyzing *aljamiado-morisco* narrative.

Performance and Participation Frameworks

The social foundations that supported the processes by which *aljamiado-morisco* narratives took on meaning differed from those that corresponded to dominant Christian narrative discourse at both the larger macro- and more reduced micro-social levels. Like Mexican border *corridos* (Paredes 1958, 1976, 1993), Egyptian Bedouin *ghinnawat* (Abu-Lughod 1986), or Western Apache historical narratives (Basso 1990), the traditional stories of the Moriscos of Castile and Aragon achieved their power — and beauty — within very localized social networks of composition, reproduction, and use. And while it is true that these local networks often enough exist within and between national borders, their operation is quite different from that of the expansive "imagined communities" (Anderson 1983) supported by powerful, often national or transnational, institutions that frame and legitimate textual genres such as the modern novel in the postindustrial West. Such cultural institutions, which exist and play a decisive role in the shaping of language use at all levels of human social life, are potent loci for the production and legitimization of language forms (Bourdieu 1991; Gal 1990). However, the local institutions that underlie and valorize the production and use of *aljamiado-morisco* narratives — the local *alfakí* (from Ar. *fqih*) responsible for religious instruction, the semi-hidden Qur'anic school within certain towns, scattered Islamic authorities such as the Mançebo de Arévalo (more and more a scarcity after the first half of the sixteenth century) — functioned and were shaped in ways that have little to do with the highly segmented national and international institutions from which Christian writers and readers sought support and legitimization. Miguel de Cervantes's work reached a wide audience within and eventually beyond Spain through the patronage of the count of Lemos and an entire system of symbolic exchange that shaped literary tastes and practices, produced and distributed print books, and afforded the possibility of gaining an audience beyond the boundaries of the Iberian peninsula. No such wider institutionally sanctioned systems of support and patronage for *aljamiado-morisco* literature were available to Castilian and Aragonese Moriscos. Islamic education was always an ad hoc process handled in most cases by marginally trained *alfakíes,* and though the participation of a small number of well-to-do Morisco book buyers and parents concerned about the religious education of their children was certainly important, such patronage was always relatively unstable and contingent upon unpredictable circumstances.

Another important distinction between the production, reproduction, and use of traditional *aljamiado-morisco* narratives and the factors that shaped book culture among the larger Christian society has to do with issues of performance and the micro-level participation frameworks that shaped specific textual events (i.e., socially embedded activities in which texts played a significant, salient role) among the Moriscos. Highly dependent upon concrete performative settings — and the collaborative/conflictive activities that take place in such settings (Bauman 1996; Duranti 1994) — for their meaning and force, traditional *aljamiado-morisco* narratives are texts whose expression is inseparable from the socially embedded activities such as literacy and religious instruction, ritual practice, and storytelling performances in the micro-level, face-to-face settings in which they were engaged. Modes of reading, and the collaborative processes by which contextualized meaning was achieved in the case of the Moriscos' traditional literature — for example, the constant back-and-forth between authorized readers and their audience in specific, often ritualized reading events — point to a much more emergent, co-constructive, and flexible form of sense-making in the absence of stable institutions of symbolic power such as those that helped to shape and support the activities of the Christian majority. Like many minority communities forced to operate within the interstices of broader social systems (migrant groups, religious minorities, and indigenous communities throughout the Americas come to mind), the Moriscos of Castile and Aragon were continuously compelled to make use of their literature in their efforts to recreate, reshape, and reproduce — over and within time — the social frameworks and activities that made up their world.

Traditional narratives, like the very traditions to which they are associated, find their force and meaning in the micro-level social settings in which they are employed (Bauman 1986, 1992). They may also have force at a larger, macro-social level, such as the power that *corridos* recorded before the start of the Mexican Revolution had to call into question, on a larger regional scale (i.e., the expansive northern border region of Mexico), the legitimacy of President Porfirio Díaz's oppressive government and challenge the imperialist leanings of the United States (Paredes 1993). It is at the local level, however, through face-to-face verbal interaction, that these stories achieve their greatest impact within the communities that produce them. Here, readers and their audience collaboratively embed narrative texts within situated activities (such as a religious celebration) that in turn give meaning to the texts themselves as an integral part of larger "language games" (Wittgenstein 1999; Duranti 1997).

Lila Abu-Lughod's ethnography of poetic performance, emotion, and social structure within a Bedouin tribe in Western Egypt (1986) illustrates the surprising power that traditional poetry can have to facilitate the reconfiguration of engendered social roles when speakers make use of them in everyday settings: "[This poetry] is formulaic, thereby disguising the identities of poet, addressee, and subject. It is fleeting and ambiguous, performed by women and youths among trusted intimates who can decipher it exactly because they already know the reciter well" (Gal 1990, 194). As part of the verbal interaction of youths and women in relatively intimate and informal settings, the *ghinnawa* poetic genre comes to serve as a potent tool by which speakers and their listeners can collaboratively construct the expression of certain emotions that would be otherwise impossible to express given the rigid honor codes upon which Bedouin society depends. The use of the *ghinnawat,* according to Abu-Lughod, reveals a striking paradox that runs through Bedouin society: while autonomy and equality between lineages is highly valued, inequality within lineages with respect to gender and generation are insisted upon. Within this moral framework, poetry becomes a "discourse of defiance [employed] mostly by those slighted in the system," that is, perhaps ironically, poetry is "exalted because a refusal to be dominated is key to Bedouin political life, [even as] it is avoided by elders because it threatens to expose the illegitimacy of their authority" (Abu-Lughod 1986, 254).

Steven C. Caton's comprehensive study of poetic performance among North Yemeni Bedouins further confirms the rootedness of traditional forms of verbal art in the daily practice of certain traditional societies:

> In many non-Western, non-literate societies . . . process is given priority over product, or, as in the Yemeni tribal case, aesthetic appreciation is balanced in a continuum stretching from the reception of the creative process (as in the *balah*) to reception of a perfected product (the *qasidah*) to reception of works of art that are perceived simultaneously as practices of composition and as finished works of art (the *zamil*). In the light of such a continuum, we begin to see how artificial, even misleading, it is to think of the work of art as an *object*. What we would call an object is really the end product of a creative process, a particular moment in a continuous practice, that has become privileged for reception in our tradition. (1990, 251–52)

Caton's notion of "poetry as cultural practice" serves to embed the expression of verbal art forms (even when converted into fixed texts, as in the case of the *qasa'id* [sing. *qasida*] recorded by Bedouin poets and distributed as far away as Sana'a, the Yemeni capital) within the daily social lives of members of the traditional Bedouin community whose "continuous practice" he studies. His micro-level analysis of activities such as weddings and other feasts in which *balah* songs are improvised and performed by tribal members (and the risks to their honor that these tribesmen run through such performance) also provides multi-layered documentation of the manner in which traditional cultures — especially within traditional Arab cultures — can place a much higher value on artistic or narrative process rather than product. Such an inversion of modern Western artistic values (ultimately adapted from Greek metaphysical and aesthetic ideals of perfection) is also an integral part of medieval Christian literary practice in Castile and Aragon (Barletta 1999, 2001, 2004; Dagenais 1994), a fact that provides yet another possible intersection with the Morisco case under consideration here.

Caton's and Abu-Lughod's approach to verbal art is helpful for an understanding of the traditional narratives of Castilian and Aragonese crypto-Muslims, for as traditional, though profoundly isolated communities of Sunni Muslims-cum-Christian converts, the Moriscos of Castile and Aragon depended upon their literature to the same extent that their distant cousins in North Yemen and Western Egypt do, though in different ways. And given the extremely dire circumstances faced by Moriscos throughout Spain, especially during the second half of the sixteenth century, when most of the extant manuscript copies of these texts were produced, it would be a grave mistake to attempt to study *aljamiado-morisco* literature of any sort without taking into consideration the function of these texts within the cultural practice — specifically modes of resistance, compromise, negotiation, and perseverance — of their communities. For the Moriscos made use of traditional narratives not only in order to preserve and guide their practice as Sunni Muslims, but also in order to deal with — within more locally negotiated Muslim moral frameworks — the increasingly difficult triple bind within which they found themselves as practicing Muslims, new Christian converts, and subjects of the Spanish Crown.

Time-Consciousness and Traditional *Aljamiado-Morisco* Narratives

If humans can be described as "desiring, suffering, death-conscious, and ...time-conscious" creatures (Fraser 1966, 17), then Castilian and Aragonese crypto-Muslims were without a doubt extraordinarily human. Their traditional narratives, which include stories of Qur'anic heroes (e.g., Abraham, Ishmael, Job, Joseph, Moses, and Jesus), miracles of the Prophet Muhammad, accounts of his life and death, tales from the earliest Muslim communities (e.g., *La leyenda de Tamin Addar* [The legend of Tamin Addar]), and moral tales set in al-Andalus (e.g., *Alhadith del baño de Ziryab* [The story of the bath of Ziryab]), reveal a profound concern with personal and communal death, and the contingency that underlay their very day-to-day existence in Spain. This concern with personal and collective death is evidenced by the large number of eschatological texts found among the roughly two hundred extant *aljamiado-morisco* manuscripts scattered throughout Europe (Chejne 1983). It is also evident, in perhaps a deeper way, through the narrative account of Mançebo de Arévalo's interview with the elder Granadan scholar Yuçe de Banegas. Yuçe, telling his guest about the tragic events revolving around the conquest of Granada in late 1491–92, describes with unmistakable grief how he saw with his own eyes "the ladies mocked, widows and married women alike...and more than three hundred maidens put up to public auction" (Harvey 1993, 219). Having created a vivid picture of the sufferings of those Granadan Muslims unlucky enough to have been caught in the ever-tightening net of Christian culture in the peninsula at the end of the fifteenth century, Yuçe continues his narrative, addressing the Mançebo directly:

> Son, I do not weep over the past, for there is no way back, but I do weep for what you have yet to see, if you are spared, and live on this land, in this peninsula of Spain.... For anybody with feelings it will all seem bitter and cruel. What troubles me most is that Muslims will be indistinguishable from Christians, accepting their dress, and not avoiding their food. May God grant that at least they avoid their actions. (Harvey 1993, 219)

Yuçe makes it clear that his principal concern has to do with the *actions* of his co-religionists vis-à-vis the Christian majority. He laments what he considers the near certainty that Muslims will assimilate themselves to Christian norms in the future, losing their cultural identity in the process. He states that what troubles him most is that "Muslims will be indistinguishable from Christians," simultaneously excluding himself — an older man — from the events of this unfortunate future. In this short passage Yuçe expresses deep concerns about the future of Spanish Muslims while simultaneously revealing an acute awareness of the end of his own life course. Admittedly, it would be too much of a generalization to equate Yuçe's religious concerns with those of all Moriscos in Spain. Even if we leave aside the minority who willfully and sincerely converted to Christianity, it is doubtful that many Moriscos would frame their future within such explicitly orthodox, Islamic terms. Nonetheless, Yuçe's comments are indicative of a prevailing sentiment of loss and concern among Muslims in Spain during the first half of the sixteenth century, a sentiment that would be encoded in the traditional texts copied and used by *alfakíes* and other Muslim scholars in the communities that dotted Castile and (especially) Aragon.

My explicit wish here is to underscore the fact that the traditional narratives of Castilian and Aragonese crypto-Muslims are anything but timeless, static, or decontextualized pieces of writing. On the contrary, these texts encode the profound time-consciousness that seems to have permeated Morisco culture throughout the peninsula. In all cases — this means in every traditional *aljamiado-morisco* narrative text with which I have come into contact — evidence of a deliberate and complex renegotiation of temporal frameworks through the implementation of traditional discourse is evident. It can be argued that narrative is itself a discursive genre deeply shaped by its own temporal character; William Labov has in fact defined it in terms of its ability to sequence phenomena: "we can define a minimal narrative as a sequence of two clauses which are *temporally ordered:* that is, a change in their order will result in a change in the temporal sequence of the original semantic interpretation" (1972, 360; italics in original). Labov's conclusions are echoed in Julio C. M. Pinto's statement that "narrative (in whatever form it may take, be it oral storytelling, fiction, or drama) is a temporal art in that it tells or recounts events in an organized fashion" (1988, 5). Given these definitions of narrative, it may seem somewhat redundant to underscore the inherently temporal nature of the traditional narratives of Castilian and Aragonese Moriscos. My point, however, is that even beyond the inherently temporal character of narrative as a genre, the workings and reworkings of time within *aljamiado-morisco* narratives (even those that do not explicitly engage traditional sources) stand out in ways that are not easily dealt with by the analytical tools of literary criticism.

Authorship and Manuscript Textuality

There is, in addition, a more practical (though no less compelling) reason for my decision to work outside of strictly literary frameworks in my analysis of *aljamiado-morisco* narratives. This reason is rooted in the tremendous problems that repeatedly come up when we attempt to apply theoretical frameworks developed for the analysis of modern print texts to premodern manuscript ones. Put another way, much of the disciplinary baggage that we bring to our analyses of textual discourse from the Middle Ages (as well as later periods, as in the case of *aljamiado-morisco* narrative) can do great violence to the material that we study, leading us down investigative paths that are at best ethnocentric and at worst simply Procrustean.

To begin with, there is the minefield of authorship. Critics frequently run into trouble when they attempt to assign authorship to texts that do not, because of the way in which they were produced (e.g., by many scribes, over time), possess "authors" as we understand the term. Efforts to identify the authors of many canonical texts from medieval Spain (the canonicity of these texts having been determined in most cases centuries after their production and only after their significant transformation from manuscript texts to scholarly critical editions) have ended in frustration not because scholars have been unable to provide reliable dates and places of production, but because they have persistently sought to identify an individual figure — a Juan Ruiz or Gonzalo de Berceo — as the sole creator of each of these respective texts. In the case of literary works such as the *Libro de Alexandre* (Book of Alexander) and the *Libro del cauallero de Dios* (Book of the knight of God, more popularly known today as the *Libro del caballero Zifar*), individual authors have been elusive precisely because these texts were simply not produced under the same conditions — or for the same uses — as those that abide elsewhere. The text of the *Zifar*, for example, states quite clearly that it was composed "under the emendation of those who might wish to and know how to emend it" and that it should "much please a person who begins something that all those who wish to and know how to emend it do so, for the more a thing is emended the more it is praised" (Madrid, BN ms. 11.309 f. 3ᵛ).[2] Commenting on this strip of text from the *Zifar*, John Dagenais has stated that "a reading of this passage from the author-oriented point of view leads to a dead end" (1994, 25). Elaborating on this point, he argues that the passage from the *Zifar* is:

> as clear a statement as we could wish for that the "work" of an "author," which we still place at the summit of our hierarchy of literary values, took second place to those written forms which we tend to de-value: commentary, continuation, *remaniement*. In fact, praise accrues to the author in direct proportion to the amount of emendation readers carry out upon his text. (1994, 25)

As Dagenais points out, we may indeed speak of medieval authors such as Dante Alighieri and Chrétien de Troyes, but this does not mean that all of the culturally specific values and practices that we assign to "authorship" are applicable to textual production and engagement in other settings, such as the scribal communities of mid-fourteenth-century Toledo, where the *Zifar* was first redacted, or the Morisco communities of sixteenth- and early seventeenth-century Castile and Aragon.

Like trying to fix the exact numeric value of pi without having continuously to add numerals to the right of the decimal point, attempts to identify medieval authors are, in many cases, simply futile and beside the point. Indeed, a number of manuscript works from the Middle Ages — most notably wisdom texts copied from Arabic, Latin, and popular sources — frequently do not present any sign that the people who engaged them during the medieval period were particularly troubled by the anonymity of those who first redacted them. Such a claim is not as radical as it might at first seem. Today we may insist on knowing who the author of a given novel or piece of short fiction is, but do we tend to worry about who first composed the off-color joke we pass on to our friends? Or do we ask our parents who first composed the traditional stories that they tell us as children? In most cases, to do so is simply wrong, and I would argue that the same is true for a larger number of textual genres than we might at first imagine. Public announcements and signs, many newspaper editorials, just about everything published in *The Economist,* maps, shared work documents, folkloric texts, and an overwhelming number of digital texts found on the Internet are all examples of written texts that we commonly use and encounter today without necessarily feeling compelled to inquire into their exact authorship. And most manuscript texts from the medieval and early modern periods, insofar as they were produced by many people over time, altered and emended by readers with the culturally defined authority to do so, and performed in social settings characterized by a high level of discursive give-and-take, are similarly far too complex to be contained by the relatively narrow modern concept of "authorship." This, as I have already mentioned, does not mean that we have to ignore issues of intentionality and agency with respect to the achieved meaning of the manuscript texts we study; rather, both are more accurately approached as distributed, collective values that take shape over time and within situated activities characterized by discursive interaction and collaboration.

Approaching Manuscript Texts as Texts

Beyond the violence that we can do to the literature we study by insisting on our own, culturally situated ideas of authorship — on the presence of some person who individually sits down with pen and paper to "make sense" of our lives in some way — literary analysis can fail us at an even more basic level. It is very difficult, after all, to engage in the careful and detailed analysis of a "text" when it exists in several practically irreconcilable versions hand-copied at various times by different communities of scribes and readers. An excellent example of the difficulty inherent in bringing traditional methods and theories of literary analysis to the study of manuscript texts is the long trail of confusion that the manuscripts collectively known as the *Libro de buen amor* (Book of good love) have left in their wake. Dagenais, in his study of the *Libro de buen amor* and the "manuscript culture" that produced and engaged it during the Middle Ages, points out in glaring detail the limitations of traditional literary criticism when confronted with medieval manuscript texts such as the three extant versions of the *Libro de buen amor:*

To make medieval literature conform to the author-text model suggested by the printed book, we must subject it to considerable brutality.
In the specific case of the *Libro [de buen amor]*, in order to produce
an authorial text that is "authentic," we struggle to create a critical
edition that, within certain limitations, will be the closest representation of Juan Ruiz's "original." The three surviving manuscripts and the
few fragments must be reduced to one "book" that can then sit on our
shelves alongside other canonical texts. Dialectal traits (for example,
the Leonese pronunciations reflected in *S* and *T*) must be corrected to
conform to the presumed dialect of the author: Castilian. Other variations are judged according to metrical rules or to usually unspecified or
ad hoc standards of logical integrity.... Marginalia — marks, jottings,
doodles, *notas* — which are part of each of these manuscripts, are, in
the case of paleographic editions, relegated to footnotes or endnotes,
and in the case of critical editions, often ignored.[3] (1994, 19)

As Dagenais points out, the tools that we commonly bring to literary
analysis, which also include our ideological dispositions regarding what,
in fact, a "book" or "text" is, can require serious revision when we
turn our attention to medieval and other manuscript texts. Summing
up his position vis-à-vis traditional modes of literary criticism and their
usefulness for scholars dealing with medieval literature, Dagenais goes
on to state:

The surviving evidence for the literary life of the Middle Ages is fundamentally different from that of the era of the printed book. And I
believe that the criticism that seeks to elucidate this literature must also
be fundamentally different. In simplest terms, this criticism must grow
out of the evidence itself. It must recognize that although medieval
people certainly read "books" by "authors," these deceptively familiar
concepts were constantly conditioned by the processes through which,
in the Middle Ages, "books" were produced and read — that is, by the
physical manuscript codex. (1994, 20)

Arguing against the use of modern and postmodern modes of literary
analysis developed to handle print literature — (Roland Barthes, for
example, goes back no further than the works of Gustave Flaubert
[1821–88] and Marcel Proust [1871–1922] in making his claims for
the utility of semiotic analysis for literary texts) — Dagenais makes the
commonsense claim that analyses of medieval texts must take into full
consideration the material and social context of their production and use.

Anthropologists and folklorists working on non-Western popular traditions of text and verbal performance have made a number of points that resonate with those made by Dagenais, suggesting that contextual issues may have more to do with textual meaning and communal sense-making through narrative across cultures than was previously thought. Keith Basso has made the argument that seemingly generalized historical narratives commonly take on a strong moral and pragmatic charge among the Western Apache, serving as a means of influencing the behavior of particular community members:

> Although I cannot claim to understand the full range of meanings that the hunting model for storytelling has for Western Apache people, the general premises on which the model rests seem clear to me. Historical tales have the capacity to thrust socially delinquent persons into periods of intense critical self-examination from which (ideally, at least) they emerge chastened, repentant, and determined to "live right." Simultaneously, people who have been "shot" with stories experience a form of anguish — shame, guilt, perhaps only pervasive chagrin — that moves them to alter aspects of their behavior so as to conform more closely to community expectations. (1990, 126)

This morally corrective feature of Western Apache historical narrative is deeply situated in contexts of performance. However (and here is where important similarities between Western Apache practices and those of medieval European lectoral communities jump to the surface), long after having been "shot" by a storyteller's performance, a member of the Western Apache community can continue to be "stalked" by the story, as it is always anchored in a specific physical locality that the rebuked person must inevitably pass by with some regularity. Giving a ride to a young woman who had been the target of a story two years before, Basso relates how, as they drew near to her camp, she became silent when they passed the place where the events of the story took place: "I pointed it out to my companion. She said nothing for several moments. Then she smiled and spoke softly in her own language: 'I know that place. It stalks me every day' " (1990, 123).

In similar ways to the historical tales told by Western Apaches, medieval morality tales, such as those embedded within the running chivalric narrative of the *Zifar*, served as effective tools to mold the behavior of those to whom they were told. Also, the physicality of the manuscript books that contained these tales, characterized by tightly regimented spatial hierarchies, gave these books the quality of land-scape and served to anchor the lessons of the text and guide the actions of readers long after formal instruction had ended. Illuminations, marginal notes, squiggles, and commentaries all served as material anchors for practices of interpretation and action (what Dagenais terms "adaptation" and "application") that were imbued with meaning through their implementation in situated activities. Suzanne Reynolds's detailed analysis of marginal glosses left in twelfth-century Latin manuscripts of Horace's *Satires* provides important information regarding medieval reading and textuality in this respect. Discussing textual glosses made by instructors to aid their students, she states:

> Ultimately, these glosses demand that we conceptualise reading in a different way. They are not the reflection of an individual's interests and desires, but an answer to the grammatical requirements of the audience — a third party — for which they were destined. Reader response is replaced by the notion of mediation; the glossator or expert reader painstakingly mediates the text for a specific purpose, a purpose shaped by the needs of a particular set of learners. (1996, 31)

In this example, glossing, itself an activity carried out within multiple networks of social interaction and signification, is embedded within a larger framework that gives it meaning and purpose: the socialization of young boys into Latin literacy. The role of glossing within this larger framework takes it well beyond the mere engagement of text by a reader (or even a group of readers). Here the larger activity — transmitting cultural as well as grammatical knowledge from expert to novice (though the actual performance of this activity was anything but a one-way street) — generates and shapes the activities of both the instructors and their students.[4] Reading, in this context, is something much broader and more powerful than textual exegesis. It is a socially embedded activity that intersects with complex processes of cultural reproduction and change. And like the morally charged Western Apache landscape, the physical layout, or "environment," of the manuscript operates as a culturally structured material anchor for the carrying-out of these processes.

We find another example of the analytical flexibility that critics must bring to non-Western textual traditions, even in contexts where minority communities have had extensive contact with Western modes of textual engagement, in Joanne Rappaport's study of reading among the indigenous communities of Highland Colombia during the period of Spanish colonial rule. Making the argument that "visuality and literacy were also intimately connected to bodily practice" within colonial Andean society, she suggests that:

> ...literate patterns were superimposed in both sacred and secular contexts upon the architectonic and topographic space within which people walked, upon the temporal and kinship space by which they traced descent, and in the ritual space of sacred precincts where they worshipped. That is, alphabetic and visual texts were ceremonially manipulated, or the categories and spatial dimensions of their organization were reproduced in non-literate genres. In this sense, we must understand literacy as transcending the producer or the direct consumer of an alphabetic or pictorial text, to include a much broader range of participants: we must pay heed to the corporeal experience of a colonial culture that was inscribed both on paper and canvas, as well as upon the land, its buildings, and the bodies of its inhabitants. (1998, 175)

It is a similar sense of embodied, locally negotiated, and participatory literacy that permeated many medieval communities, as well. Mary Carruthers's recent analysis (1998) of the role of visual texts and embodied practices such as *ruminatio* in the construction and implementation of knowledge among even very learned clerics during the High Middle Ages reinforces this idea.

The picture that emerges from this handful of examples is one of great diversity. Reading, as Shirley Brice Heath has put it in her ethnography of reading in the Appalachian region of the United States, involves different "ways of taking" that are learned rather than natural, culturally shaped rather than universal (1982, 49). And the texts that mediate all these different "ways of taking" cannot be approached as flat, featureless terrain, or as purely referential in content. Like the Western Apache historical narratives, texts (written and verbal) can intersect with various other orders of social phenomena as the people who engage them attempt to "make sense" of their lives. In the case of the Western Apache, indigenous readers in colonial Highland Colombia, as well as the long chain of lectoral communities that medievalists have grouped under the rubric "manuscript culture" (a term that implies neither shared ethnic nor linguistic traits, but rather the common use of certain material objects that mediate practice in analogous ways) the material anchors and socially embedded narrative events that make up textuality have a strong pragmatic charge that can extend well beyond the referential meaning of the written or verbal text.

Turning to *aljamiado-morisco* narrative texts, we may also ask to what extent traditional forms of literary criticism can help us to determine what these texts *meant* to the Castilian and Aragonese crypto-Muslims who copied and engaged them. To begin, it is crucial to keep in mind the fact that *aljamiado-morisco* literature is wholly *manuscript* literature and subject to all of the variations and complexities that accompany such texts as they are copied out, reproduced, and read. Furthermore, *aljamiado-morisco* narratives are, for the most part, anonymous translations of traditional narratives that had been passed along for several generations, even back to the earliest days of Islam. As such, they represent written recenterings of folkloric texts of a decidedly non-Western tradition, despite the fact that they were copied out in Castilian (with abundant Aragonese inflections). These two points — that *aljamiado-morisco* literature is both handwritten and almost wholly part of a non-Western folkloric tradition — make it difficult to imagine that traditional modes of literary analysis can help us to understand their socially contextualized meaning beyond the most superficial level. To understand the pragmatic function of these texts, or the ways in which they were agentively engaged by Castilian and Aragonese Moriscos to mediate their efforts to construct local theories about time and reality, requires another order of analysis altogether.

Let us take, as an example of what I am driving at, a brief section from an *aljamiado-morisco* text. In the opening passages of the *Estoria i rrekontamiᵞento de Ayub* (The story and tale of Job), a text that occupies folios 23ʳ–41ʳ in Madrid, Biblioteca Nacional ms. 5305, we find the following:

> In the name of God the Compassionate and Merciful. Chapter of Muhammad: The Story and Narration of Job (peace be upon him), of his trials and patience. Narrated to us by 'Abdullah ibn 'Abdul Wahab, through Umar ibn Kathir, through Saad ibn Jamir, through 'Abdullah ibn Abbas, may God be pleased with all of them that they spoke of the tale of Job (salvation be upon him) as we heard it from the prophet Muhammad (the blessings of God be upon him and peace), who said that Job (salvation be upon him) was a good and purified servant of God, was honored in the power of God (may He be praised), and gave to the poor and needy and to those in the service of God, the high.[5]

The passage significantly begins with an invocation of God in Arabic. This formula, which initiates nearly all Muslim textual discourse, is from a referential perspective empty of meaning, in that it does not move the narrative forward in any way. However, it does have a vital pragmatic function, serving to "key" the narrative (to use Dell Hymes's term) and index the larger corpus of Islamic discourse within which it seeks to be incorporated.[6] The invocation is an integral part of the narrative as a whole insofar as it keys its lectoral performance and helps to shape the context of individual lectoral events. This context-building feature is signaled also by the various other Arabic formulae found in this brief passage, such as the blessings that follow the names of holy or enlightened figures, the Prophet Muhammad, and God. These formulae (e.g., the abbreviated *s'm* or *çala Allahu 'alayhi w'çalam* [the blessings of God be upon him and peace] that follows any mention of the Prophet's name) take on meaning through their power to situate the speaker and audience within a sacred Muslim space that in part fashions the very community that utters them. From a pragmatic perspective, these formulae are potent speech acts that link their speakers to a world beyond their own and to a temporal framework beyond their historical circumstances. Incidentally, that the phrase "Chapter of Muhammad" is not followed by such a formula could indicate that this particular part of the text was not read aloud, or that the *çala Allahu 'alayhi w'çalam* was pronounced by the audience, who knew when and how to respond. Or, perhaps more logically, its omission represents a simple mistake made by the scribe who copied this or some other, earlier version of the text.

Apart from these invocations and the initiating narrative key, there is more to the opening of this tale. The phrase "narrated to us," besides indexing a collective narrator at the deictic origo ("to *us*"), situates this story of Job within an even more precise form of Islamic narrative. The Castilian *rekontónos* corresponds to the Arabic *haddathana*, a term specific (though not necessarily exclusive) to the *hadith* tradition in Islamic scholarship and law. A *hadith* (pl. *hadiith*), in the context of Islamic scholarship and jurisprudence, is essentially something that the Prophet Muhammad said or some sort of report about something he did. The reliability of these sayings and reports is of the utmost importance to Islamic scholars and authorities, who use the *hadith* as an adjunct to the Qur'an in the determination of orthodox Muslim practice. Over the years, reliable collections of *hadiith* have been compiled, whose authenticity is determined by the chain of oral transmission (*isnad*) by which they have been received (the ultimate source being the Prophet Muhammad himself). From time to time, *hadiith* are abrogated due to the fact that they are determined to be *tadlis al-isnad,* or unauthentic, because of some weak point in the chain of transmission, often enough signaled by the scholar's use of vague constructions such as "So-and-So said..." (*qala*) rather than the more precise "So-and-So narrated..." (*haddathana* or, alternatively, *akhbarana*). The use of the Castilian *recontar* in the opening passage of the *Estori'a i rrekontami'ento de Ayub,* as well as in the title of the text, is thus not casual: as the opening invocation places the text within a broad category of Muslim discourse, the use of the *rekóntonos/haddathana* construction situates the telling, and subsequent retellings, of this story within a very specific, orthodox, and authoritative genre of Islamic discourse. That the narrator follows this construction with a very authoritative *isnad* for his audience — one that goes back to Abdullah ibn Abbas, the Prophet's first cousin, and eventually, to the Prophet himself — provides even more support for this hypothesis.[7]

Taking into account, albeit briefly, a sample of the discursive elements encoded within the opening of the *Estori'a i rrekontami'ento de Ayub,* we find valuable information regarding the text's mutually constitutive relation to its performative context, as well as its place within the larger linguistic repertoire of the Moriscos. With respect to genre, we come to a more finely grained, culturally situated sense of what terms such as *rekontamiento* and *rekontar* meant as translations of Arabic terms (though why the former is paired with *estori'a* in the case of *Estori'a i rrekontami'ento de Ayub* remains something of a mystery). Moving beyond the analysis of elements specific to this text, we also find a great deal of information in the larger manuscript frame within which this text is physically situated, surrounded as it is by a series of other narrative texts, including the *Alhadith de Muça kon Yakub el Karniçero* (Story of Moses with Jacob the Butcher, ff. 1^r–4^v); *El rrekontami'ento de Çulayman* (The recounting of Solomon, ff. 68^v–103^v); *Una estori'a ke akaeçi'ó en ti'enpo de 'Iça* (A story that occurred in the time of Jesus, ff. 14^v–16^v); and the *Alhadith i rrekontami'ento de 'Iça kon la kalavera* (Story and recounting of Jesus with the skull, ff. 16^v–22^v). All of these texts make use of the terms *rekontar/rrekontami'ento* or *hadith* in some way, while two of these even offer their readers an abbreviated *isnad.*

Thick Description and the Ethnography of Reading

In spite of my contention that the present book's interdisciplinary approach to traditional *aljamiado-morisco* narrative is in many ways novel, this approach has not been conceived *ex nihilo*. In my efforts to study the temporally framed experience and actions of Castilian and Aragonese crypto-Muslims in light of related data encoded in their manuscript texts, I am necessarily building upon previous research that has been carried out in the complex field where texts and cultural practice intersect.

Two particular modes of textual analysis, both of which stem from the field of cultural anthropology, have had a particular influence on my approach to *aljamiado-morisco* texts. The first of these, Clifford Geertz's notion of "thick description" elaborated in his *Interpretation of Cultures* (1973), has had a very specific effect on the early development of the present book. For Geertz, "thick description" signifies a style of ethnographic analysis in which the researcher interprets tightly framed cultural phenomena (such as his classic example of the difference between a man either twitching his eye or winking) as signs that can reveal a great deal more about a given culture. In this, Geertz claims that the work of the ethnographer is much like that of the literary critic, in that she must employ her interpretive faculties to determine the significance of a given phenomenon within the larger semiotic system that is a given culture. This method or style of analysis is based on Geertz's definition of culture itself, a notion that he borrows from Max Weber:

> The concept of culture I espouse...is essentially a semiotic one. Believing, with Max Weber, that man is an animal suspended in webs of significance he himself has spun, I take culture to be those webs, and the analysis of it to be therefore not an experimental science in search of law but an interpretative one in search of meaning. (1973, 4–5)

For Geertz, ethnographic analysis is much like reading, in that the researcher is engaged in the interpretation of signs and larger "systems of meaning" (1973, 12). Such a hermeneutic approach is apparent in Geertz's famous chapter on Balinese cockfighting, in which he unpacks the various symbolic layers of the cockfight as one might a written text. Speaking of the symbolic meaning of the seemingly incoherent system of wagering and the animal violence embodied in the fights (paradoxical, according to Geertz, given the Balinese aversion to all other sorts of animalistic behavior), Geertz argues:

What makes Balinese cockfighting deep is thus not money in itself, but what, the more of it that is involved the more so, money causes to happen: the migration of the Balinese status hierarchy into the body of the cockfight. Psychologically an Aesopian representation of the ideal/demonic, rather narcissistic, male self, sociologically it is an equally Aesopian representation of the complex fields of tension set up by the controlled, muted, ceremonial, but for all that deeply felt, interaction of those selves in the context of everyday life. The cocks may be surrogates for their owners' personalities, animal mirrors of psychic form, but the cockfight is — or more exactly, deliberately is made to be — a simulation of the social matrix, the involved system of crosscutting, overlapping, highly corporate groups — villages, kin groups, irrigation societies, temple congregations, "castes" — in which its devotees live. And as prestige, the necessity to affirm it, defend it, celebrate it, justify it, and just plain bask in it (but not given the strongly ascriptive character of Balinese stratification, to seek it), is perhaps the central driving force in the society, so also — ambulant penises, blood sacrifices, and monetary exchanges aside — is it of the cockfight. This apparent amusement and seeming sport is, to take another phrase from Erving Goffman, "a status bloodbath." (1973, 436)

This "world in a text" approach is highly powerful and has inspired a great amount of research in anthropology as well as in cultural and literary studies. My first contact with Geertz's interpretive paradigm in fact came in the context of a graduate seminar in literary theory rather than in my later postdoctoral work in linguistic anthropology. (I was to read his work then, as well, although the approach in my anthropology seminar — the second in a series of three courses on the history of the discipline — was much more of the historical, this-used-to-be-a-highly-influential-approach vein.)

It needs to be pointed out, however, that the interpretation of cultures and Geertz's semiotic theory of culture are not without their limitations and blind spots. It is a useful lesson, in fact, to keep in mind that while Geertz and his wife (both of them admittedly "malarial and diffident" [1973, 412] upon their arrival to the Balinese village in which they would live and work) were focusing on the symbolic meaning of Balinese cockfights, Indonesia itself was being torn to shreds by CIA- and British-supported attempts to overthrow the government of President Achmad Sukarno. This "year of living dangerously," which would erupt into a full-blown coup attempt less than a decade later, receives no mention within Geertz's work in Bali, an oversight that seems odd in retrospect —

much like a researcher offering a "thick description" of systems of signification in urban Egypt in 1981 and not making any mention of the
brewing religious revolt that would culminate in Islamic Jihad's very public assassination (though an army lieutenant named Khaled al-Islambouli
was the principal trigger man) of President Anwar al-Sadat.

The blindspots in such a symbolic approach, one that constructs culture as a "web" or "text" (from the Latin *textus,* meaning "something
woven" or "fabric") rather than as a processual force negotiated between
human agents in real time, multiply when we are dealing with communities such as the Moriscos that no longer exist. To study, for example, the
complex negotiation of religious and ethnic identity in premodern Spain
by simply converting devotionary and other embodied practices into sys-
temic, analyzable "texts" that can be studied in much the same way as
any other written text is highly problematic insofar as it fails to account
for the agency — not to mention the situated and ever-fluctuating point
of view — of the people whose practices we intend to study. Similarly,
to reach conclusions about cultural practice based on purely referential
data (i.e., what texts "say") found in texts brings with it a different set of
risks and possible pitfalls, as recent critiques of historiographical work
based on Inquisition testimony have demonstrated (Rosaldo 1986).

Another shortcoming of the interpretive paradigm that I have just described is its problematic conceptualization of context. Placing the texts
under analysis and the context within which they take on meaning within
a relatively static figure/ground relation, many text-centered approaches
to cultural criticism create an artificial divide between text and context,
often resulting in a distorted understanding of both. John B. Thompson
makes reference to this artificial divide in his questioning of text-centered
analyses of literary meaning:

> To proceed in this way is to ignore the ways in which the text, or
> the analogue of the text, is embedded in social contexts within which,
> and by virtue of which, it is produced and received; it is to disregard
> the sense that it has for the very individuals involved in creating and
> consuming this object, the very individuals for whom this object is,
> in differing and perhaps divergent ways, a meaningful symbolic form.
> (1990, 135)

Taking Thompson's statements into account, what I propose in the
present study is an activity-centered approach to the traditional narratives of Castilian and Aragonese Moriscos, an approach that places

the agentive, eminently human processes of text and context formation at the center of investigative concern. This line of research is in keeping with current concerns in anthropology and folklore studies regarding the social processes through which context and discursive interaction presuppose and dynamically constitute one another. As Charles Goodwin and Alessandro Duranti put it in the introduction to their book-length study of verbal discourse and context:

> Instead of viewing context as a set of variables that statically surrounds strips of talk, context and talk are now argued to stand in a mutually reflexive relationship to one another, with talk, and the interpretive work it generates, shaping context as much as context shapes talk. (1992, 31)

For Goodwin and Duranti, as well as a host of other researchers in the social sciences (most notably sociologists working in the ethnomethodological tradition and discourse analysts concerned with micro-level accounts of talk as social practice), the mutually reflexive relation between talk (and/or text) and context revolves around the situated activities of human agents, shifting analysis away from texts per se to an account of the ways in which people make use of texts in the negotiation of, for example, local theories of reality.

This activity-centered approach has been hinted at in certain lines of literary criticism, though even here a concerted focus on texts (with context serving as an interpretive horizon), as in the case of Stanley Fish's notion of "interpretive communities" and the Constance school's version of reception theory and history, has prevailed. Perhaps one exception to this rule would be poststructuralist accounts of meaning and discourse, which tend to focus on system-wide issues of signification rather than particular textual ones. In this respect, Vincent Leitch has argued that "one important task of criticism is to connect literary discourses and genres with sociohistorical regimes, which include networks of institutions that facilitate and constitute regimes" (1991, 91). Linking "literary systems" to larger cultural and political ones, Leitch attempts to historicize literary discourse and genres; however, he does so without accounting for the processes by which such discourse, including the systems within which they operate, take shape and change. This inability to account for human agency as well as the mechanics of rudimentary social change is a classic critique of structuralist and poststructuralist accounts of culture and discourse (Bourdieu 1990; Giddens 1984), and while as a literary scholar whose training took place in American universities during the late 1980s and 1990s I have undoubtedly absorbed a host of poststructuralist tendencies (surely only some of which I am aware), it is principally because of these shortcomings that the present study bases very little on overtly structuralist and poststructuralist theories and lines of analysis.

My wish is not to split hairs here, nor is it to offer an unfair criticism of the important and influential work of cultural anthropologists and poststructuralist theorists such as Geertz and Leitch several years after the fact. Rather, I wish to point out two things. First, to engage in textual analysis with the goal of reaching larger conclusions about the culture that produced and made use of the texts under consideration necessarily implies — even if in a restricted way — the sort of semiotic, "thick descriptive" work that Geertz promotes. Second, critics need to find ways to rework such semiotic analysis so as to account for the agentive practice of the human beings at the center of textual production, reproduction, and use. There are, after all, serious limitations, as well as ethical shortcomings, to purely textual, or even semiotic, approaches to the study of culture; the human world is simply not just a text to be studied by those with the advantage of hindsight and/or specialized training in textual analysis. The human world — past, present, and future — is made up of actual human beings who act, think, interact, make mistakes, and worry about their eventual death, and I would argue that any truly "thick description" of human life however conceived must attend to this fact in some significant way. The alternative, to treat culture as a network of signs to be interpreted, and within which we are compelled to act out our limited part, inevitably makes it necessary for critics to entextualize phenomena (such as culture itself) that stubbornly resist such processes of conversion.

Another important paradigm that has influenced — perhaps in a less problematic way than Geertz's interpretive framework — the present book is the growing body of research dedicated to carrying out ethnographies of reading in a range of cultural settings. Jonathan Boyarin's edited collection of essays on this topic serves as a kind of touchstone for researchers engaged in more specific modes of text-mediated sensemaking than those described in earlier research on literacy (Goody 1986, 1987; Goody and Watt 1968; Graff 1981; Havelock 1982). As Boyarin points out, the ethnography of reading in fact implies a very different research project than that elaborated by early anthropological accounts of literacy. In his introduction to the edited volume, Boyarin explains:

> The contributors to this volume have all given reading a second glance, and find much to say about it. Their investigations take us beyond the simple rubric of "literary," which was once understood as an evolutionary advancement in the generalization, abstraction, and reliable transmission of otherwise evanescent and changeable oral communication. They all throw into question the assumption made a few decades ago, at the beginning of anthropological studies of literacy, that we could safely posit a "central difference between literate and non-literate societies" (Goody and Watt 1968). We are now coming to recognize a much more complex interplay of different forms of human communication, from lullabies to hypertext and beyond. Likewise all of their essays make it clear that the question of causality — whether it is "writing itself that makes a difference" ... or writing is merely part of the larger context — will not get us very far, not only because reading is as much part of literacy as writing, but also because "writing" and "reading," unlike the speed of light, are hardly constant at all times and places. (1993, 1)

Boyarin's statements intersect with the research findings of a number of anthropologists and sociolinguists working more or less at the time that this collection of essays was published (Besnier 1995; Duranti and Ochs 1997; Messick 1993; Street 1993, 1995). Shirley Brice Heath's earlier work in Appalachia (1983), as well as Brian V. Street's (1984) research in prerevolutionary Iran along with his critical rereading of Jack Goody's theories also provide important precursors to Boyarin's ethnographic concerns vis-à-vis reading and cultural practice.

There are several provocative and useful essays in Boyarin's edited book, though it is perhaps the work of Joanne Rappaport — which first came to my notice by way of an essay that she co-authored with Diana Digges and published in Boyarin's collection — that has most informed the present study. Looking at modes of reading in colonial Highland Colombia, Digges and Rappaport argue that "the ethnography of reading cannot be examined independently of the ethnography of writing and of ritual practice" (1993, 139). They go on to explain how the meaning of colonial-era legal contracts between the indigenous community of Cumbal and the Spanish Crown has been shaped through the text's embeddedness in ritual practices carried out over time. By situating reading within a larger framework that includes writing and copying (in the case of manuscript texts) as well as embodied activity (i.e., ritual, performed actions) in socially embedded settings, Digges and Rappaport draw a very solid connection between text-mediated sense-making and the broader range of cultural practice in which human agents engage. And they do this largely on the basis of textual, manuscript data produced centuries ago. In this respect, Digges and Rappaport's study resembles William Hanks's work on discursive hybridity and theories of cultural practice within colonial Yucatec Mayan society (2000). However, in Rappaport's later work on the ethnography of reading, she moves beyond ideas of hybridity to offer a much more detailed picture of reading in the colonial Andean setting. Focusing on the importance of embodied interaction in ritualized settings, Rappaport raises important suggestions regarding what colonial modes of reading mean for the cultural and political situation of indigenous communities today. I will be discussing Rappaport's more recent work in the next chapter. However, I have included this short overview of her critical approach, as well as that of Jonathan Boyarin, to give readers a more contextualized sense of the ideas that have informed this book.

An Activity-Centered Approach to *Aljamiado-Morisco* Narrative

With all of the issues discussed above in mind, I have sought in this book to frame traditional *aljamiado-morisco* narratives in such a way as to attend to the emergent and co-constructed nature of their meaning within Morisco communities in Castile and Aragon. Like Dagenais, I am concerned with the ways in which manuscript copies were produced and made use of within communities of readers and copyists. Like Geertz, I realize that the best way to examine the ongoing production and use of these handwritten texts is to engage in a "thick description" of these same texts, given that they are the only data available to us. And like Boyarin and Rappaport, I am committed to drawing out the uniquely human and interactional aspects of textual interpretation and use within these communities. For this reason, I have adopted — as I have mentioned above — an approach that focuses upon the manner in which human agents (i.e., members of Castilian and Aragonese Morisco communities) imbued these traditional narratives with meaning within situated activities such as ritual practice.

What I mean by "agent" in this study implies the ability of humans to act and, in a very practical sense, to make a difference in their world. My ability, for example, to pick up a bucket of water and dump it on my neighbor's head implies a form of agency. Of course, the overall meaning of this act depends upon a number of contextual circumstances that must be teased out through hermeneutic analysis — whether, for example, my neighbor's hair is on fire or he has just insulted me changes the meaning of my actions dramatically — but my ability to act (or not) is a fundamental aspect of my participation in any given social system. Also, importantly, this notion of agency does not always imply a "conscious aiming at ends" (Bourdieu 1990, 53), but rather takes into consideration the importance of unintended results, absent-minded mistakes, and practice shaped by habitus in the larger system of human practice.

My main point in defining my approach to traditional *aljamiado-morisco* narratives as an activity-centered one is to underscore the place of these texts in the complex and precarious life world of crypto-Muslims living in sixteenth- and early seventeenth-century Castile and Aragon. For one of the most salient characteristics of the Moriscos' narrative texts is the powerful manner in which these written texts encoded meaning at both the referential and indexical levels. These texts told generically regimented stories to be sure, but they also pointed to the situated, performative activities by which their readers and the larger, listening public (most Moriscos were not alphabetically literate) worked out local theories of reality, identity, and meaning.

In using the term "indexical" I follow Michael Silverstein in referring to the ways in which signs, whether verbal or written, "point to a presupposed context in which they occur (i.e., have occurred) or to an entailed potential context in which they occur (i.e., will have occurred)" (1998, 128). In the case of traditional *aljamiado-morisco* narratives from Castile and Aragon, modern readers are confronted with textual relations of contiguity across the temporal gamut: past, present, and future come together to weave a temporal fabric of human suffering, anxiety, survival, and in-group struggles for prestige and authority.

Given this revised project, to come to some understanding — even from a marked temporal and cultural distance — of how the traditional narratives of Castilian and Aragonese crypto-Muslims mediated the processes by which members of these communities built and dealt with their social world, I have been compelled to look beyond established forms of literary and textual criticism.

As a number of scholars have pointed out, in the handwritten narratives of Castilian and Aragonese crypto-Muslims, we seem to be dealing with literature that is for the most part not very "literary." A. R. Nykl, in the introduction to his critical edition of an *aljamiado* version of the Qur'anically inspired *Rrekontami^{y}ento del rrey Alixand^{e}re,* presents this commonplace in slightly different terms:

> The *aljamiado* texts have thus far received but scant attention. Literary critics have dismissed them with very brief remarks in their works, and it cannot be gainsaid that from the point of view of a literary historian their importance is, with but a few exceptions, small. They are more interesting as human documents reflecting the cultural and mental status of a foreign race speaking the language of a nation whom they had conquered at first, and who conquered them in turn: the tenacious struggle between two elements diametrically opposed in religion, customs and views concerning questions of social and political life. (1929, 14)

From an anthropological (and historical) perspective, Nykl's comments about the Moriscos as a "foreign race," as well as his framing of Christian and Hispano-Islamic cultures as "diametrically opposed" are admittedly outdated. As a great deal of recent research has shown, peninsular Muslims were always an ethnically, culturally, and even linguistically diverse community, and by the sixteenth century the communities that extended throughout Spain (with greater concentrations in Aragon, Valencia, and, before 1571, Granada) had been in cultural and physical contact with Christians for eight centuries. Also, given the numerous theological intersections that exist between Christianity and Islam (e.g., the Virgin birth of Jesus, the adventures of Joseph in Egypt, and Abraham's near-sacrifice of a beloved son as a sign of his faith), as well as the profound influence that Christianity and Judaism have had over Islamic practice, it is hard to accept the notion that the religious and social lives of Christians and Muslims — even barring the sort of contact present in the Iberian peninsula throughout the Middle Ages — are in any sense diametrically opposed. Despite these exaggerations, Nykl makes one very important point that directly coincides with the approach that I will be taking throughout this book, namely, that *aljamiado-morisco* texts are "more interesting as human documents" than as material for literary history or analysis.

To approach *aljamiado-morisco* narrative texts as human documents — that is, as handwritten texts that mediated a range of socially embedded activities by which members of crypto-Muslim communities in Castile and Aragon gave shape to and made sense of their personal and collective lives — allows us to attend to this "unliterary" literature using tools from different scholarly traditions and disciplines. Given that, as Dagenais has pointed out, we must deal with the concrete evidence before us, a full account of *aljamiado-morisco* narrative texts will necessarily focus on the manuscripts that contain them as well as on the written texts themselves. In this, our work here is not significantly different from that of the medieval literary scholar. However, in laboring to situate these texts *as socially embedded language use* within the larger context of Morisco cultural practice within Castile and Aragon, the present investigation moves into intellectual territory for the most part unexplored by literary scholars.

2

Written Narrative and the Human Dimension of Time

And know that the world is like a book, and people are like the letters, and the written pages are like the times, such that when one page finishes, another begins.
— Flores de filosofía (medieval Castilian reworking of an Arabic anthology)

This chapter will map out in some detail the activity-centered approach to traditional *aljamiado-morisco* narratives from Castile and Aragon. This approach, based on the analysis of manuscript texts and what is known about the cultural world of Castilian and Aragonese crypto-Muslims, seeks to address the ways in which members of these communities used handwritten narrative texts in their efforts to make sense of their complex and precarious existence in Spain. In order to present the details of this approach, both from a theoretical and methodological perspective, I will be drawing connections between phenomenological philosophy, ethnographic research on oral narrative, and recent research on manuscript textuality in medieval and early modern Europe.

The crucial theoretical intersection of these philosophical, ethnographic, and literary/codicological approaches is the notion that written narratives are themselves examples of socially embedded language use rather than decontextualized signs with no real link to what Edmund Husserl termed our "life-world" *(Lebenswelt)*. The idea that written texts are not necessarily different in kind from verbal utterances has been expressed by Mikhail Bakhtin in his essay on speech genres: "Our speech, that is, all our utterances (including creative works), is filled with others' words" (1986, 89). Implicit in this statement is the sentiment that the social forces and heteroglossia that give shape to speech are also present in our written words. The consequences of this argument — beyond Bakhtin's efforts to map out a "social poetics" — are to place written, creative works on the same discursive footing as spoken, even nonartistic forms of language use.

Paul Ricoeur also weighs in on the issue of written and verbal narrative, arguing that while written texts operate in ways that differ from the here-and-now of verbal discourse, they nonetheless have tremendous power to work in the life-world of those who engage them:

> Through fiction and poetry, new possibilities of being-in-the-world are opened up within everyday reality. Fiction and poetry intend being, not under the modality of being-given, but under the modality of power-to-be. Everyday reality is thereby metamorphosed by what could be called the imaginative variations that literature carries out in the real. (1991, 86)

Ricoeur's argument, based on Heideggerian ideas of being-in-the-world and temporality, reflects the almost unparalleled power that narrative — and Ricoeur is referring primarily to written narratives here — has to create possible worlds that are not immediately given to us. Our written narratives, folktales, and poems are a significant part of the means by which we create our temporally ordered world, and an integral component of any fashioning of reality: "fiction and poetry intend being ... under the modality of power-to-be."

Ricoeur's comments admittedly reflect a fairly limited and self-contained perspective on reading, textuality, and meaning, based as they are on a narrow portion of cultural data culled from modes of reading more typical of literary critics and philosophers in the modern West than of the many social groups that engage written narratives across cultures. Heath (1983) has effectively pointed out the reduced application of such a cultural paradigm through ethnographic work on reading and language socialization in working-class poor communities in the Appalachian Piedmont region of the United States. I will be discussing Heath's and others' findings later in this chapter, and I make brief mention of them here only to underscore the idea that reading — as well as other forms of textual engagement — takes a wide variety of forms across cultures and historical epochs (medievalists such as Carruthers [1990, 1998], Michael Clanchy [1979], and Dagenais [1994] have shown in great detail how modes of reading in medieval Europe could differ tremendously from those dominant in the modern West).

The point in Ricoeur's statements about texts and reality that most stands out for the purposes of developing an activity-centered approach to *aljamiado-morisco* narrative is his claim that through written narratives and poetry, "new possibilities of being-in-the-world are opened up within everyday reality." In this Ricoeur seems to echo Jerome Bruner's larger claim regarding narrative's (whether verbal or written) ability to generate "possible worlds" (1986). Bruner's theories on narrative, based on his research in developmental psychology, can be summed up in the belief as follows:

> [I]t is far more important, for appreciating the human condition, to understand the ways human beings construct their worlds...than it is to establish the ontological status of the products of these processes. For my central ontological conviction is that there is no "aboriginal" reality against which one can compare a possible world in order to establish some form of correspondence between it and the real world. (1986, 46)

For Bruner, the human mind is an integral part of the world in which we live (and vice versa), and human perception is "to some unspecifiable degree an instrument of the world as we have structured it by our expectancies" (1986, 47). Put another way, our individual and collective theories of the world — our narratives of origin, surprise, happiness, and death, etc. — shape our perception of the world around us to a greater degree than might at first be apparent. In fact, David Carr (1986) has strongly suggested that our very perception of the world always has a "beginning-middle-end" structure that closely parallels narrative structure. Carr's argument, a modification of Hayden White's theories concerning narrative as a genre that brings order to a chaotic world ex post facto, is that the world is never "out there" in some unmediated way for us. Basing his ideas on Husserl's phenomenological theories of perception and time, Carr states that the world and all of its happenings are continuously folded into complex temporal frameworks of start and finish at the very moment that we come into contact with them:

> [T]his [beginning-middle-end] structure belongs just as surely to the human events — experiences and actions — about which stories are told, and, more important, it belongs to them whether or not a story, in the sense of a literary text, is told about them at all. What is more, if we are right, this structure belongs essentially to such events; they could not exist without it. Just as the beginning-middle-end structure

requires a temporal sequence in order genuinely to be what it is, so the temporal sequence requires this sort of closure; insofar, that is, as it is a human sequence, one whose phases and elements are the stuff of human experience and action. (1986, 51–52)

Reality for us, in other words, is always a distinctly human reality and thus it is necessarily situated in temporal frameworks of, at their most basic level, "beginning-middle-end" that shape the ways in which we sense and act upon the physical world around us.

How do written narratives fit into this larger discussion of narrative, time, meaning, and human perception? Clearly it would be a mistake to posit some direct or immediate correspondence between the written texts that we compose and use to varying ends and the moment-to-moment discursive action by which our world unfolds for us. Written texts — we must take Ricoeur seriously on this point — are in meaningful ways different from verbal discourse and the face-to-face work that goes on between human beings throughout our lives and in all cultures. Although they are without a doubt more closely related than established modes of literary criticism (from Prague School formalism to French poststructuralism) have suggested, they are not the same thing. There is, for example, an important physical element to all written texts that still requires a great deal of study, as well as a whole suite of activities that surround the composition, reproduction, interpretation, and implementation of written texts. Such analysis is still for the most part uncharted territory for literary critics, although a growing number of researchers in other fields — some of them mentioned above — have begun to yield findings that promise to reshape dramatically the investigative landscape within the humanities.

The broader argument of the present book is, in light of the ambitious task of mapping out the various intersections between written texts and verbal discourse, a relatively modest one. My goal is not to convince readers of the social roots of written narrative per se, but rather to show what can be learned about these texts when we focus on how humans engage them within socially embedded activities. If I am making any sort of larger theoretical statement, it is that the uses to which members of human communities put written texts have a great deal to do with what these texts in turn *mean* — a point that seems simple enough when we are speaking about a restaurant menu or a telephone directory, but one that becomes murky when we begin to classify texts as "literary," "artistic," or "canonical" (Fish 1980). In fact, and this may sound heretical coming from a literary scholar (a medievalist, no less), literary texts do have a great deal in common with restaurant menus and telephone directories, and not simply due to the almost unbridled use of figurative language common in both the "literary" and "nonliterary" examples. From the point of view of the reader, the most significant feature that characterizes both works of "literature" such as novels and "nonliterary" works of writing such as a restaurant menu or a brochure is the fact that whenever we read a novel, consult the business listings, or peruse the daily specials, we are doing so for a purpose and always within socially embedded settings shaped by more broadly framed activities and goals.

Even when we take into consideration the most common of lectoral *topoi,* the reader sitting alone, absorbed by a novel that he or she is reading for pleasure, we are never divorced from the temporal and social situatedness of lectoral practices. There is, for example, the mere affordability of the private copy that our reader holds (and if a library copy, then we must consider the institutions that support and control access to it), and all of the socio-historical forces, on a personal as well as communal level, that have shaped his or her habitus vis-à-vis the novel as a cultural artifact containing written signs. And what about the question of time itself? As Miguel de Cervantes suggests with customary irony throughout the introduction to the *Quijote,* the *desocupado lector* (literally, that "unoccupied reader" with time to spend) is a strange thing. Such a reader is also a relatively recent creation of Western culture, as much the product of capitalist modes of production as of the ideological underpinnings of the bourgeoisie. *To read for pleasure,* that is, to be predisposed to spend time — at least at the conscious level — reading just for the sake of reading, is a highly contextualized, historically situated phenomenon. It is also, even today, an activity that remains for the most part off-limits to members of many minority communities, as well as the many millions of humans living in poverty. Reading for pleasure, put quite plainly, is an activity inseparable from issues revolving around social class and ethnicity. As Bourdieu has pointed out, people's embodied dispositions (for example, to engage a written text at all), as well as their aspirations and limitations are intricately tied up in the social world that lies beyond, though somehow also within, the written text (1990).

For the better part of the world that has something resembling regular contact with written texts — whether this means price tags, personal letters, street signs, and government forms or the classics of European literature — readers are always occupied and for the most part conscious of this occupation. Like readers and the listening public before social changes in Cervantes's time produced a class of readers that could spend time as they would money on "idle pursuits" such as reading chivalric potboilers, most of us are aware of the fact that we always read *in-order-to*. The socially embedded, *occupied* nature of reading — so even for our reader quietly absorbed by the novel though he or she is conscious only of the (culturally mediated) pleasure felt while *in acto legendi* — puts the written text on very different footing. And a critical approach that focuses on the occupied character of reading and readership, and the practices of the human agents thus occupied, similarly puts the literary project on a different terrain: rather than framing texts as motionless art objects or seemingly autonomous webs of signification, we consider written texts of all sorts as instruments that mediate human practice and interaction, as tools for communication in the social sphere. To further illustrate this point, we will turn now to Martin Heidegger's particularly lucid and rich presentation of ideas regarding instrumentality, time, and practice.

Written Narrative and the Tools of Time: Heidegger's Clock

Lecturing on time and temporality at the University of Marburg in 1927, Heidegger chose to illustrate his ideas regarding time and being-in-the-world by speaking at length about what it means to read a clock. Embedding both the instrumentality of the clock and the direction of our individual attention toward time within a practical framework of phenomenological experience, Heidegger explains:

> In using a clock, in reading time from it, we do indeed look at the clock but the clock itself is not the object of our regard. We do not occupy ourselves, for example, with our watch as such, as this particular instrument, so as to distinguish it, say, from a coin. . . . When I use a clock to read the time, I am also *not directed toward time as the proper object* of my vision. I make neither clock nor time the theme of my regard. When I look at my watch I ask, for instance, how much time still remains for me until the scheduled end of the lecture. I am not searching for time as such in order to occupy myself with it; on the contrary, I am occupied in giving a phenomenological exposition. . . . I make inquiry

of the clock with the aim of determining how much time I still have to do this or that. (1982, 258; italics in original)

For Heidegger, neither the clock *qua* clock nor time as a concept (in the Kantian sense) are what we are "occupied with" when we read the time. Instead, both time and the instrument by which we order its passing come embedded in already-existent frameworks of action, experience, and a concern for the future that Heidegger would come to term "care" (*Sorge*).

Speaking of Heidegger's notion of "care" and the fundamental role of narrative in people's lives, Elinor Ochs and Lisa Capps have pointed out that Heidegger's ideas about the "in-order-to-ness" of such cultural tools as narrative (and, by extension, the artifacts that mediate its engagement) directly address the emotionally charged and temporal aspects of individual and communal life:

> [A]nticipation has an untamed, anxious edge, which can prompt those recounting personal experience to disrupt the orderly logic of past events and voice pangs of concern for what the past means for them at present and for their uncharted future. This interpretation of anticipation is based on Martin Heidegger's phenomenological concept of temporality, wherein a primal human "Care" about death, and thus the future, infuses, organizes, and overwhelms how we remember and represent the past. In this view, past events become less remote and more intimate when people invest them with a sense of engagement and concern for what lies ahead in the life course. The past is then pulled or "stretched" into the realm of present consciousness, including trepidation about the future. In this sense, the apprehended past still endures, still *is*. This face of human time is quintessentially nonlinear, in that past, present, and future are sensed holistically. (2001, 157)

Turning to *aljamiado-morisco* narrative, evidence of the nonlinear workings of narrative with respect to both trepidation about the future and the "stretching" of the past among Castilian and Aragonese crypto-Muslims is not difficult to find. In the early seventeenth-century preface to the no longer extant *Guía de la salvación, kompuesto por Abdelkarím Juan del Rincón, para uso de sus hermanos los muçlimes* (Guide to salvation, composed by Abdelkarím Juan del Rincón, for the use of his brothers the Muslims) translated into English by Pascual de Gayangos, we find a dramatic reworking of past events, present practices, and future concerns:

God having been pleased to permit that the Moors of this country should be afflicted and oppressed with so many persecutions, allowed in his infinite wisdom that the affairs of our religion should be brought to such extremity, that it is not practised either in public or private. Prayer is laid aside and forgotten, and the few who still perform it do so secretly, and consequently with fear, and without the necessary devotion: the fast is not observed, or if so, far from the manner in which it ought to be; the accustomary alms abolished; the annual festivals and their tithes sunk in oblivion; the invocation of Allah and his beloved messenger never heard; or, if they invoke them, they do not call them by their proper names in our language. All this is owing, first of all, to the circumstances that have placed the Moors for so many years far from any spiritual advice; and secondly, to the tyranny of the Christians, who have caused them to be all forcibly baptized through fear and terror. Their books are all lost, and scarcely any remembrance remains of them; the doctors of the law are no more, some are dead, others lie in prison; the Inquisition displays against us its utmost fury and oppression, so that few parts of the kingdom are free from fire and faggot; the newly baptized Moors are everywhere seized and punished with gallies, rack and fire, and other chastisements best known to God, the master of all secrets. These intolerable torments and other calamities we have endured till the present day, for a space of seventy-six years, with greater fury and vigour than at the first beginning [sic]. Now, I ask you what knowledge can we have of religion and its dogmas, how can we serve God, if we are continually disturbed and perplexed? (Gayangos 1839, 79)

In this extended passage, Abdelkarím Juan del Rincón brings both the recent historical and traditional Islamic past together in order to construct and present theories regarding the troubling state of Islamic religious practice among Moriscos in Spain. Also significant, however, is the way in which he infuses his narrative with his worries about the future of his community, asking his rhetorical interlocutor: "what knowledge can we have of religion and its dogmas, how can we serve God if we are continually disturbed and perplexed?" These questions, which forge a complex interpenetration of past events, current practices, and a range of potential futures (none of them particularly promising), cut right to the heart of matters concerning the survival of the Moriscos as a Muslim community, at least from the point of view of the most learned and religious sectors of their society: when they are finally, fully separated from all Islamic knowledge and practice, they will quite simply cease to be. And this "ceasing to be," as Anthony Paul Kerby has pointed out, is filled with meaning and affect: "Our time — a time of indifference, a time of joy and hope, a time of despair — is bound not simply by a beginning and end, but between what can more richly be described as 'birth' and 'death'; we do not 'end,' we die" (1991, 17).

Returning to Heidegger's clock, it is possible to perceive a means of addressing in written narratives the emotional charge and "human" temporality that Ochs and Capps speak of in verbal narratives of personal experience. For that clock, an instrument by which we reckon with time submerged within the practical activities of our daily lives, mediates our contact with the temporal horizon of our existence, shapes it, and in a sense, helps us to construct and test local theories of reality (e.g., "Two hours is a long time to be sitting there watching television" or "Eating dinner at 11:00 p.m. is just too late for me"). According to Heidegger, we read a clock in order to see where we stand in relation to activities in which we are, have been, and possibly will be engaged. This means that the clock, engaged as a practical instrument or tool, cannot help us to uncover metaphysical truths about time. The clock's inability to speak to transcendental values presents no real crisis, however, for in any case, we are not looking for metaphysical truths when we "read the time." We merely inquire as to where we stand vis-à-vis the movement of the world around us. We wish to know, in very quotidian terms, "how long" we have been doing something, "how much longer" before we begin something else, and so on.

Most written narratives do not deal explicitly with time as a theme, and we generally do not read them in order to occupy ourselves with time (certain science fiction masterpieces aside). There are, nonetheless, important parallels between written narratives and the clock in Heidegger's example. The first of these parallels, and perhaps the most important for the present study, is the notion that whether we are occupying ourselves with a clock or with a written narrative text, we are engaging in an activity that is inherently saturated by context. In other words, we produce, alter, and otherwise engage written narratives in the very same social world in which we live and interact with other people, making whatever meaning we might ascribe to these texts contingent upon the activities within (and often beyond) which they are used. This point is underscored by William Hanks in his broader study of the relation between language and reality:

> This relational perspective [between verbal expressions and context]
> struggling to emerge indicates that there are many factors that come
> between language forms and reality. These include the immediate social
> setting of speech, the cultural and ideological values that participants
> bring to interaction, their cognitive activities, and particular projects.
> To posit a dichotomy between language and the world is erroneous be-
> cause it ignores these mediating factors. The more productive challenge
> from our perspective is to find a way of systematically describing the
> social embeddedness of language. (1996, 120)

Attempting to describe systematically the "social embeddedness of language" is all the more important when we speak of written language
use, given that beyond the mediating factors listed by Hanks, we must
also inevitably attend to the cultural artifacts (e.g., books, loose folios,
road signs, computer screens) through which we engage written forms
of language. The worldly, culturally structured, and situated character
of all written language use — insofar as such language use depends upon
the implementation of cultural artifacts such as paper and parchment for
its existence — in fact requires a great deal of effort to ignore. And as
I will be pointing out throughout the chapters of the present book that
deal with specific *aljamiado-morisco* texts, the individual forms taken
by the cultural artifacts that mediate narrative do matter a great deal in
our attempts to determine the contextualized meaning of the texts they
contain.

Leaving aside a discussion of the specific mediating properties of given
written language forms such as the handwritten *aljamiado* books and
loose folios of Castilian and Aragonese Moriscos, we may accept for the
moment the general hypothesis that these written forms, like their verbal
counterparts, are most fully understood when close textual analysis is
coupled with a consideration of their indexical relation to the social
processes within and by which they are produced and used. In this way,
written narratives are very similar to the clock in Heidegger's example.

In the present book I argue for an approach to the written narratives
of Castilian and Aragonese crypto-Muslims that radically contextualizes
them, embedding them within temporal frameworks of "care" and the
cultural (and agentive) practice of members of these communities. I do
this in spite of the dramatic and largely influential claims made by other
writers (e.g., Goody and Watt 1968; Havelock 1982; and Ong 1982) for
the simultaneously decontextualized nature of written language use and
the profound cognitive effects that the acquisition of alphabetic literacy

per se can have on people. As psychological work in the Vygotskian tradition — most notably Scribner and Cole's literacy research among the Vai people of Northwestern Liberia (1981) — has shown, the claims made by those who subscribe to the "autonomous" view of literacy (as it is described by Street [1984] in the course of his elaboration of a more socially rooted paradigm of literacy study) are not borne out in ethnographic studies of reading and writing across cultures. Reflecting a more situated, though not necessarily more particularistic slant on reading and writing activities in cultural settings, Heath has described literacy as a "culturally organized systems of skills and values learned in specific settings" (1980, 126). Niko Besnier, echoing Heath's comments, reminds his readers:

> Despite their microscopic form, literate exchanges articulate the larger structures in which they are embedded. For example, when literate communities are embedded in a colonial context, or when they constitute different social classes or gender groups in a complex society, the differences in their literacy activities are no longer simply instances of the heterogeneity of literacy as a mode of communication. Rather, they become part of a dynamics of domination and resistance, structure and agency, and reproduction and change. In such contexts, certain literacy activities are valued, exalted, and employed as gatekeepers restricting access to institutions and other organs of power. Others are devalued or simply not defined as literacy or communication at all.... Literacy, like many other social activities (even beyond the realm of communication), thus mediates between microscopic, person-centered, and agentive behavior and macroscopic, structural, overarching, and reproduction-centered institutions, ideologies, and similar categories. To use terminology now well established in anthropology from the work of Pierre Bourdieu, literacy activities are thus another form of habitus. (1999, 142)

By approaching literacy as a form of habitus, Besnier is able to work between the micro-level person-to-person exchanges that make up literacy practices in most settings and the macro-level structural and institutional forces that shape and are shaped in turn by human interaction around written texts.

What I would like readers to draw from this short anthropological exposition is the idea that there is much more to be gained by studying the workings of written language within social contexts and its incorporation into and shaping of the activities carried out by members of human communities.[1] Or, to continue with Heidegger's example of "reading time," we may say that just as Heidegger makes use of a clock to check, for example, how much time is left until the end of his lecture, so we make use of written narratives to mediate our actions and interactions (at the micro- and macro-levels) in the world. Even when we read silently alone, after all, we are engaging in a situated activity shaped and conditioned by a wide range of social factors, some historical and others emergent (not the least of these being the complex processes of socialization by which we have come to be "literate" members of a particular speech community in the first place).[2]

Another important parallel between written narratives and the example of Heidegger's clock is the dual nature of both with respect to time. Clocks are at once cultural artifacts designed to reflect agreed-upon ideas regarding the ordering of time (e.g., the division of a day into twenty-four sixty-minute hours) and devices that mediate our continued negotiation of culture-specific ideas of temporality and our life world. Cognitive anthropologist Ed Hutchins (1995) has spoken of clocks and other objects as material anchors for the generation of conceptual blends within situated activities, highlighting the mapping that often occurs between conceptual spaces (as time is often metaphorically understood) and physical spaces (such as the spaces between the numbers on an analog wristwatch) in human social life. According to Hutchins, the sort of conceptual blending that forms the very fabric of human cognition is in many cases supported by material structures that are both found in the world (such as stars and shadows) and culturally created (such as watches and compasses). The result of such interaction with objects in the world is a complex cognitive process that puts the material and social world in direct contact with our "inner" psychological world — showing in fact, the extent to which these objects shape the way we think and interact. It is in this very fundamental practice of "cognition in the wild" (to use Hutchins's phrase) that clocks not only reflect cultural values and practices regarding time, but also play a mediational role in the ongoing shaping of these and other cultural phenomena.

Apart from explicitly anthropological and psychological attempts to deal with narrative and human experience, there have also been important efforts in literary criticism and philosophy to understand the dynamic relations between narrative and processes fundamental to human cognition and sense-making. Beyond George Lakoff and Mark Johnson's now classic study of metaphor (1980), research into cognitive mapping has recently led Mark Turner to go so far as to theorize human cognition and meaning-making itself as a distinctly *literary* process:

> We typically conceive of concepts as packets of meaning. We give them labels: marriage, birth, death, force, electricity, time, tomorrow. Meanings seem localizable and stable.
>
> But parable gives us a different view of meaning as arising from connections across more than one mental space. Meaning is not a deposit in a concept-container. It is alive and active, dynamic and distributed, constructed for local purposes of knowing and acting. Meanings are not mental objects bounded in conceptual places but rather complex operations of projection, binding, linking, blending, and integration over multiple spaces. Meaning is parabolic and literary. (1996, 57)

According to Turner, the mapping that occurs as humans generate meaning in everyday activities involves multiple processes of projection and crossing that he sees as virtually indistinguishable from the peculiarly *literary* activity of engaging parables. In this way Turner takes narrative imagining, traditionally seen as "extra" or "optional" by psychologists and literary critics alike, and frames it as "inseparable from our evolutionary past and our necessary personal experience" (1996, 25).

Carr's philosophical work on narrative (especially historiographical narratives) and human experience/action, of which I have already briefly spoken, similarly reframes narrative imagining as a central feature by which humans encounter and act in the world. Carr argues that the separation of "reality" from "narrative accounts of reality" is fundamentally misleading, given that our contact with phenomena always possesses, at its root, the structure of narrative:

> A double error is committed by those who associate beginning, middle, and end only with the narration (rather than the events narrated) and then go on to consider this relation atemporal because the written text, as a collection of marks or sentences, is all there at once. A text is no different from anything else: without time it can have no beginning, middle, and end. Its sentences are spatially arranged and some may be logically interconnected, and its pages are numerically ordered, but unless it is gone through temporally it neither begins nor ends. It just sits there on the shelf. And its only middle is a spatial point equidistant from its edges.
>
> But the more serious mistake is the one which identifies the beginning-middle-end structure exclusively with the narration in the first place. As we have seen, this structure belongs just as surely to human events —

experiences and actions — about which stories are told, and, more important, it belongs to them whether or not a story, in the sense of a literary text, is told about them at all. What is more, if we are right, this structure belongs essentially to such events; they could not exist without it. (1986, 51–52)

For Turner, our brains work in ways that can be described as literary; for Carr, our experience of and actions in the world are always temporally structured as "events" with the sort of beginning-middle-end structure described a century ago by Husserl. For this reason, there can be no distinction between what we see as reality "out there" and our narrative accounts of that reality, for whatever we mean by "reality" (or, in historiographical terms, "what really happened") *always* implies a distinctly situated, human reality that is shaped and given meaning by what Gary Saul Morson has termed "the human dimension of time" (1994, 4). Or, to use the language of philosophical hermeneutics, our existence as historically situated beings-in-the-world makes it so that we cannot experience the world around us (or ourselves) in any other way except as a finite series of temporal, narratively structured phenomena. Speaking in general terms of the integral role that narrative (whether oral or written) plays in the shaping of human life, Ricoeur has made the argument that "the common feature of human experience, that which is marked, organized, and clarified by the act of storytelling in all its forms, is its *temporal character*" (1991, 2; italics in original). If we take Ricoeur's point seriously, then we are everywhere and in myriad ways reckoning with the human dimension of time when we occupy ourselves with narrative, whether verbal, written, or some combination of the two.

These ideas regarding human cognition, time, narrative, and the physical objects that mediate socially embedded processes of sense-making are crucial for an understanding of *aljamiado-morisco* literature as a social phenomenon. Basic questions, such as, "Why did the Moriscos continue to produce narrative texts in *aljamiado* given the dangers inherent in such activities?" take on new, more subtle, shades of meaning. Rather than seeing the narrative texts of Castilian and Aragonese crypto-Muslims as literary works that merely *reflected* cultural dispositions and ideologies, we begin to comprehend the powerful pragmatic charge that these handwritten texts had — how fundamentally *useful* they were to the people who engaged them. As mediators of practice, as material anchors for the socially embedded processes by which members of Morisco communities reckoned with their temporal existence, the handwritten narrative texts that we study are extraordinarily effective cultural tools.

But understanding the importance (and ramifications) of considering the human dimension of time in our analyses of *aljamiado-morisco* narrative texts is not the same thing as having a method for studying these texts in light of such understanding. For this reason, I would like to devote the rest of this chapter to a discussion of methodological considerations. In particular, I will be speaking of two processual framings that have greatly influenced the manner in which many social scientists have come to approach narratives and text in general. The first of these methodological framings involves inquiring into the dynamic connections in force between written texts and the cultural practice of human communities by focusing jointly on the texts themselves and the varied processes by which they come to be, are altered, resituated, reused, and applied in settings seemingly unrelated to the act of reading. In other words, rather than focusing on texts and their contexts (e.g., cultural, historical, political, etc.), researchers in a growing number of fields have instead begun to focus on written texts and the ongoing process of "contextualization" that gives them shape.

Contextualization

The current focus on contextualization has as its primary stimulus the theoretical work of folklorist Richard Bauman and anthropologist Charles L. Briggs, who have argued that a concerted shift "from the study of texts to the analysis of the emergence of texts in contexts" represents a central component of sufficiently nuanced approaches to verbal art in fields such as linguistics, folklore, and anthropology (1990, 59). Based on earlier ethnography of communication research by sociolinguists such as Dell Hymes (1972, 1974) and John Gumperz (1982), such a shift involves an expanding critical focus from purely referential analysis (what or how does a given strip of talk or writing mean?) to include a consideration of how verbal and written texts mediate discursive interaction (how do human agents make and use texts to construct their social world?) in a very explicit way. A central aspect of this expanded focus, inspired largely by the work of the Bakhtin Circle, is — as I have mentioned in the previous chapter — a reevaluation of both the concept of context itself and its role within the social construction of reality.

William Hanks addresses the question of context and its relation to cultural and linguistic analysis in his book-length study of language and communicative practices. Beginning the chapter (aptly titled "Saturation by Context") he writes:

> What is context? Everything and nothing. Like a shadow, it flees from those who pursue it, evading the levels and categories of theory, and pursues those who try to flee from it, insinuating itself as the unnoticed ground upon which even the most explicit statements depend. If you are persuaded by the phenomenological concept of incompleteness, then context is inexhaustible. The more you try to specify it, the more blank spots you project, all in need of filling in. Ultimately, context is nothing less than the human world in which language use takes place and in relation to which language structure is organized. How we describe it and what properties of organization and duration we ascribe to it depend upon what we focus on. In other words, because context is so pervasive, "context" is necessarily a theoretical construct. (1996, 140)

As a theoretical construct, a metalinguistic abstraction in most forms of native and analytical expression, the notion of context needs to be examined with some thoroughness and flexibility. Hanks, concerned with addressing context as it reveals itself in actual speech events, argues against Saussurian and Chomskyan approaches to context and linguistic forms, maintaining that their methods lead to a sort of infinite regress:

> In its strong versions [linguistic] formalism presumes that the encoded meaning of a sentence is transparent, however vague its implications when used on a given occasion. The Chomskyan sentence is either anomalous, unequivocal, or ambiguous, in which case it is associable with a limited number of possible semantic readings. And the tacit assumption is that fully competent speakers intend just one reading for their utterance. Thus, we add to the form features of context that serve to disambiguate it and nail down its core meaning. This view is akin to the Chomskyan program for studying performance: Start from forms that in no way depend upon the situations of their production, define them, and then observe what happens when they are realized in actual situations. The situations are never explored beyond their providing frames for the occurrence of the forms. If Saussure had discussed the study of *parole*, it is likely he would have said something similar.
> This approach leads to an impossible task, however, because you never know when you have added enough context to fix the meaning.

> And moreover, for every meaning that arises in a context, there is always another context in which the meaning would be different. (1996, 140–41)

What underlies Hanks's remarks is the need not for new analytical tools to fix the meaning of linguistic forms or texts within contexts, but an entirely new vocabulary for dealing with the meaning of linguistic forms as an integral component and product of social practice. "As long as we start from the analytic division between linguistic form and use, the problem [of indeterminacy] remains insurmountable" (Hanks 1996, 141). Hanks's main point, that the continued separation of *langue* and *parole* (not to mention the perceived primacy of the former over the latter) creates a situation in which meaning will always be indeterminate, is especially true of written texts, whose form depends, as I have argued above, to such a great degree upon their use in socially embedded settings. One could characterize, in fact, much poststructuralist criticism — but especially that of Jacques Derrida — as a *reductio ad absurdem* argument against the primacy of *langue* and the indeterminacy that the separation of *langue* and *parole* ("competence" and "performance" in the Chomskyan paradigm) creates.

The indeterminacy of context is a particularly vexing problem for analyses of historical discourse (such as the handwritten texts of Castilian and Aragonese Moriscos), as it is the very reconstruction of the local networks of textual production and use that give shape to context that is absent. We have written texts, but no community. How to work backward to establish the local networks of language use that gave meaning to the texts that we study? This is no simple task given the recent reconceptualization of context and its relation to discourse that I have just sketched out. Nonetheless, it is a mistake to shrink from this analytical challenge. To claim defeat and focus solely on the internal structure of the manuscript texts of the Moriscos is to miss the point that these texts drew (and continue to draw) their force and meaning from their continuous and dynamic relation to social contexts whose generation they themselves helped to construct. In other words, by leaving aside the question of context, we take in the trees, but miss the forest altogether.

And there are, after all, methodological clues available to us if we seek them out. Excellent examples of highly provocative and thorough examinations of historical discourse, culture, text, and context can be found in Joanne Rappaport and Tom Cummins's study of colonial Andean textuality and its embeddedness in ritual practice (1998) and Digges and Rappaport's aforementioned analysis of literacy, orality, and ritual practice in Highland Colombia (1993). At the very conclusion of their study on the idea of written media and cultural practice in colonial Quechua-speaking society, Rappaport and Cummins argue:

> What our small example demonstrates is that literacy is a strategy intrinsic to Spanish colonization in the Americas (as well as in other parts of the globe). What is to be found in its legacy, the myriad of documents, is not a neutral gathering of data to be ordered and analyzed. Documents, visual as well as textual, and the technologies used to produce them, are social and cultural forms that are variously enacted. To think of a signature as a relic or the king's signature as a *quillca* [a Quechua term that suggests a sort of intersection between written historical record, sculpture, and painting] suggests that much more is at stake than the neutral transcription or rendering of something. Media and genre intersect in unexpected ways. Not only do they refer to each other in an intertextual series, but they socially overlap in the rituals of colonial religion and administration. They become things in the colonial world that operate at a variety of levels and in so doing are both transformed and transforming. This gives documents a certain agency or efficacy that exceeds the intentions of their authors. We therefore suggest that one of the key issues before us is to begin to think of the relationship between the visual and the written as a condition of colonial praxis that is never static or stable. (1998, 24)

Like Don Kulick and Christopher Stroud's (1993) ethnographic study of the native inversion of literacy practices brought to Papua New Guinea by Christian missionaries, Rappaport and Cummins's article provides an in-depth sense of how seventeenth- and eighteenth-century Quechua-speaking communities contextualized features of Spanish colonial documents within local speech genres in a manner wholly unintended by Spanish officials. Working from textual data, but with a flexibility and attention to concrete detail with respect to the documents that serve as the material support for these texts, Rappaport and Cummins are able to produce a rare and valuable portrait of indigenous cultural practice during the colonial period.

The implications of such an approach to emergent context in historical settings, as well as the "efficacy" that written documents of various genres and orders can possess in new social settings, are potentially far-reaching within the study of literature and textual studies in general. One of the main effects that such a rethinking of context has had within anthropological approaches to poetry and verbal art is to shift analytical focus away from normative, generic rules of composition and/or interpretation and place it squarely on the fluid give-and-take always in force between participants in text-mediated discourse:

> Contextualization involves an active process of negotiation in which participants reflexively examine the discourse as it is emerging, embedding assessments of its structure and significance in the speech itself. Performers extend such assessments to include predictions about how the communicative competence, personal histories, and social identities of their interlocutors will shape the reception of what is said. Much research has focused on the way this meta-level process is incorporated into the textual form of performances, particularly in the case of narratives. (Bauman and Briggs 1990, 69)

Within this framework, poetic texts derive their full meaning through situated acts of performance in which participants collaboratively generate/embed specific texts, or sets of texts, within the flow of discursive interaction.

Judith Irvine's ethnographic study of Wolof insult poems (*xaxaar*) in rural Senegal provides an excellent example of research concerned with the contextualization of poetic texts. She insightfully maps out the ways in which shifting participation frameworks (who is speaking? to whom? who is present? whose words are being spoken and by whom?) and deictic fields — personal and temporal — function as contextualizing features that give meaning to these poems in performance, situating them in the social life of the community. With respect to the texts themselves, Irvine places them in relation with the ever-growing body of conversational commentary and gloss that accompanies them:

> Perhaps one would want to say that the independence, or pragmatic transcendence, of this set of utterances — what makes it a transferable object — is what gives it a sense of "textuality." But if so, it is a textuality that presupposes the conversational moments it purports to transcend. . . . As the chain of discourse progresses, the "transcendent" text carries traces of its history along with it, as the conversations in which it is repeated provide new reportable material that add to its significance. (1996, 156–57)

Such an ethnographic observation has important implications for the study of *aljamiado-morisco* literature, for it is through active relation with analogous "chains of discourse" that the handwritten narrative texts of Castilian and Aragonese crypto-Muslims derived their social force. Similar to Dagenais's ideas regarding "adaptation" and "application" in medieval reading (1994, 56–79), the processes by which *aljamiado-morisco* narrative texts were copied, recopied, emended, performed, and applied are interrelated and central aspects of what these texts meant in any contextualized sense.

A new focus on the details of this process of contextualization (hinted at in broader strokes by earlier philological work and theories of reception) has dramatically altered the sorts of questions researchers working with texts (including written texts) ask. As Michael Silverstein and Greg Urban argue in the introduction to their edited book on contextualization and ethnographic practice:

> The text-artifact does indeed have a physical-temporal structure, precisely because it was originally laid down, or sedimented, in the course of a social process, unfolding in real time.... We seek the durational event of the laying-down process, insofar as traces of the original co(n)text in which a discourse fragment was configured are available to us. So what we are looking for is not the denotational text simply and directly, but rather indications of more originary interactional text(s) of inscription. We seek the residue of past social interaction carried along with the sign vehicle encoding the semantic, or denotational, meaning in denotational text. (1996, 5)[3]

These statements are partially echoed in Francisco Rico's arguments regarding manuscript study and performance:

> The most complex versions and performances are by definition inaccessible to us, but there is nothing more simple than to compare the versatility of the copies to which we do have access. There is also nothing more understandable: each copy could not but reflect the impulse that had given it origin. (1996, 251)[4]

The argument implicit in both Silverstein and Urban's, as well as Rico's, comments is that text-artifacts can be approached as the residue of socially embedded, discursive interaction. To cite Rico, each medieval text-artifact ultimately "could not but *reflect* the impulse that had given it origin." Like Silverstein and Urban, Rico posits that "the text implied and mobilized an unwritten context and gave rise to an activity" (247).[5]

For Silverstein and Urban, it is the "impulse" to which Rico refers, as well as the socially bounded mechanics by which it is transformed into text, that serve as their explicit object of study.

The question that remains, however, is whether the text-artifacts that Silverstein and Urban describe serve only as "residue of past social interaction" or if they also had, and still possess, the power to shape future social interaction in turn.[6] Are text-artifacts merely "residue" in the Ongian sense, or do they also operate within the "complex, multidimensional web of interrelationships" that link other texts such as those performed in folkloric settings, to "culturally defined systems of meaning and interpretation and to socially organized systems of social relations" (Bauman 1996, 141–42)? Clearly the term "artifact" itself is problematic, as it fixes the written text within an already-occurred past as a more or less lifeless thing, a sedimented product of ephemeral social processes that have passed and left only an object for interpretation behind. Within this framework, the written word is the scuff mark left on the floor, not part of the dance itself.

There is validity to this formulation of the "text-artifact," but only as a part of a larger picture. For while written texts serve as the residue or endpoint of certain processes, they may also function, as I have suggested above, as integral components in the performance of a wide range of other discursive activities. Like Heidegger's clock, written texts are always engaged "in order to . . . "; meaning that written texts — whether we see them as artifacts or not — inevitably find their full expression and meaning in situated activities. One of these activities, of course, is the complex procedure by which one manuscript copy becomes another manuscript copy (the central focus of Dagenais's call to refocus medieval literary study on "lecturature"), or how an orally transmitted text finds its way into written form. Clues of similar processes of contextualization are found within the manuscripts that contain *aljamiado-morisco* narrative texts: marginal notes, lectoral commentaries, code-switching between Castilian, Aragonese, and Arabic, even the quality of the paper upon which texts are written tell us a great deal about the processes by which copies of books came to be and became new copies in turn.

A focus on contextualization and its encoding within *aljamiado-morisco* manuscripts also tells us a fair amount about how these books were read, interpreted, and made use of within the communities that held them. It is only a matter, as Dagenais has argued, of focusing on the concrete evidence before us, though perhaps in heretofore unthought of ways.

Traditionalization

The process of contextualization is one that unmistakably deals with the human dimension of time, and analyses of contextualization within and across particular settings can lay out in surprising, micro-level detail the movement "through time" of handwritten texts from copy to copy. There is also another, related way in which researchers have focused on texts — specifically traditional ones — as contextualized elements of social interaction. This analytical focus, referred to as *traditionalization* by Richard Bauman in his study of Icelandic legends of the *kraftaskáld* (1992), is of particular use to scholars dealing with *aljamiado-morisco* literature, given its focus on the complex issues that underlie the implementation of traditional texts — such as the majority of narrative texts produced by Castilian and Aragonese Moriscos — within novel settings. Bauman defines traditionalization in the following terms:

> Tradition, long considered a criterial attribute of folklore, is coming to be seen less as an inherent quality of old and persistent items or genres passed on from generation to generation, and more as a symbolic construction by which people in the present establish connections with a meaningful past and endow particular cultural forms with value and authority. Thus, the focus of attention is the strategic process of traditionalization rather than a quality of traditionality that is considered to inhere in a cultural form conceived of as akin to a persistent natural object. (128)

The simultaneously backward- and forward-looking process by which members of human communities engage texts from the past (importantly, a past they somehow understand as their own) in such a way as to construct them as authoritative and "traditional" works not only to shape the very traditionality of the texts themselves, but also to grant legitimate authority to activities and discourse in the present.

The fact is, we often make use of "traditional" texts (such as folkloric and patriotic songs) in order to shape our future, or at least mitigate our anxiety about it. One need only cast a glance back to the frequent performances of "God Bless America" in the wake of the September 11, 2001, terrorist attacks in New York City and Washington, D.C., to see the powerful role that traditional texts can have in moments of communal crisis and doubt, especially when these texts are sanctioned by institutions such as elected governments recognized to have legitimate authority. In addition, we should also take note that the ways in which "God Bless America" was used and performed in the weeks following the attacks (as bodies were pulled from the rubble of the World Trade Center and a national anthrax scare began to cause new worries) also served to change — perhaps indelibly — the contextualized *meaning* of that particular song for many Americans: a song once associated with childhood civics lessons and school assemblies was quickly transformed into something of a national prayer. And while a little ironic distance from patriotic songs and flag waving amid national crises is probably healthy, even cynical observers (myself included) could not help but sense that an old song was taking on something very new as three-hundred-pound NFL linemen sang it, weeping, before a game. Or that this old song was being used precisely because it was so old, and the fear so new.

Turning to the details of Bauman's study, we find a similar, if less dramatic, account of the ways in which texts produced and reproduced in contemporary settings make use of traditional discourse in order to achieve a wide range of goals, both consciously and otherwise. The *kraftaskáld* were magical poets from Iceland who were believed to have had the power to affect the future through the sheer force of their verses, which they made up in moments of emotional excitement. Bauman, working with audio-recorded data collected in the late 1960s by Icelandic folklorist Hallfreður Örn Eríksson, analyzes a story told by an elderly informant, Jón Norðmann, about a *kraftaskáld* named Páll Jonsson who lived during the first half of the nineteenth century.[7] In Norðmann's narrative, Páll Jonsson engages in a poetic debate with a seasonal fisherman in which Jonsson issues a magical verse calling for his adversary to meet his end face-down in the wet sand and for his body to be found with its tongue missing. According to Norðmann, who heard the legend from his father, who had heard it in turn from Jonsson's daughter, this is precisely what happened to the fisherman: he drowned while sailing to the mainland and was found without a tongue (the theory being that a shrimp had eaten it).

Norðmann's telling possesses, according to Bauman, all of the thematic and formal features of a *kraftaskáld* legend. However, Bauman calls on his reader to look a bit more deeply at Norðmann's telling itself:

> From an agent-centered point of view . . . looking at Mr. Norðmann's
> storytelling as social practice, other questions must arise. What we have
> in this text is Mr. Norðmann directly and explicitly engaged in an act
> of symbolic construction, drawing the links of continuity by which he
> may tie his story to past discourses as part of his own recounting of
> it. This is the act of traditionalization, and it is part of the process
> of endowing the story with situated meaning. "The traditional begins
> with the personal" (Hymes 1975, 354) and the immediate here, not
> with some objective quality of pastness that inheres in a cultural object
> but with the active construction of connections that link the present
> with a meaningful past. (1992, 136)

The story as Norðmann tells it includes a string of other tellings
(i.e., Jonsson's daughter to Norðmann's father, Norðmann's father to
Norðmann, Norðmann to Erícksson), a move that serves to authenticate
Norðmann's telling: "If the original event is reportable, Mr. Norðmann's
direct connection with it through the links with his father and Páll's
daughter establishes and enhances the legitimacy of his claim to report
it himself" (Bauman 1992, 137).

In like fashion, the recounting — even in written form — of traditional
Islamic narratives among members of crypto-Muslim communities in
Castile and Aragon relies upon a direct connection to previous narra-
tors (referred to in Arabic as an *isnad,* or "chain") for its legitimacy
and authority in concrete settings. The written texts themselves, which
make full semantic use of the generic term *hadith* ("story," but also a
specific form of religious legal discourse), and begin with very solemn
invocations to God in Arabic, key the process of traditionalization,
often encoding previous traditionalizing events, much in the same way
that Norðmann embeds previous tellings of the Páll Jonsson legend in
his own.

As we shall see in subsequent chapters of the present study, the handwritten narratives of Castilian and Aragonese crypto-Muslims embed a
wide range of traditional forms, formulae, and discourse. Far from any
model of author- or text-centered "literature," these narratives found expression and meaning through inherently situated processes of collective
sense-making. The twin foci of contextualization and traditionalization
allow us to focus on these processes while not losing sight of the concrete manuscript evidence before us. Rather, they help us to attend to
the dynamic, socially embedded, and contingent nature of this literature

while digging even more deeply into the manuscript texts copied out by Morisco scribes.

The narrative texts of Castilian and Aragonese crypto-Muslims take us well beyond traditional literary analysis and into a decidedly anthropological realm. Framed this way, our investigation ceases to be occupied with explaining the *meaning* of these texts as some sort of autonomous or intrinsic value with only the most provisional links to cultural practice. Rather, it begins to inquire into these texts' socially embedded meaning(s) as handwritten narratives used by members of a string of loosely related communities over time. In short, we begin to ask how *aljamiado-morisco* narratives helped to give form to the lives of the people who engaged them — a subtle change of focus that makes all the difference. And as with the historical tales of the Western Apache, a sufficiently nuanced understanding of these narratives inevitably takes into account the integral role that the "human dimension of time" plays in the construction of contextualized meaning and the "sense" that Castilian and Aragonese crypto-Muslims made of their world.

3

Contexts of Rediscovery,
Contexts of Use

*. . . and we feel assured . . . that the Morisco literature, although the pro-
duction of a degraded and oppressed nation, and laying claim only to
an ephemeral existence, is highly deserving of the scholar's investigation, since it is embellished with all the wild flowers of their country,
and sparkles with true Arab genius.*
— Pascual de Gayangos (1839)

"A true America waiting to be discovered."[1] These are the words
that Serafín Estébanez Calderón (1799–1867), a prominent nineteenth-
century writer, political figure, book collector, and committed Arabist,
uses in his address at the Ateneo de Madrid on November 12, 1848,
to characterize the potential value of the *aljamiado-morisco* texts that
had been turning up in private collections and in areas of rural Spain
once inhabited by communities of crypto-Muslims.[2] Speaking at the ceremony inaugurating Pascual de Gayangos's chair in Arabic at the Ateneo,
Estébanez was likely unaware of the ominous associations that his America metaphor might engender, even prior to Spain's ignominious loss of
its last Transatlantic colonies in 1898 and its ill-fated incursions into
Morocco during the first quarter of the twentieth century. He must have
known, however, how the texts to which he was referring had come to be
lost or hidden in the first place, and of the prolonged human tragedy —
forced conversion, marginalization, and expulsion — that was encoded
in their folios.

Estébanez goes on to claim enthusiastically that the study of *aljamiado-
morisco* texts "would provide much material for the writer of customs
and the novelist, who would have a theme of great newness, being able to
separate themselves from the road worn down by imitation of the French"
(Galmés de Fuentes 1978, 190).[3] It may be somewhat hard to imagine how
Spanish novelists of the nineteenth century might have found inspiration

in the traditional narratives and Qur'anic commentaries that make up the bulk of *aljamiado-morisco* texts, especially given the fact that so few transcriptions of these texts existed. The image, for example, of Benito Pérez Galdós (a voracious reader and certifiable graphomaniac) plowing through the narrative texts of sixteenth-century Hispano-Muslim communities as research for a new novel of Spanish customs and manners — even in a historical setting — does seem to be a bit of a stretch. The truth is, to understand Estébanez's literary call-to-arms one must accept that his enthusiasm for these materials could at times seem over the top, even to his contemporaries. Speaking before the Real Academia Española in 1878, just eleven years after Estébanez's death, his nephew, Antonio Cánovas del Castillo, characterizes his deceased uncle's interest in *aljamiado-morisco* texts as a sort of benign madness: "surely no one has looked at this *aljamiado* literature with such special affection as Estébanez. It seemed in him a mania at times, albeit an inoffensive one, as literary manias tend to be" (61–62).[4] Estébanez was also the author of two moderately popular *costumbrista* novels dealing with Moorish themes (*Cristianos y moriscos* [Christians and Moriscos] and *Cuentos del Generalife* [Stories of the *Generalife*]), a fact that provides a little more insight into why — especially given his perceived *manía* — Estébanez would seek to promote *aljamiado-morisco* texts as rich resources for novelic and poetic work in Castilian over two centuries after the Moriscos' expulsion from Spain.

Estébanez was in many respects a singular personality, whose imaginative literary interest in Hispano-Arabic culture set him apart from more academic scholars such as Gayangos, Pablo Gil, Francisco Guillén Robles, Eduardo Saavedra, and, later Miguel Asín Palacios. However, he was also, in a very profound sense, a man of his time; and his enthusiasm for *aljamiado-morisco* literature — as well as the underlying motives for this enthusiasm — intersected with that of more highly trained Spanish Arabists in important ways. First, we must consider that in the decades between Spain's war of independence from the French and the formation of a short-lived republic inspired by unmistakably French ideals, Spain's cultural and intellectual elite often found itself scrambling to define and highlight what was inherently "Spanish" about Spain and its national culture. In this climate (which extended, in different forms, well into the twentieth century) folk culture, regional customs and literature, and even the Islamic past came to serve as effective tools for nation building. Hispano-Arabic culture, seen after the medieval Christian reconquest as an undesirable, foreign "Other," began to be reimagined in the nineteenth century as an integral component of what set Spain apart from its European neighbors — a historical point of view that Américo Castro would refine and express systematically in the middle of the twentieth century. While scholarly efforts and government support of serious investigations often did not match the perceived importance of this cultural effort vis-à-vis Spanish Islam, Estébanez's comments, both about the artistic utility of *aljamiado-morisco* texts and the need to move away from the "camino trillado por la imitación francesa," have their full meaning — along with his own intellectual caprices — within this context.

Perhaps the most interesting aspect of Estébanez's comments, apart from how these comments function within his not so subtle attempt to reconfigure and embed *aljamiado-morisco* texts within mid-nineteenth-century ideologies and practices of literary production (a complex process of recentering that incidentally characterizes much of what Morisco scribes and *alfakíes* did with the traditional Islamic material they inherited, as well), is the unintended irony that saturates his words. For example, it is at once striking that Estébanez frames *aljamiado-morisco* texts as somehow utterly Spanish, in essence glossing over the fact well known to him and to his colleagues at the Ateneo that these texts were considered inherently subversive and even criminal by Christian authorities in the sixteenth century. This is admittedly a rhetorical maneuver facilitated by the passing of two centuries without the social tensions between Christians and Muslims that prompted the Moriscos' expulsion (and the presence of much more powerful tensions between Spain and France by 1848); however, this fact does only a little to reduce the level of irony inherent in any attempt to recast crypto-Islamic texts — some of which openly expressed a desire to see Spain fall to the Ottoman Turks and have its Christian community punished for its cruel sins and spiritual blindness — as raw material for novels representative of "Spanish" themes and discourse.

Critical reevaluations of Hispano-Muslim (and Jewish) culture within the larger context of the Spanish nation-state such as those that underlie Estébanez's comments are difficult to carry out successfully, even in light of the rigorous historiographical revisionism of Américo Castro and his students (many of whom, such as Samuel Armistead, Carroll B. Johnson, and Francisco Márquez Villanueva, continue to work in American universities). Serafín Fanjul, professor of Arabic literature at the Universidad Autónoma de Madrid and a vocal skeptic of Castro's theories, has expressed the reservations of a significant portion of European and American academics with respect to the role of Semitic culture in the literary activities of medieval and Golden Age Spain as presented by the Castro school, arguing:

> Américo Castro and his hallowed followers have constructed for Spaniards the fiction of Christian converts (Jewish ones or Muslim ones, the same holds true for both) who infiltrate the cultural media of the age and infect them with their own *identity* — will it not be noticed that this is an extremely recent concept? — inoculating these media with a concern for "living as one deconstructs oneself" [*vivir desviviéndose*], a criticism of the dominant system of values, fear of the Inquisition, caste consciousness, the search for fame..., which can only be explained, according to Castro and his followers, by the Semitic origins of these authors; they sell "the literature of the Spanish Golden Age within the frame of a *conflictive society* — What society is not conflictive? — of caste confrontation; and in all the literature there would be, under the surface, a settling of accounts among Old Christians (the *Romancero*, the chivalric novel, the comedies of Lope de Vega, and Francisco de Quevedo belonged to this group) against New Christians." The *converso* (Jewish) origins of Santa Teresa or Mateo Alemán (both good Catholics) support stupendous generalizations, forgetting that the ones most interested in showing themselves to be loyal servants and addicts of the dominant culture and ideology were these same New Christians (2002, 58).[5]

Fanjul's critique of the theories of Américo Castro and his followers (Luce López Baralt, a former student at Harvard University of Francisco Márquez Villanueva, receives the brunt of his more pointed attacks) is admittedly less than fair. He presents Castro's theories as extreme and general, as a brilliant but hopelessly flawed response to a dominant trend in Spanish historiography that all but denied the significance of Semitic culture within the peninsula throughout the twentieth century (Sánchez Albornoz 1946, 1956). However, the majority of Castro's work — as well as that which he inspired — is much more subtle than Fanjul claims, and less prone to "stupendous generalizations" (Blackmore and Hutcheson 1999; Gilman 1972, 1989; Márquez Villanueva 1973, 1975, 1977, 1991; Johnson 1978, 2000). Nonetheless, it is difficult to defend Estébanez's comments along these same lines, given that he is not making the argument — as Castro and his students have — that mainstream Castilian works of literature such as *Don Quijote* and

Guzmán de Alfarache were in some profound sense shaped by *converso* ideologies and concerns; rather he is making the much more radical point that his contemporaries could employ their genius to convert *aljamiado-morisco* texts into mainstream Castilian products by simply recontextualizing them within nineteenth-century Spanish literary genres such as *costumbrista* novels and poetry. On another level too — as I have briefly alluded to above — there is a kind of elegant parallelism to the fact that Estébanez's efforts to resituate and revalorize *aljamiado-morisco* texts within the literary practices and values of Spain at a specific time in its history mirror the very processes of recontextualization by which crypto-Muslim scribes and readers in sixteenth-century Castile and Aragon were able to make use of much older, traditional Islamic materials in social settings radically different from any encountered by Muslim communities before them.

His arguments about the potential uses of *aljamiado-morisco* literature aside, what Estébanez could not have known was that the texts that he considered to be such a potentially rich, exploitable continent would fail so utterly to meet his or anyone else's lofty expectations. Far from a "true America waiting to be discovered," the texts of Spanish crypto-Muslims turned out to be more of a difficult and unpredictable land of largely anonymous and folkloric texts that were for the most part very difficult to read or understand except by specialists. A brief survey of research devoted to *aljamiado-morisco* literature throughout the nineteenth century shows exactly how limited critical interest in these texts was during this period, despite the momentary excitement generated by the discovery of new collections of Morisco books in Aragon during the last quarter of the century.

The earliest scholarly accounts of the *aljamiado* literature produced by Spanish crypto-Muslims were those of Pascual de Gayangos. Gayangos (1809–97) trained as an Arabist in France before serving in Spain's foreign office and eventually as professor of Arabic at the Universidad Complutense de Madrid, a post he held until 1881, when he was called to public office. His influence on subsequent generations of Spanish Arabists is difficult to overestimate, as are his material contributions to Spanish archives: the bulk of the *aljamiado-morisco* texts held by both the Biblioteca Nacional and the Biblioteca de la Real Academia de la Historia in Madrid were once part of his personal collection, as were many other rare manuscripts (Roca 1904; Galmés de Fuentes 1998).

Gayangos published a number of scholarly articles on Spanish and Hispano-Arabic literature while working in England between 1836 and 1843, including an 1839 study of *aljamiado-morisco* literature based largely on his growing personal collection of manuscripts. This early effort, published in the *British and Foreign Review* (entitled "Language and Literature of the Moriscos") is generally held to be the first modern scholarly study of Morisco literature and culture, although its principal goal seems to be to review Louis Vardot's *Essai sur l'histoire des Arabes et des Mores d'Espagne*, which had been published six years earlier in Paris. In this article Gayangos uses language not so different from that employed by Estébanez: he praises the poetic skills of Morisco writers, challenging his readers to compare "a sonnet of Garcilaso, the Petrarch of Spain, with the true Morisco romances [i.e., ballads], and he will soon perceive the immense advantage which, in point of simplicity and feeling, these small compositions possess over the best contrivances of the Castilian poets" (83). Such comments have their historical and political setting, as evidenced by Gayangos's comments on the state of Arabic studies in Spain during the mid-nineteenth century. Not mincing his words, Gayangos laments:

> [A]lthough the peninsula seems to be the place most fit for the culti-
> vation of the Arabic language and antiquities, — since it still retains
> many of the customs and manners introduced by the conquerors, with
> a language which owes a great deal of its richness and flexibility to
> the Arabic [*sic*] besides one eighth of its words, and a history, which,
> for a period of eight centuries, is intimately connected with that of the
> Arabs, — it is perhaps the only country in Europe where this study has
> been entirely neglected. No efforts whatsoever have been made by the
> government to increase the stock of books written in that language;
> and had it not been for the capture of two vessels with the emperor of
> Morocco's library, it becomes a matter of doubt whether Spain would
> have possessed a single Arabic MS. (65)

The scholarly and governmental neglect to which Gayangos refers provides an important backdrop to the energy that Arabists — even less scholarly ones such as Estébanez — brought to the *aljamiado-morisco* texts to which they had access. In the mind of a devoted Arabist such as Gayangos, these *aljamiado-morisco* texts, written in Castilian but unmistakably linked to the Arabic literature of the Andalusi period, could serve as a sort of bridge — a way to increase interest in and knowledge of Hispano-Arabic culture while simultaneously focusing on texts that were firmly part of the Castilian cultural heritage. Gayangos was not alone in presenting *aljamiado-morisco* texts in this way, as we shall see later in this chapter.

More than a decade after this first study, Gayangos published an edition of two Islamic legal treatises for the Real Academia de la Historia entitled "Tratados de legislación musulmana: *Leyes de moros del siglo XIV* y *Suma de los principales mandamientos y devedamientos de la Ley de Çunna* por don Içe de Gebir, Alfaquí mayor y muftí de la aljama de Segovia, año de 1462" (Treatises of Muslim legislation: The fourteenth-century *Leyes de Moros* and *Summa of the principal commandments and obligations of the Law of Sunna* written by Içe de Gebir, al-Faqi and Mufti of the Muslim community of Segovia in the year 1462) (1853). This work was followed in the same year by his "Glosario de las palabras aljamiadas y otras que se hallan en dos trabajos y en algunos libros de moriscos" (Glossary of *aljamiado* and other words found in two works and in a selection of Morisco books), published again by the Real Academia de la Historia. Gayangos's important early work on *aljamiado-morisco* literature failed to inspire a great number of followers, though he did manage to pique the interest of George Ticknor, who at Gayangos's suggestion included long passages on Morisco poetic texts in the final volume of his *History of Spanish Literature* (1849).

Beyond the attention afforded *aljamiado-morisco* literature by Gayangos and Ticknor, studies of these texts were infrequent and for the most part fragmented (e.g., Lord Stanley of Aderley's editions of the poetry of Muhammad Rabadán, published over the span of five years in the *Journal of the Asiatic Society*). On December 29, 1878, however, Eduardo Saavedra delivered his landmark *discurso* before the Real Academia Española, a comprehensive study of what was known about *aljamiado-morisco* literature at that time. Saavedra, a former student of Gayangos, published his *discurso* in the same year through the Real Academia Española along with a thorough survey of *aljamiado-morisco* literature and long citations of transcribed texts. The printed piece also contains eighty-seven pages of appendices with descriptions of the *aljamiado-morisco* manuscripts that were known to exist in 1878 and a glossary of terms found in them (published within this same volume is the aforementioned response to Saavedra's *discurso* delivered by Antonio Cánovas de Castillo in which the latter eulogizes Estébanez). Saavedra's study, despite its having been written over a century ago, continues to be a fundamental resource for scholars and students interested in the *aljamiado* literature of the Moriscos. Many modern studies, most notably Anwar Chejne's *Islam and the West: The Moriscos* (1983) and much of Alvaro Galmés de Fuentes's work, depend to a great extent on Saavedra's late nineteenth-century scholarship and his conclusions regarding the nature of *aljamiado-morisco* literature.

Six years after Saavedra's *discurso* before the Real Academia Española, a new collection of *aljamiado* books was found in rural Aragon (Almonacid de la Sierra), prompting new studies of the literary materials contained within the salvaged books. Francisco Codera Zaydin's "Almacén de un librero morisco descubierto en Almonacid de la Sierra" (Storehouse of a Morisco bookseller discovered in Almonacid de la Sierra) (1884), and Pablo Gil, Julián Ribera, and Mariano Sánchez's *Colección de textos aljamiados* (1888) are important examples of these. The latter, a book-length edition of *aljamiado-morisco* texts copied out by hand in Arabic script, is preceded by a short prologue and a guide for the reader unfamiliar with reading Arabic letters. The underlying purpose of this edition, besides stimulating a more general interest in the study of Hispano-Muslim culture, is to provide a sort of lectoral bridge for Spanish students of Arabic:

> Our study is meant, in the first place, to assist in the greatest and most immediate way students of the Arabic language, in order that they may quickly overcome any reading difficulties and quickly continue on to other readings, also accustoming themselves to, from the beginning, the singular turn of the Arabic sentence, something retained within almost all the translations made by our Moriscos. (1888, v)[6]

As a means to gaining greater familiarity with Arabic script and syntax, the *aljamiado* texts of the Moriscos were seen by Gil, Ribera, and Sánchez as a powerful tool. That they framed these texts as a kind of pedagogical means-to-a-greater-end also says much about specialized perceptions regarding the literary and culture worth of the *aljamiado-morisco* texts themselves: seen as a Romance-language reworking of Arabic literature (one that largely preserves Arabic syntax), *aljamiado-morisco* literature could serve as an effective means of bringing students to more complex and sophisticated Andalusi texts written in Arabic. In this respect, the texts of Castilian and Aragonese crypto-Muslims were seen as a teaching tool or a "way in" for students looking to engage Hispano-Arabic literature from a much earlier period. It should also be mentioned that besides the explicitly pedagogical uses to which Gil,

Ribera, and Sánchez's study seeks to put *aljamiado-morisco* texts, there is another motivation for their study (which I will be discussing later in this chapter), namely, a desire to increase awareness of *aljamiado-morisco* literature in general so that the dramatic and mostly preventable destruction of Morisco manuscripts that took place in Aragon in the 1880s would not be repeated.

Another important nineteenth-century figure within the small subfield of *aljamiado-morisco* studies is Francisco Guillén Robles. Like Estébanez, a native of Málaga (and official historian of the city after the publication of his 1874 *Historia de Málaga y su provincia* [History of Málaga and its province]), Guillén Robles studied Arabic at the University of Granada with Francisco Javier Simonet and in 1881 was appointed Arabist to the National Library in Madrid. With unfettered access to the National Library's significant Arabic-language holdings (*pace* Gayangos), Guillén Robles was able to put together a tremendously comprehensive *Catálogo de los manuscritos árabes existentes en la Biblioteca Nacional de Madrid* (Catalogue of Arabic manuscripts extant in the National Library of Madrid) (1889), which includes descriptions of a number of *aljamiado* manuscripts, as well as short transcriptions of some of these texts. Also worth noting, from the point of view of increasing access to *aljamiado-morisco* texts, was Guillén Robles's three-volume *Leyendas moriscas sacadas de varios manuscritos existentes en las bibliotecas Nacional, Real y de don P. de Gayangos* (Morisco legends taken from various extant manuscripts in the National Library, the Royal Library, and the Library of don P. Gayangos) (1885), as well as his shorter *Leyendas de José, hijo de Jacob, y de Alejandro Magno, sacadas dos manuscritos moriscos de la Biblioteca Nacional de Madrid* (The legends of Joseph, son of Jacob, and Alexander the Great, taken from the Morisco manuscripts of the National Library of Madrid) (1888). These collected folktales, translated into modern Castilian and subsequently republished in paperback during the early 1990s by Editorial Sufi (Madrid), provide a potentially very wide group of readers with access to Morisco narrative texts, although the radical linguistic reworking of these texts makes such access somewhat superficial.

During the last years of the nineteenth century, Saavedra published his comprehensive "Indice general de la literatura aljamiada" (1889), and the journal *El Archivo* published two articles on Morisco literature in its 1890 volume, one a transcription of a Morisco sermon on the end of the world (Chabas 1890) and the other a study of Puey de Monçon's

Las coplas del peregrino (The verses of the pilgrim) (Gil 1890). In Italy, Emilio Teza produced a study in 1891 of an *aljamiado* manuscript that turned up in Florence ("Di un compendio del Corano in espagnolo con lettere arabiche [manoscritto fiorentino])," while Mariano Pano y Ruata offered his book-length analysis of Puey de Monçon's *The Verses of the Pilgrim* entitled, *Las coplas del peregrino de Puey Monçon, viaje a la Meca en el siglo XVI* (The verses of the pilgrim by Puey Monçon, a journey to Mecca in the sixteenth century) (1897).

These studies, mostly philological transcriptions and general surveys of *aljamiado-morisco* literature for nonspecialists, make up the published corpus of *aljamiado-morisco* studies carried out in the nineteenth century. And while the aggregate number of articles and monographs on *aljamiado-morisco* literature increased dramatically during the twentieth century, the scope of analysis did not expand a great deal. The study of *aljamiado-morisco* texts — a subfield within a subfield according to the manner in which literary studies in Spanish and Arabic are divided up in the American and European academy — has continued to focus predominately on philological work, the drafting of critical editions of *aljamiado* texts, and more or less general presentations of Morisco language and literature. There have been some notable exceptions to this rule, as López Baralt's collected work on both individual texts and issues related to Morisco textual culture, as well as Consuelo López-Morillas's studies of versions of the Qur'an owned and used by Moriscos (1981, 1982, 1990) and research on Morisco scribes (1986, 1984) near the end of the century demonstrate. These two scholars, as well a handful of others (Francisco Márquez Villanueva's essay on Miguel de Luna [1991] certainly deserves mention here) have shown in considerable detail the richness of cultural and literary data encoded within *aljamiado-morisco* texts. Nonetheless, there has remained in place a sharp contrast between the large and growing number of in-depth historiographical works devoted to the Moriscos and the relatively small number of narrowly defined studies of Morisco literature that have been produced since Gayangos first began to write about *aljamiado* texts in 1839.

Alvaro Galmés de Fuentes, a scholar who has published over thirty articles and books on Morisco literature, offers an interesting case in point regarding the uses to which modern scholarship has put *aljamiado-morisco* literature. Speaking in 1972, over one hundred years after Estébanez's address before the Ateneo and Gayangos's initial work on *aljamiado-morisco* texts, Galmés de Fuentes describes at length the epistemological breach that he feels separates modern scholarship from Estébanez's approach. Addressing a group of international scholars convened for a six-day conference on *aljamiado-morisco* literature (a conference marked by the simultaneous occurrence of a total solar eclipse and the participation of prominent scholars such as Samuel Armistead, Emilio García Gómez, L. P. Harvey, Ottmar Hegyi, and Reinhold Kontzi), he engages Estébanez's words directly:

> Today we are surely very far from the Romantic appraisal of Morisco-Aljamiado literature. When in the first half of the nineteenth century some of the Moriscos' texts are discovered and put into circulation, the mentality of the nineteenth century extols the value of such writings in terms with which we cannot completely agree today. (1978, 189)[7]

Galmés de Fuentes addresses a very different audience than that to which Estébanez spoke, and at a very different (though by no means more certain) time in Spain's history. Nonetheless, he chooses to begin his survey of *aljamiado-morisco* literature (subtitled, "El interés literario") by reading portions of Estébanez's 1848 address and commenting on it. Galmés de Fuentes's intention in doing this is twofold: on one hand, he wishes to point out the epistemological distance — inevitably framed as progress — that separates him and his audience from Estébanez and his; on the other, he means to underscore and provide his own ideas regarding the reasons for the fact that nineteenth-century enthusiasm over the rediscovery of something as simultaneously exotic and inarguably Spanish (i.e., not French) as the *aljamiado* narratives of the Moriscos was almost immediately frustrated.

Focusing on Galmés de Fuentes's first point, we may ask exactly to what extent the intellectual ideologies that inform research on *aljamiado* texts and Morisco culture in general today differ from those that moved nineteenth-century scholars to study and write about this material. Clearly Galmés de Fuentes is right to point out that Estébanez's statements are not convincing, though there is considerable evidence — such as Cánovas de Castillo's weak defense of his uncle before the Real Academia Española in 1878 — that his arguments were no more convincing to nineteenth-century audiences. And if by "the mentality of the nineteenth century" Galmés de Fuentes also means to include Gayangos, Ribera, Saavedra, and Gil, then there really is little that separates Galmés de Fuentes's own approach to *aljamiado-morisco* literature from that of the century that precedes his own. It is a mistake, in other words, to take Estébanez's view as that of his contemporaries; while there is much in his words that undoubtedly situates him within a particular moment in Spanish history, he does not represent the majority of those scholars and writers who dealt with *aljamiado-morisco* texts during the nineteenth century. On the contrary, when we read the work of Gayangos or Saavedra, we get the sense that much modern philological work on *aljamiado-morisco* literature is but a continuation of nineteenth-century research projects.

Galmés de Fuentes's second point is a much less problematic one. He argues that critics ceased paying much attention to the *aljamiado-morisco* texts because there did not exist any once-hidden Hispano-Muslim masterpiece to be published: "Naturally, today whoever hopes to find in *aljamiado-morisco* literature a novelistic Potosí or an Islamic Cervantes, a Shakespeare or Erasmus, is on a critical path that does not lead to the correct understanding of the intrinsic literary values and enchantment that our texts contain" (1981, 439). And not only were the *aljamiado* narratives of the Moriscos less than inspiring from a modern literary point of view, these and other texts that were being discovered and perused offered no clear window onto the cultural world of sixteenth-century Spanish Islam. In fact, the *aljamiado* literature that surfaced throughout the course of the nineteenth century (and into the twentieth) required — as I have stated above — for the most part a great deal of scholarly effort to be understood even at the most literal level, and this effort quickly began to seem disproportionate to any possible payoff.

That the contents of all those folios of Arabic-script Castilian and Aragonese text could not sufficiently kindle the collective imagination of Spanish novelists, playwrights, and poets — though the human drama of the Moriscos themselves had inspired a number of creative works during the seventeenth century[8] — is, according to Galmés de Fuentes, cause for the relative lack of interest shown in *aljamiado-morisco* literature throughout much of the twentieth century:

> Naturally, at no time today may we consider *aljamiado* texts as a source of inspiration for new literary creations. It is, in part, for this reason that *aljamiado* literature, after a euphoric reception in the nineteenth century, was forgotten. Only occasionally would a specialist pay

momentary attention to it, although these texts were frequently appreciated only from a purely linguistic perspective or as the basis for investigations into the exotic. (1978, 190)[9]

The literature of the Moriscos, apparently neither sufficiently *literary* to warrant inclusion in the Hispanic canon, nor intriguing enough to serve as a foundation for new literary works based upon them, had thus been transformed — in a very short time, relatively speaking — from a metaphoric new continent of potentially endless cultural riches to the marginalized hunting ground of dialectologists and dabblers.

Whether we share this admittedly harsh judgment of the way in which *aljamiado-morisco* texts were studied throughout the 124-year period that separates Galmés de Fuentes's presentation from Estébanez's or not, we can agree that neither the Romantic vision of these texts as "virgin territory" to be exploited, nor the scientist posture adopted by modernist philology are able to do much justice to the literature of sixteenth- and seventeenth-century Spanish Islam. Throughout this book I will be employing what I see as more productive and nuanced approaches to this literature, and I have discussed the comments of Estébanez and Galmés de Fuentes principally in order to provide brief interconnected examples of how the narrative texts of Castilian and Aragonese crypto-Muslims have been framed over the past two centuries. Beyond this framing, characterized by varying levels of critical (and semi-critical) treatment and analysis, the fortunes of *aljamiado-morisco* texts have in many ways mirrored those of the Moriscos themselves throughout the roughly one-hundred-year period between their forced conversion and expulsion.

Contexts of Rediscovery

The very manner in which modern scholars have come to have access to *aljamiado-morisco* literature provides a dramatic example of both how uncertain and even dangerous the situation was for Castilian and Aragonese Moriscos in early modern Spain, as well as how important their written texts could be to them. Throughout the sixteenth century and into the first decade of the seventeenth, members of Morisco communities in Castile and Aragon actively copied, recopied, and read texts dealing with Islamic faith, practice, and folklore. Writing for the most part in *aljamiado,* the scribes that produced these books did so for a relatively small group of readers that in most cases did not extend beyond the members of their own community.[10] And while it is well known that Spanish law forbade the Moriscos from making or owning such books — especially in the wake of stringent laws regulating language and cultural practice among the *cristianos nuevos de moros* (new Christians once Muslims) passed during the middle of the sixteenth century — these and other prohibitions, as well as the best efforts of local parish priests and the Inquisition, did not seem to slow down in any significant way the activities of crypto-Muslim scribes and readers in Castile and Aragon.

At present, archives in Spain, England, France, and Italy hold more than two hundred *aljamiado* books produced by Morisco scribes. The majority of these books, as well as an even greater number of unbound folios, were discovered by accident in rural Aragon well over two centuries after the expulsion of the Moriscos from the Iberian peninsula. The rest, originally scattered throughout Europe and North Africa during the first years of the Morisco diaspora, have made their way into Spanish archives through the energetic efforts of Spanish scholars to procure them from private collectors in Morocco and Tunisia, as well as in England and France. With regard to the rediscovery of the majority of *aljamiado-morisco* books now located in Spain, the large cache of codices and loose papers found by construction workers in 1884 under the floor of a dilapidated house in Almonacid de la Sierra (Aragon) provides a good example of how they came to light. As Pablo Gil, Julián Ribera, and Mariano Sánchez describe it in the introduction to their 1888 edition of selected *aljamiado* texts from this collection:

> ...the children of Almonacid de la Sierra, in the midst of some childish celebration, made bonfires with piles of Arabic and *aljamiado* papers and books that some brickmasons had found — carefully stowed away and placed, one by one, in cloth pouches underneath a wooden floor — as they worked to demolish the wooden floor and the plaster one beneath it. Fortunately,...the Reverend P. Fierro of the Escuelas Pías of [Zaragoza], who happened to be living in Almonacid, intervened in time. (1888, vii)[11]

Not considered of any particular value by the workers at the site, the books — approximately four hundred of them by Gil, Ribera, and Sánchez's estimate — had been removed from their hiding place and tossed into the growing piles of rubble alongside the house. The majority of these were lost or destroyed in the children's bonfire. A few dozen of these books and some of the unbound folios were salvaged by Fierro, and these eventually became the property of Gil, then the dean of the Faculty of Philosophy and Letters at the University of Zaragoza. Moved by their desire to prevent any further destruction of undocumented *al-jamiado* and Arabic books by those unaware of their value, Gil, Ribera, and Sánchez published transcriptions (in Arabic script) of some of these documents, including a copy of the now well-known *Alhadith del baño de Ziryab* (Story of the bath of Ziryab). Upon Gil's death, the books and papers found in Almonacid de la Sierra were put up for sale, though only one of these — "a volume of motley materials acquired at a price too high to admit any profit" (un tomo de materias abigarradas que adquirió a precio excesivamente elevado para realizar ninguna ganancia) (Ribera and Asín 1912, ix) — was actually purchased by an antiquarian from Madrid who knew little of the book's contents. In 1910, the rest of Gil's collection of Morisco books and papers were moved to the Biblioteca de la Junta para la Ampliación de Estudios Históricos in Madrid where they are still located.[12]

Between the enthusiastic book-burning efforts of the Inquisition (as well as those of the occasional gang of Aragonese children) and the common crypto-Muslim practice of hiding books in ingeniously secure places within and around their homes, one can only imagine the exact number of *aljamiado* books that have been lost over the past four centuries. Gil, Ribera, and Sánchez provide a handful of examples of Morisco books being used as kindling for cooking fires. A particularly grievous example of such book burnings took place in Morés (Aragon) during the last quarter of the nineteenth century:

> ...there was a house whose hearth was fueled on long winter nights, and its stews heated up for some months, with the parchments, papers, and books bound in leather and wood that had been found in the partial ruins of a house. (1888, vi)[13]

There is no way to know with any exactitude how many *aljamiado* books were reduced to ashes over the months that they served to stoke household fires for heat and cooking in Morés. One can imagine, however, that their numbers must have reached the hundreds (e.g., three books a day over roughly ninety days adds up to 270 books), and that among them were copies of several important works. Found in the ruins of a dilapidated house, these books survived the Inquisition and nearly three hundred years of often-violent history only to be destroyed by the material exigencies of a cold Aragonese winter.

Pascual de Gayangos, whose personal collection of *aljamiado* texts has enriched the holdings of both the Biblioteca Nacional in Madrid and the Biblioteca de la Real Academia de la Historia, makes similar comments about books having been found in the walls of homes, under false floors, and even in the recesses of caves. Such is the case of one manuscript copy of the *Hadith de Yuçuf* (now located in Madrid, BRAH under the signature ms. 11/9409 *olim* T-12), which was rediscovered during the second half of the nineteenth century in a cave near Morés, Aragon, along with several other moisture-damaged books and a small stock of rusted firearms (Johnson 1974, 13). Moriscos from this community, flouting Spanish law forbidding them to possess either Islamic texts or weapons, had kept both hidden, though close at hand.

Another interesting example of the rough fortunes of *aljamiado-morisco* books before, during, and after the expulsion of the Moriscos from Spain is the case of a collection of Muslim prayers and legends currently held in the French National Library in Paris (ms. Arabe 1163). Joseph-Toussaint Reinaud, president of the French Société Asiatique from 1847 to 1867 (a post formerly held by Gayangos's teacher, Silvestre de Sacy) describes this manuscript in the following way:

> Manuscript in Arabic characters, in Spanish. The volume made up part of the Llorente Collection of manuscripts, within which it was listed as number 19. It belonged to a Spanish Moor named Rodrigo el Rubio, a native of the area of Albeta, Aragon, who, due to the simple fact that he owned this book was brought before the Inquisition in 1567. See the detailed notice of this volume placed within the Llorente collection along with a calamus or reed still stained with ink, which must have served as a support. Signed, Reinaud. (Saavedra 1878, 145–46)

Rodrigo el Rubio no doubt suffered a severe punishment for owning a book containing Islamic material (or even written in Arabic script), as the possession of such books was considered conclusive proof of the accused's adherence to Islam. Henry Charles Lea notes the case of Nofre Blanch and his wife, Angela Carroz, two Moriscos brought before the Inquisition of Zaragoza in 1607 after a book and some papers in Arabic were found under their bed in the course of an official search:

> Each declared that that the articles had belonged to an uncle of the husband and that they were ignorant of the contents. Both were tortured without confessing and were sentenced to abjure *de vehementi*, to 100 lashes apiece and a year's imprisonment, with the addition of a ten ducat fine on the woman. (Lea 1901, 131)

A more disturbing case involving the possession of a book written in Arabic script (the distinction between books in Arabic and *aljamiado* is not made by the Inquisition) is that of Isabel Zacim, a ninety-year-old woman brought before the Inquisition of Valencia when a copy of the Qur'an was found in a chest in her home. Although she denied knowledge of its presence in her home, and there was no other evidence against her, the Inquisition still managed to impose a punishment upon her.

> As she was ninety years old she was spared torture and scourging but appeared in a Valencia *auto de fe* of 1604, abjured *de vehementi*, was exposed to a *vergüenza pública* — parading through the streets on an ass with an inscription setting forth her name and offense — imprisonment till she should be instructed in the faith, and the inevitable ten ducat fine. (Lea 1901, 131–32)

The imprisonment of a woman of such an advanced age, as well as the imposition of such a heavy fine (with 10 gold ducats one could buy roughly 20 sheep or 370 two-pound loaves of bread in the late sixteenth century; and there are cases of rural schoolteachers receiving annual salaries of 5,000 maravedís, the equivalent of roughly 13 ducats) demonstrates the seriousness with which the Inquisition dealt with Moriscos possessing books containing Arabic script. One can only imagine that Rodrigo el Rubio faced much harsher penalties, including torture and scourging (usually one hundred lashes across the back), imprisonment for a year, a ten-ducat fine, and public humiliation.

Rodrigo el Rubio's book, unlike its original owner, seems oddly enough to have been fairly well treated by the Christians who took it from him. It contains over 171 folios, on which are written a variety of religious texts, mostly having to do with Muslim prayers and religious practices, some corresponding to particular times of the Muslim year. Saavedra lists its contents as the following:

1. (f. 1): Sura 99 of the Qur'an
2. (f. 2): This is the virtue of the day of Assura [Muharram 10]
3. (f. 5^v): This is the virtue of the day of al-Jumu'a [Friday]

4. (f. 10^v): On March 7 was the twenty-seventh day of Ramadan.

5. (f. 12): The *hadith* of the Prophet, when he ascended to the heavens.

6. (f. 61): These are the sayings of Bias, which are the following, and in order for them to be well understood, the reader must keep in mind that every wise man speaks with him: Look at yourself in the mirror / each day that you should live / and take from me this advice / If you judge yourself to be handsome / without finding any flaws in your looks / then so also may your actions be above reproach / If you see yourself as ugly / then work like the light / with nobility of habit.

7. (f. 80^v): The writing of the sayings ended on the final day of March 1563.

8. (f. 82): Chapter on how one must deal with a person who is about to die, whether the sick person is a man or a woman.

9. (f. 83^v): In the year 1566, September 10, I took possession of the garden of Lope Jimel; Pellares of Alberite wrote up the transfer letter, which is in his notes and can be found there should it ever be necessary.

10. (f. 91): First sermon of *Paxku^{w}a*.[14]

11. (f. 93): Reminder of the proper way to do prayer.

12. (f. 110): Second sermon of *Paxku^{w}a*.

13. (f. 114): God said in his Qur'an, "I tested Abraham."

14. (f. 120): Chapter on one who moves away from or has ceased to perform prayers due to stupidity, and repents afterward.

15. (f. 132): Chapter on what a Muslim man or woman should know when his/her mother or father dies.

16. (f. 136): The petition that a man should make to God.

17. (f. 138): Remembrance of those days in which God put harm on the Jews.

18. (f. 139): On the chosen days of the moon.

19. (f. 140): It was related by Atrima ibn Abén....

20. (f. 158): These are the months of the year, with their virtues.

21. (f. 171): A very honored preaching for the month of Shaban.

(1878, 146–47)[15]

In light of the interrelatedness of its contents, this book can hardly be considered a miscellany in any strict sense. In fact, two significant strings run through the texts contained within Rodrigo el Rubio's manuscript book: a serious preoccupation with ethical/pragmatic issues, and an explicit reckoning with time within the larger ethico-moral framework laid out by these texts. Item 20, for example ("These are the months of the year, with their virtues"), explicitly embeds time within a Muslim framework not only of belief, but of practice, given that the *alfadilas* of each month correspond to religious practices (prayer, fasting, performing ablutions, etc.) carried out by the faithful. The short poem by Bias, too, accentuates the intertwined issues of time and practice, highlighting the human dimension of time that expires not with any sort of unfelt "ending," but with death ("each day that you should live..."). That this section reports in poetic form the authoritative words of Bias ("the reader must keep in mind that every wise man speaks with him...") in order to engage these themes offers a sort of microcosmic example of the larger practice of *aljamiado-morisco* literature: traditional narratives function to help readers and a larger listening public shape their individual and communal actions within various intersecting temporal frameworks, all overshadowed by a keenly felt sense of personal and collective mortality.

That a book containing material so apparently unacceptable to the Inquisition should have been preserved represents one of the many paradoxes that surround the *aljamiado-morisco* literature to which modern scholars have access. While the majority of books confiscated by the Inquisition and other Christian authorities were summarily destroyed, there remained a small quantity of texts valuable enough in the minds of Christian authorities to escape immolation. What value Inquisition officials saw in Rodrigo el Rubio's manuscript book is hard to determine, although given the relatively loose grip that the Aragonese Inquisition had on its own resources, it may be unnecessary to consider this as a possibility. It is relatively easy to imagine, after all, that the book might have simply slipped through the fingers of Christian authorities and into the possession of someone who thought it possible to make some use of it, even if just as a way to make some quick cash from a book collector with a taste for the exotic. In almost all law enforcement bureaucracies there is this sort of leakage — police lockup facilities in major U.S. cities periodically "lose track of" confiscated items ranging from firearms to uncut heroin, and even items as large as Russian submarines have been known to fall into private hands since the breakup of the Soviet Union. A 171-folio manuscript book is, within this larger context, a relatively easy item to let slip through the cracks, especially if light-fingered functionaries (with keys to temporary storage facilities) play their expected part.

While the circumstances that surround the preservation of Rodrigo el Rubio's manuscript book in 1567, its incorporation into the Llorente collection, and eventual cataloguing within the Bibliothèque Nationale de Paris (where scholars with an interest and minimal academic credentials can read it at their leisure) are unknown, it is possible to suggest hypotheses regarding the course that the book has taken over the past nearly five centuries. My own pet theory — based on similar cases involving Arabic and *aljamiado* manuscripts — is that Rodrigo's book was stolen from the Inquisition and then sold to a book collector in Spain or France. Many years later, after the book had changed hands several more times, Llorente came into possession of it as part of a single or collective purchase, after which it became the property of the Bibliothèque Nationale.

Thinking in this way about the messy trail that leads from late sixteenth-century Zaragoza to late nineteenth-century Paris (when the book became part of the Bibliothèque Nationale's collection) it becomes difficult not to put our own analyses of *aljamiado-morisco* manuscript texts within a much more pragmatic, perhaps less altruistic, perspective. For in a broad sense, we represent nothing more than the latest link in the long chain of hands that have brushed across the folios of manuscript books that only narrowly missed being destroyed on at least one occasion. I will be speaking about our own scholarly contact with *aljamiado-morisco* literature (a narrative of conscious hindsight and open concern for the future), as well as potential future approaches to these texts, in the concluding section of this book. In what remains of the present chapter, I would like to focus on some of the uses to which Castilian and Aragonese crypto-Muslims put their narrative texts in the years that preceded their expulsion from the Iberian peninsula.

Morisco Contexts of Use

Turning our attention back to the case of Almonacid de la Sierra, we find further examples of the significant textual activity in which Morisco communities engaged. A small hamlet located approximately thirty miles southwest of Zaragoza, Almonacid de la Sierra was, according to Inquisition records, a small center of Morisco book production, reproduction, and use. This argument corresponds to the larger claim made by Juan B. Vilar, who points out:

> The traditional thesis, according to which the Moriscos formed an illiterate minority with a residual culture more verbal than written, can no

> longer be sustained in light of the numerous studies produced during the past fifty years, especially those dealing with libraries and literary contributions, as much in Arabic as in *aljamiado* Castilian. (1996, 180)[16]

Given the widespread nature of Morisco book ownership and use, especially in rural Aragonese communities, it is hardly surprising that such a large repository of *aljamiado-morisco* books should have been found in Almonacid de la Sierra. Jacqueline Fournel-Guérin, in her seminal study of Morisco book culture in Aragon, cites the case of Miguel Cajal, who testified before the Inquisition of Zaragoza that he had been asked by other Moriscos to transport a small collection of books in Arabic (or perhaps in *aljamiado*) from Caspe to Almonacid de la Sierra, and that there were readers in Almonacid waiting for these books (1979, 247). Also telling — as a concrete account of narrative texts held by a member of the community of Almonacid de la Sierra — are the two collections of *historias de moros* (Moorish narratives) found in the home of Gerónimo Mediana by the Inquisition in 1603 (Fournel-Guérin 1979, 255). The picture that emerges, when we take into account historical records as well as the hundreds of books and loose folios found in Almonacid de la Sierra near the end of the nineteenth century, is the presence of a brisk handwritten book trade in even the smallest of Aragonese *pueblos,* with readers and scribes energetically defying the orders of Christian authorities with respect to the reproduction and reading of Islamic texts.

If Inquisition records are any indication of the extent to which Moriscos in Aragon were engaged in the production, purchase, and use of Islamic books in *aljamiado* and, to a lesser extent, Arabic, one can legitimately speak of a definable book culture among the Aragonese Moriscos: of the 900 guilty verdicts handed out by the Inquisition of Zaragoza between the years 1568 and 1620, 409 were due to the possession of books in "Arabic" (it is unclear whether Christian authorities were aware that the largest number of books that they were finding were actually written in Castilian) or having to do with Islam. And of these 409 guilty verdicts, only 3 were given during the six-year period between the Moriscos' final expulsion from Spain and 1620 (Fournel-Guérin 1979, 243). The general picture that emerges from these Inquisition proceedings, that roughly half of all crypto-Muslims found guilty by the Inquisition of Zaragoza over a forty-six-year period were charged, *inter alia,* with owning Islamic texts, provides a strong indication of the relatively widespread nature of book ownership among the Aragonese Moriscos. And while the possession and use of Islamic works in Arabic and *aljamiado* — as well as some copies of texts in Latin characters — may not justify the classification of sixteenth-century Castile and Aragon as a sort of archipelago of Morisco "textual communities" as Brian Stock (1983) has defined the term, books and the texts they contained clearly played a large role in the cultural life of both Castilian and Aragonese crypto-Muslims.

Looking at the ritual practice of the Moriscos as it was carried out throughout Spain during the sixteenth century, we see an even larger range of activities within which the narrative texts that form the central focus of this book would have played an important part. We may take as an example of such ritual practice the yearly celebration of the Prophet's birth, which fell on the twelfth day of *Rabi'a I* according to the Hijri calendar used by Moriscos in their religious observance.[17] The celebration of this holiday (*paxku^{w}a*) consisted of a range of devotionary acts that would take place throughout the day. Led by their *alfakíes,* members of Morisco communities would most often join in a day of fasting, prayer, and almsgiving. As part of the celebration too, stories related to the birth and life of the Prophet would be told. These storytelling activities, the texts of which are encoded in the manuscripts we study today, provided a means by which even those who did not own books themselves or know how to read *aljamiado* were able to engage traditional Islamic narratives in group settings characterized by religious worship and the conscious affirmation of Muslim institutions within their community.

As in the case of the narratives related to the Virgin of Guadalupe analyzed by Patricia Baquedano-López in her ethnographic study of religious instruction among Mexican-American children in Los Angeles, California (1997), traditional *aljamiado-morisco* narratives would have been powerful mediators by which Castilian and Aragonese Moriscos negotiated, questioned, and aligned themselves with their communal and personal identities. For ritual practice, far from a static, repetitive exercise of timeless practices, has been shown in numerous studies over the past two decades to serve more as a platform for improvisation and the co-construction of meaning through face-to-face interaction (Drewal 1992; Duranti 1994; M. Goodwin 1990).

In approaching *aljamiado* narratives in light of their role within the cultural practice of Castilian and Aragonese crypto-Muslims, it is necessary to keep in mind that these narratives were used to mediate face-to-face interaction and the construction of social reality within communities that constantly lived, as Bernard Vincent has suggested, "under the watchful eye of a dominant Other" (1999, 302). It is also important to deal with the fact that the *aljamiado-morisco* texts that we study were composed, recopied, and read by people who were at once profoundly Muslim and wholly Spanish. This (at least) two-sidedness of Morisco culture throughout the peninsula provides enormous challenges for scholars wishing to understand their culture and history. As Harvey has pointed out, to be a crypto-Muslim in sixteenth-century Spain meant dealing — on a daily basis — with the paradoxical and dangerous fact of having been, in a sense, exiled within one's own homeland:

> [I]t was the misfortune of the Moriscos to be the first large population of orthodox Maliki Sunni Muslims to find themselves in a situation in which their continued existence in their homeland depended upon their willingness to conceal their true beliefs, not just with respect to one isolated incident, but regularly and throughout their lives. (1993, 212)

This sense of internal exile would have been especially acute for Granadan Moriscos, who, after the failed uprisings of 1568–71, were forced by the Spanish Crown to leave their native Granada to be resettled in communities throughout Castile and the rest of the peninsula. The Moriscos of Aragon fared somewhat better due to the significant support and protection they received from the landowning nobles who employed them, but this protection also had its limits. The limits of such protection, and the negotiation of the perilous and shifting interstices that existed between the Christian and larger Muslim worlds within which the Moriscos operated, are what give real, socially embedded meaning to the *aljamiado-morisco* literature that we study. Indeed, the narratives that make up a great part of this literature (almost all of which are loose recontextualizations of traditional Islamic material) put us into direct contact with literature that quite literally served as a discursive resource for the very survival of Spanish Muslims as a minority population in Renaissance and Baroque Spain.

4

The Prophet Is Born,
Muslims Are Made

*The great basic idea that the world is not to be viewed as a complex
of fully fashioned objects, but as a complex of processes, in which apparently stable objects, no less than the images inside our heads (our
concepts), are undergoing incessant changes . . . ultimately constitutes a
progressive development.*

— Friedrich Engels, *Ludwig Feuerbach*

In the previous chapters, I have mapped out a basic theoretical framework for an activity-centered approach to *aljamiado-morisco* literature.
Beginning with a discussion of the inherent interdisciplinarity of this
mode of literary analysis, I concluded by defining what it means to
place Morisco scribes and readers, as human agents, at the center of textual study. Rooted in what Gary Saul Morson has termed the "human
dimension of time" (1994, 10), the activity-centered approach I am suggesting focuses on the uses to which Morisco readers and scribes put
aljamiado texts within their social world and the ways in which culturally embedded forms of temporality were encoded in *aljamiado-morisco*
narratives.

Now I will look at a specific *aljamiado-morisco* text, the *Libro de
las luces* (Book of lights), and its implementation within specific cultural activities carried out within Morisco communities in Castile and
Aragon. Focusing on two specific sections of this long and frequently
recopied (though scarcely studied) *aljamiado* text, my goal is to present
a detailed account of two cultural processes encoded within the *Libro de
las luces*. These processes, which I have chosen to term "mediation" and
"evocation," find full expression in the pragmatic intersection between
the written text and its use in concrete social settings shaped by time-
consciousness and the very human concern — expressed in no uncertain

79

terms by Morisco readers and scribes — for individual and collective survival.

The *Libro de las luces* is a translation of *Kitab al-anwar*, believed to have been written by Abu al-Hasn al-Bakri, "a somewhat mysterious figure supposedly active in Iraq during the second half of the thirteenth century" (una figura algo misteriosa a quien se supone activo en Iraq en la segunda mitad del siglo XIII) (López-Morillas 1994, 26). Its principal theme is the genealogy, birth, and life of the Prophet of Islam, Muhammad. The *Kitab al-anwar* has as its direct source the *Sirat rasulullah* (Biography of the messenger of God) written by Muhammad ibn Ishaq ibn Yasar and reworked by 'Abd al-Malik ibn Hisham during the first half of the eighth century (precisely as Islam was taking root in the Iberian peninsula). It appears, however, that al-Bakri greatly expanded and novelized several sections of the *Sirat rasulullah* in keeping with the rich folk tradition that by his time revolved around the events of the Prophet's life.[1] We may take as an example of the changes wrought by al-Bakri a comparison of the passages related to the birth of Muhammad in the *Sirat rasulullah* and the *aljamiado* translation of the *Kitab al-anwar*.[2] First, we consider ibn Ishaq and ibn Hisham's text:

> After [Muhammad's] birth his mother [Amina] sent to tell his grand-father 'Abdu'l-Muttalib that she had given birth to a boy and asked him to come and look at him. When he came she told him what she had seen when she conceived him and what was said to her and what she was ordered to call him. It is alleged that 'Abdu-l Muttalib took him... in the... Ka'aba, where he stood and prayed to Allah thanking him for this gift. Then he brought him out and delivered him to his mother, and he tried to find foster-mothers for him. (Guillaume 1955, 70)

The scene in which 'Abd al-Muttalib, the Prophet's grandfather, takes the infant Muhammad ('Abdullah, the Prophet's father, had died during his wife Amina's seventh month of pregnancy) to the Ka'aba is preceded in the *Libro de las luces* by an extended discussion between the angels, the birds, the clouds, and a *k^{a}lamador* (a sort of heavenly authoritative voice). Their discussion revolves around the issue of who should care for the newborn Prophet, given that it was the custom in seventh-century Arabia for mothers to employ wet nurses to care for their infant children:

> ...and the clouds said, "We have more right to care for him, as we move through the air between the earth and heaven. We will take him

throughout the earth and to all of its *anazeha,* for we know the good fruit trees from which he will eat, and the good springs from which he will drink. We will give him water blessed for its *al-arsh.*" The angels said, "We have more right to care for him, and more honor and favor from our Lord." The birds said, "We have more right to care for him, as we will carry him on our wings away from all the vices of the world." And they heard a *kᵃlamador* who said, "Stop this talk, for God has already ordained that he is to be cared for by Halima, daughter of Abi Duwayb al-Ça'adiyya." And he said, "The Prophet (PBUH) came from a chaste marriage untouched by adultery. Since Adam (PBUH), [the Prophet's line] has been untouched by the adultery of the unbelievers. And the Prophet (PBUH) was born on Monday, the twelfth day of Rabi'a al-Awwal, after the coming of the company of the elephant, and fifteen years after the fracturing of the house of Mecca." And once the angels' three-day visitation [of the Prophet] was over, the people were allowed to go to see him. And the first to see him was 'Abd al-Muttalib, and he saw [the boy] with his hands held high to heaven and looking upward, and the house was filled with light. Seeing this, [the boy's] grandfather smiled and said to Amina, "Fortunate are you above all women, for your son is truly a marvel." (Madrid, BRAH ms. 11/9414 *olim* T-18 ff. 102ᵛ–103ʳ)[3]

The passage from the *Libro de las luces,* an extensive amplification of the narrative presented by ibn Ishaq and ibn Hisham, reflects the strong impulse — already well developed in Muslim communities by the thirteenth century — to folklorize the events of the Prophet's birth and life.

With respect to the *aljamiado-morisco* version of the *Libro de las luces,* we are unable at present to speak with much detail about the ways in which it alters al-Bakri's text. However, given that most *aljamiado-morisco* translations of Arabic works follow the original quite closely (even, in some cases, bending Castilian syntax to the breaking point) we can suppose, provisionally, that the *aljamiado* version of the *Libro de las luces* does not reflect much of a departure from the Arabic one. Of course, the only way to move beyond this investigative impasse is to consult manuscript copies of the *Kitab al-anwar* possibly held in Middle Eastern or North African archives, given that, as López-Morillas points out (1994, 26), there currently exists no edited version of al-Bakri's text. The lack of an edited version of the *Kitab al-anwar,* as well as the possibility that there are no extant manuscript copies of the work, presents a seemingly insurmountable obstacle for the analysis of the *Libro de las luces* as a textual translation of the *Kitab al-anwar*. How much of the *Libro de las luces* is taken directly from al-Bakri's thirteenth-century version of the *Sirat rasulullah*? How much of the *aljamiado-morisco* version has been added by Morisco scribes and copyists?

To these questions I would add a methodological one: what sort of analysis is facilitated by the comparison of the *Libro de las luces* and its Arabic original? First, such a comparison is a necessary part of any consideration of the textual features of the *Libro de las luces* as they relate to the work's composition. By way of example, we may look at 'Abd al-Muttalib's last statement to Amina upon having finally visited his newborn grandson: "Blessed are you over all women" (De bu^wena ventura erex sobre todax lax mujerex). One of the striking intertextual features of this passage is that it closely mirrors a line from the "Ave Maria" (Blessed are you among women), an extraordinarily important prayer in the Catholic faith from the early medieval period to the present day. Always popular in medieval and early modern Christianity, the "Ave Maria" gained even more currency in Counter-Reformation Spain as a response to the Protestants' questioning of the cult of Mary in the Catholic Church. Mary is also a central figure in Islam; however, the mention of her being "blessed above all women" because of her son's spiritual qualities is not part of the Qur'anic tradition.

If 'Abd al-Muttalib's words to Amina reflect a sixteenth-century addition to the Arabic text, then the intertextual relation between Amina and Mary takes on even more significance. The idea, for example, that a Morisco scribe would create a discursive link between the Christian (rather than the Muslim) Mary and Amina suggests a complex ideological and discursive hybridity that gave shape to textualized notions of the Prophet Muhammad for Castilian and Aragonese Moriscos. It can also be argued that because the *aljamiado-morisco* version states that Amina is "blessed...*above all women*" that her role as the mother of the Prophet supersedes that of Mary as the mother of Jesus. In short, if this line is an *aljamiado* addition not present in al-Bakri's text, then it reflects a significant testament to the complexity of the tensions and influence that existed between Christians and Muslims in sixteenth-century Castile and Aragon.[4] Conversely, if this line is a direct translation of al-Bakri's Arabic text, it merely reflects — with respect to its composition — the complex intertextual web that joined folkloric Islamic narratives to their Judeo-Christian counterparts, at least within Arab culture, during the Middle Ages.

The status of the line cited above (i.e., whether a direct translation, a significant reworking, or wholesale addition to al-Bakri's version) is of great importance if our goal is to make sense of the ideologies and processes that underlay the composition of the *aljamiado-morisco* version of the *Kitab al-anwar.* Such information, however, is of only marginal concern if we wish to understand the manner in which the *Libro de las luces* was actually engaged over time by members of Morisco communities. What I mean by this is that long after any *aljamiado* translation of al-Bakri's *Kitab al-anwar* was first redacted, the text — now refashioned as the *Libro de las luces* — continued to be shaped and took on meaning within social contexts characterized by a great deal of activity (and talk) around the text. Given the prevalence and importance of such discursive activity over time, the first redaction of the *Libro de las luces* can tell us only very little about the contextualized meaning and use of the text. After all, it was through the recopying activities of the *Libro de las luces'* readers (and their listening, participatory public) over time that the text took on contextualized meaning, both at the denotational and pragmatic level.

Given that our primary concern is not the text of the *Libro de las luces* per se, but rather its recontextualization and use within Morisco communities, we may leave aside issues of composition in favor of a focus on the socially embedded *engagement* of this and other texts by Morisco readers.[5] We are able to analyze the *Libro de las luces* as a text that at once *mediated* certain social processes and activities within Morisco communites (such as the carrying out of ritual activities and religious education) and *evoked* cultural and moral frameworks that in turn helped to shape collective theories of reality. In other words, regardless of the details surrounding the original redaction of the passage that describes Amina as "blessed above all women," we know that in the second half of the sixteenth century this passage — along with the rest of the *Libro de las luces* — was actively recopied and performed in Morisco communities in just the form that we have it. Our focus, then, moves from the authorial or translational impulse that this and other passages might have reflected to a consideration of how crypto-Muslim readers in Castile and Aragon engaged it and put it to use.

Text, Mediation, and Situated Activities

The first theoretical frame that concerns us is the idea of mediation. By this term I mean to focus on the ways in which passages of the *Libro de las luces* were employed to mediate (and thus, give shape to) the performance of specific, socially embedded activities within Morisco communities in Castile and Aragon. The idea of *mediation,* given central importance within Marxist notions of culture, has an important place within the more general study of language and culture. Duranti, attempting to delineate theories of culture that have informed linguistic research in anthropology, speaks of the critical tendency to view culture itself (and thus, language) as a system of mediation:

> Culture organizes the use of tools in specific activities, such as hunting, cooking, building, fighting, remembering the past and planning the future. In each case, people's ability to appropriate, exploit, or control nature or their interaction with other human beings is augmented or simply modified by the use of tools. Our relation with the world, however, needs not always be mediated. If it starts raining while we are sitting in a park and our hair and face gets wet, the relation between us and nature becomes more direct, less mediated (we still have our clothes and our thoughts). If we pull out an umbrella, however, by trying to control nature's impact on part of our body, we modify the potential consequences of a natural phenomenon to fit our needs or limitations. In this case, our relation with nature is mediated by a specific tool, the umbrella, which, in this case, represents culture. (1997, 40)

This view, which frames both material and symbolic elements of culture as tools employed by humans to control or shape our relation to nature (as well as to each other), focuses upon language primarily as an instrument that we employ in order to act in the world. Of course, tools not only facilitate activities; they also shape and limit our practical possibilities: an umbrella may allow us to keep dry in a rainstorm; however, it also forces us to walk in the rain with only one hand free. In just such a way, the language we use not only facilitates a certain range of activities; it also structures and places limits on our thoughts and actions, as research on linguistic relativity and systems of deixis has shown (Hanks 1990, 1996; Lucy 1993; Whorf 1956).

Turning our attention to texts and the physical, culturally structured objects (e.g., codices and loose manuscript folios) that contain them, we begin to see the utility of this notion of mediation for our analysis of Morisco narrative and temporality. For in questions of written discourse, we are always dealing with the symbolic aspects of culture in conjunction with material ones: if language mediates our relation to the physical world and to each other, then the material, built objects through which we encounter certain forms of language use likewise have a mediational function with respect to time and cultural practice. This point was underlined in the middle of the last century by Edward Sapir, who argued:

> To knock on a door is a substitute for the more primitive act of shoving it open of one's own accord. We have here the rudiments of what might be called language. A vast number of acts are language in this crude sense. That is, they are not of importance to us because of the work they immediately do, but because they serve as mediating signs of other more important acts. (1949, 164)

Central to Sapir's argument regarding rudimentary language and human activity is the question of time: "they are not of importance to us because of the work they immediately do, but because they serve as mediating signs of other more important acts." These "more important acts" inevitably take place in what is framed as a potential or even desirable future for participants. What is interesting however, is that these "more important acts" in the future take on significance within a temporal framework of action and experience that moves across the theoretical boundaries that separate past ("door-knocking" as an already established genre of activity), present (the concrete act of knocking *this time*), and future (what one hopes to achieve — at various levels — through knocking). In a very direct way, we have returned once again to Heidegger's point regarding the temporally situated "in-order-to-ness" of reading a clock and Husserl's discussion of the thick present. In Sapir's example of knocking on a door, we are similarly engaging in this act in order to reckon with and shape events in the future, not in order to consider the door as such (i.e., we are not, primarily anyway, testing its strength or appreciating the craftsmanship that went into its production). Generally, we knock on a door *in order that* those inside will open it soon afterward. We may also knock in certain ways to communicate anger, authority, humor, or familiarity, thus further shaping the future actions of those inside (e.g., causing them to hurry, or to prepare for a warm, friendly greeting).[6] There is a strong element of time consciousness in such a use of the door, as opposed to the much more immediate and direct act of kicking in the door or crashing through a wall. Like the language games discussed by Ludwig Wittgenstein (1999 [1958]) or the tendency of conversational narratives of the past to "step into the future" (Ochs 1994), knocking on a door can be seen as an example of the use of an established "discursive" genre to shape events and moral stances in an as yet unrevealed future.

In similar fashion to Sapir's door example, the activities that revolve around written texts always imply time-consciousness and processes of discursive mediation. In picking up a book, whether to compose, recopy, or read the text within it, I am always doing so *in order to* perform some activity within a social context shaped, in turn, by my implementation of the book as cultural artifact. As Pierre Bourdieu would argue, even the cultural predisposition (or *habitus*) to pick up a book in the first place implies our agentive participation in systems of practice that structure our social world, even without any conscious "aiming at ends" on our part (1990, 53). And when our engagement of written discourse involves other human participants imbued with varying levels of agency and subjectivity (as was often the case with handwritten texts shared by members of communities in medieval and early modern Europe) the mediational power of these texts grows exponentially.

With regard to time and temporality, written texts can serve as effective tools that facilitate and put boundaries on the discursive back-and-forth that in turn gives shape to collective theories of the past, present, and a range of possible futures. This point is key for any contextualized understanding of *aljamiado-morisco* narrative. As doors are designed to shape and channel our movement in and out of built structures, as well as the access that we have to interior and exterior spaces around these structures, so written discourse (and the material artifacts that contain it) functions to shape and facilitate a wide range of activities carried out in concrete social settings across the human dimension of time. Of course, written texts are much more complex than doors, and the language found within books and analogous cultural artifacts is almost always much more subtle than any "knock-knock-*knock*" on a door. However, the situatedness — both in time, place, and practice — of both examples binds them together.

Turning our attention back to the *Libro de las luces,* we are able to see with some specificity how individual copies of this written text mediated the socially embedded actions of readers and the listening public within Castilian and Aragonese Morisco communities. Looking at Madrid, BRAH ms. 11/9413, we find, on folio 120ᵛ, an interesting group of marginal annotations that suggests the institutionalized activities within which this text was employed, as well as the participation frameworks that surrounded its use.

The text on folio 120ᵛ deals with a conversation between 'Abd al-Muttalib and his son Abu Talib about the rearing of Muhammad and the special powers that the young prophet possesses:

> ... the children of 'Abd al-Muttalib were of many mothers, and as Abu Talib and Abdullah had the same mother, Abu Talib raised Muhammad (PBUH). 'Abd al-Muttalib said to him: "My son, Abu Talib, take my grandson Muhammad (PBUH) with goodness, peace, spirtual blessings, and good fortune, for if you live you will see wonders in him. My son, when you prepare food, do not let anyone eat it until Muhammad puts his hand on it, and you will see his spiritual blessings and wonder." Abu Talib replied, "I will do this if God wants it." His father then said, "You already know that there are many children in my house and at times I can provide only little to eat. When Muhammad (PBUH) puts his hand on the food it increases and is blessed for all.⁷

The connection between spiritual blessings (*baraka*) and food (*viᵞenda/ vivanda*) in this passage revolves around the special powers of Muhammad to increase both. As a metonymic reference to Islam itself, the Prophet serves as a figure for ritual religious practice before a meal: as Muhammad places his hand on the food, so should a devout Muslim pray over it, an activity that implies specific embodied practices and postures.

In the lower margin of this folio, we find a series of notes written by five different Arabic hands that gives a different sense of this text's meaning. The first note, moving right to left, reads: "Today we will give." Beside this prediction, written in a much broader hand, a direct object is added: "the letter." To the left of these, written in thin, hurried strokes, we find: "Dinner." Next to this, in yet a different hand, a reply: "I've already had dinner." Then, in a long note that creeps up the inner margin and onto the next folio, the textual conversation closes with: "Well, let's dance, and we'll give the letter." The exchange can be represented in the following way:

Hand	English	Spanish
2	Today we will give	Hoy daremox
1	the letter	la karta
3	Dinner	Çena
4	I've already had dinner	Ya he çenado
5	Well, let's dance, and we'll give the letter	Pu^wex bamox a bailar i daremox la karta

None of these note hands corresponds to that of the text. Also, there is a sloppiness to the writing, combined with certain orthographic errors (e.g., not connecting a medial *yaa* to the *lam* that follows it). From these features, we can conclude that these notes were not written by any *alfakí* or other learned Morisco. Rather, these notes reflect the at times playful back-and-forth of students reading the *Libro de las luces* as part of their religious education.

Little is known about the religious instruction of Castilian and Aragonese Moriscos, though we do know that it was general practice for crypto-Muslim parents to send their teenage boys to local *alfakíes* to learn about Islam (Cardaillac 1979). It is also known that an important part of the teaching practices of these *alfakíes* included literacy instruction in *aljamiado,* which implied the use of Islamic texts. In fact, a large number of extant *aljamiado* manuscripts speak to, *inter alia,* the instructional, socializing activities within which they were used. Such use is generally made evident through the didactic theme of the text itself (the *Breviario çunni* of Içà de Gebir and the literary output of the Mançebo de Arévalo being good examples of these).

In part through the socially embedded discursive practice of reading and writing, local *alfakíes* worked to convert young boys into young Muslims. And what the lectoral notes at the bottom of folio 120^v of BRAH ms. 11/9413 provide us with is concrete evidence of the use of narrative texts such as the *Libro de las luces* in the religious instruction of Morisco boys, as well as the use of the physical space within these books by students to mediate their own, less structured, discursive interaction. We cannot know with certainty whether the five boys who wrote in the margins of BRAH ms. 11/9413 were all present as they marked up the margins of this book, though it is possible to construct at least a hypothetical timeline for them. First, it is most likely, from its placement with respect to the text and the other notes — as well as its starkly different hand — that "karta" was the first note written on the folio. Afterward, someone seems to have added "Hoy daremos" before it to complete the phrase. The time between this first and second note might be significant; however, the temporal distance between the second and the remaining three notes seems to close considerably, as each refers to a temporal frame in the very near future or the recent past. The second note situates itself within a specific, though relative timeframe: "*Hoy* daremos" (*Today* we will give). The other notes, though quite possibly written on *today*s that differ from that of the first or second note, maintain the proximal and relative timeframe introduced by the second.

The third note seems to relate both to the text itself — which, as I have already mentioned, is about food — and to the reader's own desires. He writes "çena" (dinner), as though the text were making him hungry; however, he is also possibly responding to the idea of "giving the letter" on that day, arguing that he is more interested in eating. The fourth note is a direct response to the third; the reader answers his colleague, responding that he has already had dinner and has no interest in dining again: "ya he çenado" (I've already had dinner). Finally, the fifth reader attempts to resolve the impasse by suggesting some dancing before they "give the letter." What it means to "give the letter" is unknown; however, we may imagine that it is somehow associated with their studies. Whatever the particulars of their interaction, it remains clear that young Morisco boys in Castile and Aragon studied the *Libro de las luces* as part of their religious education, and that they at times used the margins of shared manuscript codices to mediate their own "unofficial" discursive interaction (perhaps while the *alfakí* had his back turned or was otherwise occupied).

Looking at the use of the *Libro de las luces* as an instructional work, we begin to see the ways in which this handwritten text mediated cultural practice within local, quasi-institutional settings in Morisco communities. The point that I wish to emphasize, based on the presence of the marginal notes in BRAH ms. 11/9413, is that the *Libro de las luces* was engaged by Morisco readers of differing levels of expertise and authority within socially embedded activities. These activities served a range of ends that undoubtedly changed over time; however, a relatively stable use to which the *Libro de la luces* was put had to do with processes of language socialization carried out by *alfakíes* as they sought to make their young students part of the larger Muslim community. By language socialization, I mean the process by which people become members of given communities through the acquisition of language and the cultural information encoded in such an activity. Elinor Ochs, who together with Bambi B. Schieffelin has pioneered this field of research within anthropology, defines language socialization as research that examines "how language practices organize the life span process of becoming an active, competent participant in one or more communities" (1999, 230). What such research entails is an account not only of the specific discursive features of interaction between neophyte and veteran interlocutors, but also how these features relate to larger, cultural practices and beliefs. In the case of Morisco *alfakíes* and their young students, it implies an account of how the uses to which these interlocutors put handwritten texts and books relate to and even shape broader cultural phenomena.

What specifically does it mean to consider the *Libro de las luces* as a written text engaged within the larger process of language socialization? As I have argued at the beginning of this chapter, such a focus situates the text within the daily cultural life of human agents, forging a direct analytical link between written narrative and the social world of the Moriscos. As young Morisco boys learned to read and write *aljamiado,* became familiar with popular Islamic narratives and their ritual uses, and gained familiarity with the Qur'an and the distinct religious practices of Sunni Muslims in sixteenth-century Castile and Aragon, they simultaneously became full members of their communities — possessing not only the knowledge that placed them within their social groups, but also an identifiable, relatively stable form of habitus that corresponded to such groups over time. These forms of habitus, systems of internalized dispositions that structured Morisco cultural practice even as the activities carried out by members of Morisco communities gave these dispositions their shape within constantly changing contexts, both structured and were structured by the instructive activities that took place around and within the folios of the *Libro de las luces.* In other words, the *Libro de las luces* was not only made use of within Morisco communities in Castile and Aragon, but was made use of in specific, culturally structured and structuring ways.

Beyond the use to which the *Libro de las luces* was put within the process of language socialization in Morisco communities throughout Castile and Aragon, there is evidence that this text was employed in other sorts of activities as well. In the rest of this chapter, we will be returning to the passage of the *Libro de las luces* that describes the miraculous events that occur after the birth of the Prophet, linking this passage to its engagement within specific forms of ritual paractice in the crypto-Muslim communities of Castile and Aragon.

"El Nacimiento del Profeta" and Its Manuscript Context

Before presenting an interpretive analysis of the text of the section of the *Libro de las luces* that deals with the birth of Muhammad (= "El nacimiento del Profeta") and its place within Morisco ritual practice, it is necessary to offer a detailed description of the textual fragment that characterizes the Prophet as the product of a *kaxami^yento kaxto xin adulteri^yo* (a chaste marriage free from adultery). Present in four of the five extant manuscripts, the selected fragment presents significant variations with respect to the textual elements that make up the passage in each manuscript. A consideration of these variations makes it possible to consider the fragment as a textual index within each manuscript that partially illustrates the manner in which reading and writing, among other forms of social practice, served in crypto-Muslim communities as a tool to negotiate and define cultural life.

The textual fragment in question is directly preceded within the frame of the narrative, as I have mentioned above, by a debate between the clouds, the angels (*los almalakes*), and the birds, in which they argue over who should be in charge of the early care of the newborn Muhammad. The whole passage, as it reads in BRAH ms. 11/9414 f. 103^r is as follows:

> And they heard a *k^alamador,* who said, "Cease all that, as God has already ordered that he is to be cared for by Halima, bint Abi-Duwayb Assadiyya." And he said, "The Prophet (PBUH) came from a clean marriage untouched by adultery. Since Adam (PBUH), the adultery of the ignorant has not touched me/him." And the Prophet (PBUH) was born on Monday, on the twelfth day of Rabi'a al-Awwal, fifteen years after the coming of the company of the elephant and the forging of the house of Mecca...."[8]

There is some confusion in this and other versions of the text, as it is unclear whether the statement regarding the "clean marriage" that produced the Prophet is presented by the *k^alamador* or by the newborn Prophet himself. In both BRAH ms. 11/9414 and Real Biblioteca ms. II/3225 the text reads very clearly, *no me tokó adulteri^yo* (the adultery...did not touch me), suggesting that it is the Prophet who speaks in these lines. In addition, it is more than a little difficult to frame the dialogue within this passage (neither manuscript uses punctuation or otherwise divides dialogue from the narrative frame), given that it is unclear how to divide it up. It is possible, for example, to read, "And he [i.e., the k*a*lamador] said, 'The Prophet...'" or "And the Prophet said...," given that in both Old Castilian and Arabic (the latter's syntax persistently runs through *aljamiado* prose) it is common for sentences to begin with conjunction-verb combinations, as in "Y dijo annabi..." or "Wa qala al-nabi..." (Orduna 2001). Also, there is a parallelism created between the "i dixo annabi" (and the Prophet said) of the passage's beginning and the "i naçi*y*ó annabi" (and the Prophet was born) that follows it. This evidence, which runs against the in some ways more logical reading of the passage that situates the k*a*lamador as the sole speaker (López-Morillas 1994, 79), will be considered later in this chapter. For the present, I would like to present the variations that appear in each manuscript copy of "El nacimiento del Profeta" in order to give readers a concrete sense of the texts actually engaged by Morisco readers in Castile and Aragon.[9]

In all five extant manuscripts of the *Libro de las luces,* the narrative context that precedes the appearance of the k*a*lamador is identical: "And they heard a k*a*lamador who said..." (Y oyeron un k*a*lamador ke dixo...). The first variations between these manuscripts appear with the words uttered by the k*a*lamador:

(1): "...cease those [arguments] — he said — as God already has someone to care for him'..." (...dexalos dixo ke ya ti*y*ene Allah ki*y*en lo k*i*ri*y*e...) (Madrid, Biblioteca Nacional ms. 4955, f. 118*r*).

(2): "...leave each other be, as God already has someone to care for him..." (...lexadvos xe*y*er ke ya ti*y*ene Allah ki*y*en lo k*i*ri*y*e...) (Madrid, Real Biblioteca ms. II/3225, f. 137*r*).

(3): "...cease this dispute as God has already decided that he is to be cared for by Halima, bint Abi-Duwayb Assadiyya..." (...dexadvos de do exa dixtuta ke ya ti*y*ene Allah ke a de xe*y*er k*i*ri*y*ado por mano de Halima fija de Abi Duwayb al-Ça'adiya...) (Madrid, Biblioteca de la Real Academia de la Historia ms. 11/9410 f. 264*v*).

(4): "...leave each other be, as God has ordered that he is to be cared for by Halima, bint Abi-Duwayb Assadiya..." (...lexadvos xe*y*er ke ti*y*ene Allah ordenado ke a de ser k*i*ri*y*ado por mano de Halima fija de Abi Duwayb al-Ça'adiya...) (Madrid, Biblioteca de la Real Academia de la Historia, ms. 11/9413, f. 106*v*).

(5): "...cease all that, as God has already ordered that he is to be cared for by Halima, bint Abi-Duwayb Assadiyya..." (...dexadvos dexo ke ya ti^yene Allah ordenado ke a de xe^yer k^iri^yado por mano de Halima hija de Abi Duwayb al-Ça'adiya...) (Madrid, Biblioteca de la Real Academia de la Historia, ms. 11/9414, f. 103^r).

Manuscripts (1) and (2) dramatize the dialogue between the *k^alamador* and his interlocutors in ways that go beyond that of the other copies. In both manuscripts, after the *k^alamador* says that God has already decided who is to care for Muhammad, the angels, clouds, and birds ask him the following: "...and who will care for him?" (...y ki^yen será?). It is as a reply to this collective question that the *k^alamador* responds: "Halima, the daughter of abi Duwayb al-Ça'adiyya." These conversational turns lend a bit of suspense to the narrative, though they also render it closer to the narrative style of performed theatrical texts (Briggs 1988). In this, the formal aspects of these two texts index the performed character of the text — something that runs throughout the *Libro de las luces*. In manuscripts (3), (4), and (5) this specific system of narrative turns is absent. In these, the *k^alamador,* without the discursive intervention of the other characters, continues announcing the name of Halima as part of his original conversational turn.

In all of the manuscripts, with the exception of (3), the *k^alamador* introduces the fragment that speaks to the genealogy of the Prophet. Once the *k^alamador* makes clear the special circumstances that surround the conception of Muhammad, he — or in mss. (2) and (5), possibly the Prophet himself — proclaims:

(1): "...the Prophet (PBUH) came from a chaste marriage..." (...annabi 'sm xali^yó de kaxami^yento kaxto...).

(2): "...[the Prophet (PBUH)] came from a chaste marriage..." ...([annabi 'sm] xali^yó de kaxamie^ynto kaxto...).

(4): "...the Prophet Muhammad (PBUH) came from his chaste marriage..." (...annabi Muhammad 'sm xali^yó de su kaxami^yento kaxsto...).

(5): "...[the Prophet (PBUH)] came from a chaste marriage..." (...[annabi 'sm] xali/ó de kaxami^yento kaxto...).

Manuscript (3) does not include this utterance, which suggests — together with a greater incorporation of Arabic lexicon and syntax in (3) — that this qualification of the Prophet's "chaste" genealogy is an addition made in later copies of the *aljamiado* translation of the *Kitab al-anwar.* This textual addition is significant not only for questions having to do with the text's compositional process, but also for more complex questions related to the text's performance within specific contexts of ritual practice. It is possible, in fact, that the socially embedded use of "El nacimiento del Profeta" shaped the form of the text itself, giving it a character meant to respond to Christian claims and beliefs regarding the birth of Jesus and the "illegitimacy" of Muhammad as a prophet.

Speaking to the clean ancestry of Muhammad, the narrator lends theological specificity to his claims when he explains, in four of the five manuscripts, that not only was the marriage that produced Muhammad *kaxto,* but that in it there was no adultery of the "ignorant ones" (*torpex/jehilex*):

(1): "...without the adultery of the ignorant ones..." (...xin adulteri*ʸ*o de lox torpex...).

(2): "...without adultery since Adam...the adultery of the ignorant ones has not touched me..." (...xin adulteri*ʸ*o dexde Edam...no me tokó adulteri*ʸ*o de lox torpex...).

(4): "...without the adultery of the ignorant ones..." (...xin adulteri*ʸ*o de lox *jehilex.*...).

(5): "...without adultery since Adam...the adultery of the ignorant ones has not touched me..." (...xin adulteri*ʸ*o dexde Edam...no me tokó adulteri*ʸ*o de lox *jehilex*...).

Manuscripts (1) and (4) are similar insofar as in neither does there exist any mention of the figure of Adam; nevertheless, they differ superficially in their specific qualification of adultery. In (1) the word *torpes* is used, while in (4) we find the term *jehilex*. This fact suggests an equivalence between the term *torpe* and the Arabic *jahil,* or "one ignorant [of Islam]" — a fact that further suggests that other Romance terms such as *kaxami*ʸ*ento kaxto* and *adulteri*ʸ*o* are themselves Arabic calques, or at least words that denote specific Islamic values.

Manuscripts (2) and (5) have in common the inclusion of the figure of Adam and the transcription of the indirect pronoun *me*. This *me* seems to emphasize the performative and conversational character of this narrative in much the same way that the narrative turns between the *kᵃlamador* and the clouds, birds, and angels in (1) and (2) do. In (2) and (5) this discursive back-and-forth is achieved through an explicit framing of the Prophet as an active participant in the conversation, notwithstanding his tender age of three days.

In spite of what we find in the manuscript copies of the *Libro de las luces,* it is necessary to mention that there is a certain logic to the decision made by Consuelo López-Morillas, in her partial edition of manuscript 11/9414 of the Biblioteca de la Real Academia de la Historia, to substitute *le tokó* for *me tokó* (1994, 79). From the narrative point of view, her transcription seems more coherent if we think that the narrative is driven by the *kᵃlamador:*

(2): " ... he came ... without adultery since Adam ... the adultery of the ignorant ones did not touch him ... " (... xaliʸó ... xin adulteriʸo dexde Edam
 ... no [le] tokó adulteriʸo de lox torpex ...).

(5): " ... he came ... without adultery since Adam ... the adultery of the ignorant ones did not touch him ... " (... xaliʸó ... xin adulteriʸo dexde Edam
 ... no [le] tokó adulteriʸo de lox *jehilex* ...).

For López-Morillas, the *me tokó* construction that frames the infant Muhammad as a participant in this conversational episode renders the narrative disjointed, causing the utterances on either side of it to lose syntactic coherence and meaning. López-Morillas opts for the reading: "Y dixo [el kᵃlamador]: El annabi ... salió de kasamiento kasto sin adulterio desde Adám. ... No le tocó adulterio de los jahiles" (1994, 79). In so doing, she breaks up the narrative line into two distinct sentences, both uttered by the *kᵃlamador.*

But there is no punctuation in either of these manuscripts, making it very possible that the line that López-Morillas breaks up into two separate parts was not read in this way. In fact, it is the very lack of punctuation, together with the placement of the text on the folio, that makes possible the "substitution" of *me* for *le* in both cases. Looking at the placement of the text on the manuscript folio in (2) and (5), it is possible to see how the line-by-line division of the text could facilitate — in part — the substitution of *me tokó* for *le tokó:*

(2)
... oyeron un kᵃlamador ke
dixo lexadvox xeʸer ke ya tiʸene Allah
kiʸen lo kⁱriʸe dixieron i kiʸen dixo Halima fija
de Abi Duwayb al-Ça'adiya y dixo annabi ('asm)
{f. 137ᵛ}

xaliʸó de kaxamiento xin adulteriʸo dexde
Edam alayhi al-çalam no me tokó adulteriʸo de lox
torpex i naçiʸó annabi. ...

(5)

...y oyeron un kᵃlamador ke dixo: Dexadvox dexo
ke ya tiʸene Allah ordenado ke a de xeʸer kⁱriʸado por mano
de Halima hija de Abi Duwayb al-Ça'adiya. I dixo: El annabi s'm
salió de kasamiʸento kaxto xin adulteriʸo dexde
Edam ('alayhi al-çalam) no me tokó adulteriʸo de lox jehilex i naçiʸó
el annabi ('alayhi al-çalam) diʸa de lunex a doze diʸas de Rabi'a
al-Awwal....

In the first example, there is a change not only from one line to the next in the middle of the *kᵃlamador*'s utterance, but also a change from the recto to the verso side of folio 137. In other words, there is a very large, physical space between the first clause, "i dixo annabi 'asm" and the next ("Xaliʸó de kaxamiʸento xin adulteriʸo ... "). After this jump from one side of the folio to the next, there is also a line jump between "xin adulteriʸo dexde" and "Edam alayhi al-çalam no me tokó" that adds to the confusion. In (5) there is no change from one side of the folio to the next, but this manuscript preserves the line jump between *dexde* and *Edam*. Given this physical gap, and the already difficult syntax of the passage, it is perhaps easy to see how the scribes of (2) and (5) could get a bit lost within the syntax of the utterance and copy it out replacing a *lam* (the first letter of *le*) with a *mim* (the first letter of *me*). Adding to the difficulty of these lines is the *aljamiado-morisco* manner of copying out the word *xaliʸó*: to the final *yaa* (which is not written in the hard-to-miss manner of the Arabic final *yaa,* but as a longer version of the letter's medial form) is added a *dama,* a vowel marker that signifies, in this case, the long *o* sound. Given its appearance in the inner margin of folio 137ᵛ in (2), the *dama* is easy to miss. And if it is missed, *xaliʸó de* (he came from) becomes *xalí de* (I came from).

There are other reasons for the substitution of *me* for *le* in this passage. For if it is a scribal error (and I believe it is), it is one that provides, on one hand, concrete textual data regarding the ways in which at least two copies of the *Libro de las luces* were read within Castilian and Aragonese Morisco communities. On the other hand, these slips of the pen also provide important evidence of the view that these scribes had of the Prophet Muhammad. To them, a narrative presentation of Muhammad as a participant in a conversation about his lineage is entirely possible and even logical in some sense. We are, in this case, far from the official Muslim view of the Prophet, but we are not far at all from the text of the Qur'an.

A deeper understanding of these manuscripts' framing of the newly born Muhammad as a participant in a conversation about his lineage is possible if we take into consideration the Qur'anic account of the birth of Jesus. A prophet born out of wedlock to a virgin mother, Jesus must immediately come to the defense of his mother as she presents herself and her newborn child to the rest of her community. In Sura 19:29–33, Mary's neighbors accuse her of having behaved immorally. Mary responds to their accusations by having them speak to her son. Taken by surprise, they express their doubts about the infant's ability to speak. Then the infant Jesus speaks, showing not only his miraculous powers, but his unique relationship with God:

29. But she pointed to him. They said: How should we speak to one who is a child in the cradle?

30. He said: I am indeed a servant of Allah. He has given me the Book and made me a prophet:

31. And He has made me blessed wherever I may be, and He has enjoined on me prayer and almsgiving so long as I live:

32. And to be kind to my mother; and He has not made me insolent, unblessed.

33. And peace on me the day I was born, and the day I die, and the day I am raised to life.

Given this miracle of Jesus in the Qur'an, and the (at the very least) problematic relation between Jesus — as both a central figure of Islam and an ominous reminder of Christian power in Spain — and Muhammad for the Moriscos, it is in a sense logical that a similar miracle could be ascribed to Muhammad in the *Libro de las luces*.

The miracle of early speech is all the more important for Muhammad, for it is his role as a reciter, and therefore a speaker, of God's word that singles him out. When the archangel Gabriel appears to him for the first time in the hills outside of the city of Mecca, the word *iq'ra* (recite) is the first that is revealed to him. Because he was ordered by God to speak His word to the Meccans and the rest of humanity, the gift of speech is central to the special powers of Muhammad and the very axis about which his relationship with God revolves. That for the Moriscos this power of speech should be at least as powerful — and God-given — as that possessed by Jesus makes a good deal of sense given the complex position of resistance in that the Moriscos found themselves as practicing Muslims who were also Christian converts living in a rapidly hardening Christian state.

Cultural Evocation and Ritual Performance

Having looked at the "El nacimiento del Profeta" portion of the *Libro de las luces* as a text employed in instructional activities carried out between Morisco *alfakíes* and adolescent boys, we have also considered its relation to broader categories of belief and practice among the Moriscos (e.g., the relation between the figures of Jesus and Muhammad and the important role of speech within the Muslim faith). Finally, it is necessary to consider the text of "El nacimiento del Profeta" in the context of the ritual activities within which it was used. These ritual practices, which were frequently mediated by verbal as well as written narratives, involved a much larger portion of the Morisco community and thus allow us to consider the role of narrative in the practice of a wider swath of Morisco society, including its engagement by women.

According to Francisco Guillén Robles, Morisco communities in Aragon read sections of the *Libro de las luces* as part of their celebration of various religious festivals (1889, 39). The book as a whole, as Fournel-Guérin asserts, was one of the more widely read texts within Aragonese Morisco communities:

> Next to the Qur'an, the precepts of which accompany the faithful in their daily life, one finds among the books seized by the Inquisition biographies of Muhammad, polemical texts aimed at denigrating the Christian religion, prayer manuals, and Muslim prophecies.... Many new Aragonese converts were also condemned [by the Inquisition] for having read a book entitled *De las luces* dealing with the Muslim religion. (1979, 250–51)[10]

The section of the *Libro de las luces* that I have termed "El nacimiento del Profeta" was read in ritual settings within Morisco communities during the yearly festival of the birth of Muhammad (*Mawlid al-Nabi*), celebrated on 12 *Rabi'a al-Awwal* (the twelfth day of the third month of the Islamic calendar). Due to the thematic similarity of *Mawlid al-Nabi* to Christmas, the Christian celebration of the birth of Jesus, various Islamic legal authorities have from the medieval to the modern period censured the festival, citing the need for Muslims to be reminded of the wholly human character of the Prophet.[11] For these authorities, the celebration of the birth of the Prophet simultaneously reflects an erroneous understanding of the status of Muhammad on the part of many Muslim communities and an all too close relation to the religious practice of Christians. Such anxiety about Christian practice was without a doubt a concern for Morisco *alfakíes* and other Spanish Muslims pushed into a difficult corner at the beginning of the sixteenth century, as evidenced by the aforementioned words of Yuçe de Banegas, an elderly Granadan Morisco interviewed by the Mancebo de Arévalo in the latter's *Sumario de la relaçion y ejercicio espiritual:* "What troubles me most is that Muslims will be indistinguishable from Christians, accepting their dress, and not avoiding their food. May God grant that at least they avoid their actions...." (Harvey 1993, 219).

Such palpable anxiety regarding the imminent conversion of Muslims to Christianity did not, obviously, prevent Castilian and Aragonese Moriscos from celebrating *Mawlid al-Nabi* up until their expulsion at the start of the seventeenth century. What we know about these celebrations — that is, beyond the public reading of narratives dealing with the Prophet's birth and life such as the *Libro de las luces* — comes from earlier Muslim accounts of the festival, such as the *fatwa* produced by Imam Jalal al-Din al-Suyuti (b. 1445 CE), a late medieval Egyptian commentator of the Qur'an:

> In my view the Meelad Shareef, Celebration of the Birthday of the Noble Prophet (*sallal laahu alaihi wasallam*) is in fact such an occasion of happiness on which people assemble and recite the Holy Quran to the extent that is easy. Then they relate the prophecies concerning the appearance of the Noble Prophet (*sallal laahu alaihi wasallam*) that have been transmitted in Ahadith and Athar, and the miraculous events and signs that took place on his birth. Then food is set before them and according to their desire they partake thereof to satisfaction. This festival of celebrating the birthday of the Noble Prophet (*sallal laahu alaihi wasallam*), is a Bid'ah Hasanah (a good innovation) and those arranging it will get blessings, since in such a celebration is found the expression of joy and happiness at the greatness and eminence of the Noble Prophet (*salall laahu alaihi wasallam*) at his birth. (2004, par. 6)

The textual activities that al-Suyuti describes — reading from the Qur'an, narrating the miraculous events that surrounded the birth and life of the Prophet — are significant first because they explicitly foreground the use of these texts within the cultural practice of Muslim communities. However, they are important also because they strongly suggest that we should expand our understanding of who read *aljamiado-morisco* narratives to include women and possibly even small children, who would have at least been present while narratives of the Prophet's birth and life were read out loud during the celebration of *Mawlid al-Nabi* and most likely other religious festivals as well. Modern historians such as Lea (1901), Vincent and Domínguez-Ortiz (1978), and Fournel-Guérin (1979) have documented the possession of books by Morisco women, though they have been able to say very little about their actual reading practices. Given the almost certain participation of Morisco women in the celebration of a range of religious festivals and ceremonies within which texts of varying sorts were read aloud or narrated, it seems important to begin to tease out as much as possible the ways in which not only time and temporality, but issues as fluid and complex as gender, were encoded within *aljamiado* texts and negotiated in part through their engagement.

Focusing on the issues of time and temporality as we are, it is possible to see the Moriscos' use of traditional Islamic texts within situated activities — such as the yearly celebration of the birth of the Prophet — as a means of connecting themselves, in a mediated though wholly embodied way, to the larger Muslim world shaped and conditioned by God's revelation to Muhammad and the coming (but when?) Day of Judgment. This Islamic world, with roots in God's act of creation and his early willingness to forgive Adam's transgressions, extends outward in time to the final day of God's creation and his judgment of the wicked and the faithful. It is immediately and forcefully indexed, as an order of reality and a temporal frame that subverts and transcends the Christian order, through readers' engagement of traditional narrative texts such as the *Libro de las luces* in the course of ritual activities and celebrations.

The indexical function that traditional Islamic texts possessed within Morisco communities runs parallel to the great power that these texts had to evoke a world that at once transcended and mitigated the daily fears faced by crypto-Muslims in sixteenth- and early seventeenth-century Spain. This specific notion of *evocation*, first introduced by Roger M. Keesing in an article dealing with the advantages and drawbacks inherent in a particular vein of symbolic anthropological research, speaks to the far from uniform processes by which cultural *texts* (as framed by anthropologists such as Clifford Geertz and Sherry Ortner) take on meaning within human communities. He argues:

> What, then, about a culture as a system of *meanings?* Kwaio culture as text — the symbols deployed in ritual and in everyday life and talk — is there to be "read" by native participants. But the *meanings,* or at least many of the deeper meanings a symbolist would want to uncover, are not there *as part of the text.* Many of these meanings need not be

shared and public, need not be understood by those who *live* Kwaio culture, follow its guidelines and procedures, stay within its boundaries. Meanings, we might better say, are not in the cultural texts, not inherent in cultural symbols, but *evoked* by them. Some meanings are shared and public, others are not. They are, to change the image back again, deeper layers of the onion. What symbols mean to native actors depends upon what they know. (1987, 164)

Keesing's argument is significant in that it foregrounds the processes by which native actors generate and express local theories of knowledge and meaning. As Marilyn Strathern puts it, Keesing's focus on meaning as something reflexively generated by human actors (that is, they themselves have opinions and take stances with respect to it) in situated activities such as, in the case of the Moriscos, religious and literacy instruction, book production, and ritual practice, essentially "evaporates [his] dilemma between the search for deep meaning and avoiding interpretations that are too deep. We can be content with acknowledging [a native actor's] own powers of extrapolation" (1987, 173).

Theoretically and methodologically, the change of focus suggested by Keesing is of extraordinary importance within anthropology (Clifford and Marcus 1986). Keesing situates the meaning of cultural "texts" not within the texts themselves, but within the dialogic intersection between the researcher's observations and the diverse theories that native actors themselves provide.[12] Shifting to a research paradigm that focuses on the dialogic relation between the interpretive efforts of scholars (over time) and those of native actors/readers is of particular significance for scholars of medieval and early modern literature. Given the tremendous quantity of metadiscursive and indexical discourse contained within manuscripts — especially those produced and shared by a more or less well defined and stable community — it is entirely possible to fold the native voices in and around the manuscript texts that we study into our own analyses. In the case of the *Libro de las luces,* this means taking seriously the marginal notes left by readers and considering the texts within the situated activities in which they were engaged, even if we have access only to a very generalized sense of these activities.

It is crucial to keep in mind that Keesing's argument, similar to Pierre Bourdieu's criticism of theories that see language as a symbolic treasure equally shared by all members of a culture (1991), does not go so far as to dissolve into relativism; his point is not that each native actor will interpret a given text or situation according to the dictates of his or her own psyche. Rather, he is suggesting that knowledge is always socially embedded and that it is never evenly distributed or uniform, even within the most egalitarian societies.[13]

We gain a sense of the situated nature of cultural meaning, as well as the distributed and irregular understanding that abides in Morisco social contexts, by considering once again the different manuscript versions of "El nacimiento del Profeta." Returning to our analysis of the substitutions that occur between *me tokó* and *le tokó* that frame the three-day-old Prophet as a conversational participant in manuscripts (2) and (5), we may consider how these textual features might have served to evoke meaning for Morisco readers.

As I have already argued, the substitution of *me* for *le* in manuscripts (2) and (5) provides important evidence regarding the view that the scribes of these manuscript copies had of the Prophet Muhammad. To begin with, this reframing indexes the belief that the infant Muhammad could have participated in a conversation about his lineage within the generic confines of traditional Islamic narrative and ritual performance. It also constructs an intertextual relation between this account of the Prophet's birth and the Qur'anic account of the miracles that surrounded the birth of Jesus. There can be little doubt that the figure of Jesus, whether in his Qur'anic or biblical avatar, presented the Moriscos with difficult hermeneutical and practical challenges. For example, how were they to reconcile the privileged place of Jesus within the Islamic faith with their need to distance themselves as much as possible from Christian beliefs and practice? The answer to this question lies within the minute details of Morisco cultural practice in concrete social settings, details that have been encoded, at least to a partial extent, within the manuscript books that they produced and engaged within these activities. It is in this way that a consideration of the individual manuscript copies that represent the miraculous birth and infancy of the Prophet as evocations of cultural meanings within Morisco communities takes us to a more dynamic, contextualized, and dialogic understanding of the meaning of *aljamiado-morisco* narratives.

Meditating on the utility of manuscript copies as sources for sociohistorical data, we may return to Rico's lament: "By definition, we have no access to the more complex oral versions and performances..." (1996, 251). Nevertheless, and as if it were his intention to open up an avenue of investigation where he had just claimed there was no entry, Rico finishes this same sentence by beginning to map out a means of at least partial access: "... but there is nothing more fundamental than to compare the versatility of the copies. Nothing, either, more understandable: each copy could not but reflect the impulse that had given it origin..." (1996, 251).[14] Weaving Rico's brief argument together with what we have seen in the *aljamiado-morisco* manuscript copies of the *Libro de las luces,* we may see how individual manuscript copies do more than "reflect" the discursive practice of Castilian and Aragonese Moriscos. They serve, in fact, as a resource for the continuous negotiation of this practice. As an evocation of the finite range of culturally embedded meanings and as a mediating resource for the performance of various activities — all of them intricately intertwined with culturally embedded notions of time and temporality — the *Libro de las luces* is much more than a static text somehow encoded with meaning. It is, rather, a rich locus of interaction and practice.

5

A Morisco Philosophy
of Suffering and Action

And when his Lord tried Abraham with certain commands he fulfilled them. He said: "Surely I will make thee a leader of men." [Abraham] said: "And of my offspring?" "My covenant does not include the wrong-doers," said He.

—Qur'an 2:124

One of the first things that catches modern readers' attention when looking at *aljamiado-morisco* narratives in their manuscript context is that these narratives are frequently part of a large collection of texts bound within the same codex. Analogous in a very general way to modern literary anthologies or course readers used by university professors, the overwhelming majority of *aljamiado-morisco* manuscripts in fact contain a number of texts, many of which are not, strictly speaking, narrative in form. An example of such an anthology is Toledo, BCLM ms. 395, an *aljamiado-morisco* manuscript copied out near the end of the sixteenth century, which contains the following texts:

ff. 1–41: Muhammad's answers, based on the Qur'an, to questions related to theology, liturgy, and natural science

ff. 41–58: Litany

ff. 58–60: On the revelation given to Muhammad by the angel Gabriel

ff. 66–71: Rhymed explanation of an ejaculatory prayer written as an amulet

ff. 75–87: Laws on inheritance[1]

There is a definite religious current running through all of these works, though they all differ with respect to both form and function. The first 41 folios of the manuscript seem to be a sort of compendium of practical, though divinely authoritative, knowledge from the Qur'an that was perhaps meant for the use of a local *alfakí* or other Islamic authority. Folios 41–60, however, provide very specific knowledge regarding religious devotion and the nature of Qur'anic revelation. The rhymed explanation of a prayer written as an amulet that occupies folios 66–71 more than likely served some sort of medicinal function (or perhaps, in keeping with popular Islamic beliefs and practices, it was meant to ward off evil), though further study of the text would be necessary in order to determine its contents and possible use. The last text, dealing with Islamic inheritance laws, falls squarely within the framework of texts copied and used (even to the present day) by local and itinerant *qawad,* or Islamic judges, who since the earliest days of Islam have been charged with the authority to settle disputes — such as those surrounding issues of inheritance — within Muslim communities. And while such juridico-religious activities were vigorously prohibited by Christian authorities by the second half of the sixteenth century, there is evidence, from Inquisition records to *aljamiado-morisco* manuscripts such as Toledo, BCLM ms. 395, that suggests the widespread presence of men carrying out the work of such judges within Morisco communities throughout Castile and Aragon (García-Arenal 1978). Approached from the point of view of its socially embedded use, Toledo, BCLM ms. 395 seems to have been a tremendously practical anthology — a sort of manual of specialized religious and legal knowledge that most likely served to mediate a number of official and quasi-official activities within and between specific Morisco communities.

Turning to the contextualized meaning of traditional *aljamiado-morisco* narratives within such anthological books, we find a different, though no more or less complex, suite of uses and meanings. John P. Hawkins has addressed this issue in his 1988 article entitled "A Morisco Philosophy of Suffering: An Anthropological Analysis of an Aljamiado Text." In this study, Hawkins makes the argument that many *aljamiado-morisco* anthologies work to present an "integrated theme" in spite of their being "miscellaneous assemblages" (200). Focusing on Madrid, BN ms. 4953, a late sixteenth-century *aljamiado-morisco* anthology containing a number of traditional narratives, Hawkins argues that a coherent theme runs through the manuscript's several texts, serving to create what he terms a "coherent Morisco philosophy of suffering" (200). Hawkins presents his argument through a detailed textual analysis of the individual (but not necessarily separable, in his view) manuscript texts found in Madrid, BN ms. 4953, concluding:

> The text is not an unordered collection of legends and other religious
> sermons; it is, rather, a treatise. Clearly, the meaning of the tales is
> not to be found in the legends themselves. Rather, meaning is to be
> found in the relations between the legends and their emerging logic,
> and in the parallels between the legends and the current Morisco social
> situation. Thus the text is not a miscellany, though it is a compendium,
> for it reveals an integrated argument and an intimate relationship to
> the Morisco society. (1988, 213)[2]

Focusing on a particular facet of the intertextual relations in force between the texts contained in Madrid, BN ms. 4953, Hawkins situates
these texts' meaning within a larger web of signification that compre-
hends both the manuscript book as a whole and its reception among
Morisco readers, who experienced the book, according to Hawkins, as
a cohesive whole. Dividing the manuscript into sixteen sections (corresponding to the sixteen individual texts found within it), Hawkins
concludes his analysis of these sections in the following way:

> We see that the book offers the Moriscos a means of understanding
> their suffering. Suffering is a part of life, just as death is. Moreover, suf-
> fering brings certain benefits. First, the sufferer receives rewards from
> God. Secondly, the faithful and patient sufferer draws the persecutor
> toward the true religion. Thirdly, to be a faithful practitioner of Islam
> is a form of receiving God's blessings; the suffering does not imply that
> God does not bless. On the contrary, suffering is the means ordained
> by God through which one can wage Holy War on Christians. Each
> section builds on the logic of the previous sections and strengthens
> the argument. In the last sections, the book takes on an apocalyp-
> tic tone, discussing death extensively and offering magical means for
> drugging the Christian in order to pacify him and make him a believer.
> Finally the text makes a fleeting reference to the possibility of military
> salvation. (213)

Framed within the larger historical context of extreme tension between
crypto-Muslims and Christians in late-sixteenth-century Spain, Hawkins
reads Madrid, BN ms. 4953 as a book comprised of a series of sections
that gradually but persistently build to an apocalyptic crescendo from
the first to the final folio.

Hawkins's argument is a provocative one, though it rests upon a
thoroughly idiosyncratic reading of the textual material at hand. His
mention, for example, of a portion of the text near the end that offers
a "magical means for drugging the Christian in order to pacify him and

make him a believer" seems not to take into consideration the fact that this same recipe appears as part of a larger section on the curing of various other maladies, including headaches, toothaches, and demonic possession. Even in the specific section dealing with some form of induced conversion one struggles, in fact, to find the "apocalyptic tone" suggested by Hawkins:

> And the Prophet said: Gabriel (peace be upon him) told me that if an unbeliever drinks [this magic drink], God will take the misbelief from his heart and put within it [true] belief and whoever has misbelief in his heart, or worry, or forgetfulness, or envy, or malice and drinks it, God will tear it from his heart and cure him of it. (f. 135ʳ)[3]

While it is certainly possible to imagine that for Morisco scribes and readers the term "unbeliever" could mean a Christian, it could just as easily point to Muslims who had strayed from the straight path of Islam or Jews (those of *banu Israel,* in *aljamiado-morisco* texts). The former group has been defined according to varying criteria in distinct communities throughout the history of Islam (the current marginalization of Shi'a Muslims in places such as Pakistan where Sunni practice is dominant and the violent clashes between secular and more fundamentalist Muslims in Turkey, Egypt, and Algeria provide contemporary examples), while the Qur'an, as well as many *aljamiado-morisco* texts, specifically addresses the shortcomings and supposed obstinacy of the latter.

Before framing the social and religious conflicts of the Moriscos in terms solely of their problems with Spanish Christians, we should keep in mind that in all religious communities — from colonial Jamestown to seventh-century Medina, first-century Jerusalem, and sixteenth-century Almonacid de la Sierra — there can be extreme dissent and social tension. This tension, which often enough revolves around differing interpretations and applications of sacred texts, can lead both to symbolic and physical violence. And while it is true that a common outside enemy can forge strong bonds between members of a religious community or religiously defined nation-state for a time, the internal divisions that frequently split these communities never fully disappear. Within Muslim Iberia this sort of tension was more the rule rather than the exception (Chejne 1974; Fletcher 1992; Guichard 1993). It is important to keep in mind that the Andalusi poet Ibn Quzman was not interested in attacking Christians or even Jews in his strophic *azjal;* instead he was, for the most part, lashing out at the Almoravids, a group of militant Malikite Berber Muslims from Morocco that has seized power in Córdoba. Also, the Caliphate of Córdoba, the crowning political achievement of peninsular Islam, collapsed in 1031 CE due to internal power struggles and very local conflicts, not because of Christian military advances. In fact, it can be argued that it was the fall of the caliphate that made possible the military gains of Christian kings throughout the latter half of the eleventh century and the eventual Christian reconquest of the peninsula. Taking into account these examples, it becomes necessary to look beyond crypto-Muslim/Christian polemics in our efforts to understand the meaning of books such as Madrid, BN ms. 4953; for even within Muslim communities — especially those populated by Moriscos whose knowledge of Islamic practice, law, and devotion was often tenuous at best — the utility of a magic drink that could immediately bring about religious orthodoxy and orthopraxy (from the perspective of those invested with the legitimate power to define both) would be hard to overestimate.

In spite of the shakiness of Hawkins's specific arguments regarding the meaning of Madrid, BN ms. 4953 (it is worth mentioning, in passing, that he also bases his interpretations on the very problematic assumption that Moriscos would be reading their manuscript books from start to finish, as modern readers might do with a literary work), there is a great deal of value in his broader hypotheses. Suffering, like death, is indeed an integral part of human existence, and human attempts to theorize and emplot our being-toward-death are perhaps at the root of what it means to be human (Bruner 1986; Capps and Ochs 1995; Carr 1986; Kerby 1991; Ochs and Capps 2001). And central to the theorization and emplotment of suffering and death is a culturally structured reckoning with the human dimension of time. In this manner, Hawkins's work is important for the ideas developed in the present book, namely, that time, suffering, death, historical consciousness, concern for the future, and modes of action all intersect with the practice of producing and engaging handwritten narrative texts within the crypto-Muslim communities of Castile and Aragon. While such concerns and practices are not unique to the Moriscos, their particular situation within early modern Spain — both with respect to dominant Christians, the larger Muslim *umma,* and each other — makes their use of *aljamiado* books all the more important for an understanding of their communal habitus with respect to written texts:

> Considering the risks that the Morisco incurred by possessing, reading, listening to, or copying any Aljamiado document, such a book must have had a message worth the risk. To the degree that Manuscript 4953 of the Biblioteca Nacional de Madrid helped the Moriscos confront life and find strength, it merited the risk. (Hawkins 1988, 213)

Ultimately for Hawkins, the contextualized meaning of Madrid, BN ms. 4953 is intricately related to its ability to articulate ideologies held by the wider Morisco population and to mitigate the particular suffering of this population at the hands of the Spanish Crown.

While I wholeheartedly agree with Hawkins's point that *aljamiado-morisco* manuscripts related in profound ways to the life-world of the communities that produced and made use of them, I wish to develop a bit further the notion of "suffering" that he sketches out in only the most general terms. Hawkins elaborates an idea of "suffering" that speaks directly to the larger political/religious crisis within which Morisco scribes and readers undoubtedly found themselves in Habsburg Spain. According to Hawkins, the texts in Madrid, BN ms. 4953 work together to elaborate theories of suffering held by those members of the Morisco community that produced and engaged that particular book. This point is not all that different from what I have argued throughout this book, namely, that modes of cultural practice are encoded within the manuscript texts produced and engaged by members of Morisco communities. There is, however, a much deeper and more immediate level at which these books — and the texts that they contained — spoke to socially embedded concerns and practices within the Morisco communities of Castile and Aragon.

Much of what we must inevitably analyze within the *aljamiado-morisco* narratives that we study — especially in light of their inclusion within larger collection of texts — has to do with the ways in which these texts encode and *help give shape to* cultural practices that are not consciously expressed or aimed at by those members of Morisco communities that in some way engaged *aljamiado* books. Like the systems of embodied predispositions elaborated by Bourdieu in his definition of habitus, much of what human agents in fact do (and say) lies beyond frameworks of rational action or deliberate efforts to achieve some goal (1990, 53). This of course does not mean that our goal is to explore the psyche (or, more popularly in medieval studies, the *mentalité*) of Morisco scribes and readers along the lines of a psychoanalytic or

semiotic paradigm. Rather, we must speak to Morisco cultural practice, specifically to the ways in which the Morisco readers and scribes
in Castile and Aragon made use of written narrative texts to give form
to their social world, a world defined by temporal situatedness and the
very human need to make sense of that temporality.

In order to address in a deeper way the relation between text, time,
and the social world of the Moriscos, it is necessary to expand Hawkins's
framework of "suffering" along its vertical axis, beyond the surface-level
project of combating Christian dominance through some text-mediated
form of civil disobedience. It is also necessary, however, to expand
Hawkins's framework along its horizontal axis. For another important
aspect of what we must consider in any analysis of *aljamiado-morisco*
narratives in light of their relation to the social world of Castilian and
Aragonese Moriscos moves us beyond the general notion of "suffering" as articulated by Hawkins to a more specific notion of suffering
and action that is embedded in more deep-seated principles of human
experience of and *movement through* the world.

David Carr develops a philosophical framework for considering
human experience and action within temporally embedded settings that
suggests a narrative beginning-middle-end structure for such experience
and action. He argues that:

> ...experienced time [i.e., time understood within its situated, human
> dimensions] is a structured and configured time. Our experience is di-
> rected towards, and itself assumes, temporally extended forms in which
> future, present, and past mutually determine one another as parts of a
> whole. (1986, 31)

Moving beyond an analysis of "passive experience," Carr goes on to
describe how action — especially when what we do involves the mediation of language — is shaped by the very same sense of "structured
and configured time." Basing his approach in large part on Heideggerian
theories regarding the projective character of human existence (*Entwurf-
charakter*), Carr argues that "when we are absorbed in an action the
focus or direction of our attention, the center of our concern, lies not
in the present but in the future; not on the tools, as Heidegger says,
but on the work to be done" (1986, 39). What does this mean for our
understanding of *aljamiado-morisco* narratives? It means that in order to
understand the ways in which *aljamiado-morisco* narratives intersected

with and helped to shape the social world of Castilian and Aragonese Moriscos, we must address the question of how these handwritten texts encoded (and mediated the continuous negotiation of) more deeply rooted modes of configuring temporally embedded experience and action among the Moriscos. In other words, how do the temporal and discursive frameworks at work within and between *aljamiado-morisco* texts (in the case of anthological books such as Madrid, BN ms. 4953) intersect with and help to shape larger theories of experience, practice, and time within the Morisco communities of Castile and Aragon? I will be addressing this and related questions throughout the rest of this chapter by way of an analysis of a specific *aljamiado-morisco* narrative and the extant manuscripts in which it is found.

The Text of the *Alhadith del xakrifixi'o de Isma'il*

Throughout the rest of this chapter, I will be analyzing a specific short narrative text produced and actively read throughout Morisco communities in Castile and Aragon. This text, the *Alhadith del xakrifixi'o de Isma'il,* is found in two extant manuscripts, both produced near the end of the sixteenth century in rural Aragon. In both cases, the *Alhadith del xakrifixi'o de Isma'il* is found within manuscript codices that contain a number of other texts: Madrid, BRAH ms. 11/9409 (*olim* T-12), an 86-folio compendium containing a large quantity of narratives, including a version of "El nacimiento del Profeta" studied in the previous chapter; and Madrid, Junta 25, a manuscript described in its catalogue as a "Miscellany of bilingual Qur'anic suras and prayers in aljamiado" (Ribera and Asín 1912, 110) that contains 184 folios of primarily religious texts, many of which deal with the performance of religious celebrations such as the *'Eid al-Adha,* during which the *Alhadith del xakrifixi'o de Isma'il* was read publicly (the *Alhadith del xakrifixi'o de Isma'il* is in fact found within a larger text entitled *Khutba* [Sermon of] *'Eid al-Adha*). I will be discussing in some detail the relation between the multiple texts found within Madrid, BRAH ms. 11/9409 in a later section of this chapter: however, I would like to begin by offering an overview of the text of *Alhadith del xakrifixi'o de Isma'il* itself.

One of the striking characteristics of *aljamiado-morisco* narrative is its tendency to take stories and even whole verses from the Qur'an and recontextualize them within novel discursive settings. Like the Christian "thematic preaching" popularized throughout the later Middle Ages, *aljamiado-morisco* narratives are in many cases extensive amplifications of specific Qur'anic suras.[4] Frequently embedding the devotional practices associated with the lectoral performance of specific passages of the Qur'an within *aljamiado-morisco* narratives, Morisco scribes effectively generated hybrid literary genres that at once indexed devotional practice and divine revelation (through the Qur'an and its performance) and the narrative negotiation of the realities suggested by both. Like a gloss on God's word that implies both word and action, narratives that expand upon the Qur'an place narrative practice within the daily life and practice of crypto-Muslim communities, serving to give shape to human action, belief, and understanding. Central to this process is, as I have argued throughout this book, a reckoning with the human dimension of time.

The *Alhadith del xakrifixi'o de Isma'il* is a traditional *aljamiado-morisco* narrative dealing with God's request of Abraham that he offer a bloody sacrifice of his most beloved son as proof of his faith. In the *aljamiado-morisco* version of the story, we find not only a richly embellished recontextualization of a Qur'anic Sura but also a number of elements that speak directly to the issue of time and Morisco efforts to give it cultural form.

Christian readers will be familiar with the story of Abraham's test of faith from Genesis 22:1–14, although in the biblical story it is Isaac, rather than Ishmael, who faces death (a continuing point of contention between Muslim and Judeo-Christian religious scholars). The biblical text reads:

1: After these things God tested Abraham, and said to him, "Abraham!" And he said, "Here I am."

2: He said, "Take your son, your only son Isaac, whom you love, and go to the land of Moriah, and offer him there as a burnt offering upon one of the mountains of which I shall tell you."

3: So Abraham rose early in the morning, saddled his donkey, and took two of his young men with him, and his son Isaac; and he cut the wood for the burnt offering, and arose and went to the place of which God had told him.

4: On the third day Abraham lifted up his eyes and saw the place afar off.

5: Then Abraham said to his young men, "Stay here with the donkey; the boy and I will go yonder and worship, and come again to you."

6: And Abraham took the wood of the burnt offering, and laid it on Isaac his son; and he took in his hand the fire and the knife. So they went both of them together.

7: And Isaac said to his father Abraham, "My father!" And he said, "Here I am, my son." He said, "Behold, the fire and the wood; but where is the lamb for a burnt offering?"

8: Abraham said, "God will provide himself the lamb for a burnt offering, my son." So they went both of them together.

9: When they came to the place of which God had told him, Abraham built an altar, and laid the wood in order, and bound Isaac his son, and laid him on the altar, upon the wood.

10: Then Abraham put forth his hand, and took the knife to slay his son.

11: But the angel of the Lord called to him from heaven, and said, "Abraham, Abraham!" And he said, "Here I am."

12: He said, "Do not lay your hand on the boy or do anything to him; for now I know that you fear God, seeing you have not withheld your son, your only son, from me."

13: And Abraham lifted up his eyes and looked, and behold, behind him was a ram, caught in a thicket by his horns; and Abraham went and took the ram, and offered it up as a burnt offering instead of his son.

14: So Abraham called the name of that place The Lord will provide; as it is said to this day, "On the mount of the Lord it shall be provided."

In the Qur'anic narrative of Abraham's test (Sura 37:101–13), it is Ishmael — Abraham's son by his servant, Hagar — who faces sacrifice at the hands of his father:

101: So We gave him the good news of a forbearing son.

102: But when he became of age to work with him, he said: O my son, I have seen in a dream that I should sacrifice you: so consider what you see. He said: O my father, do as you are commanded; if Allah please, you will find me patient.

103: So when they both submitted and he had thrown him down upon his forehead,

104: And We called out to him saying: O Ibrahim,

105: You have indeed fulfilled the vision. Thus do We reward the doers of good.

106: Surely this is a manifest trial.

107: And We ransomed him with a great sacrifice.

108: And We granted him among the later generations (the salutation),

109: Peace be on Ibrahim!

110: Thus do We reward the doers of good.

111: Surely he was one of Our believing servants.

112: And We gave him the good news of Isaac, a prophet, a righteous one.

113: And We blessed him and Isaac. And of their offspring some are doers of good, but some are clearly unjust to themselves.

As is apparent from these two passages, there are many critical differences between the biblical and Qur'anic versions of this story of Abraham. The most important of these, from a theological perspective, is the identity of the boy in question.[5] Within the Islamic tradition, a large body of commentary and gloss (*hadith*) has developed around the Qur'anic account of this event, a tradition that has its parallel in the equally large *Mishna Torah* tradition in Judaism. Referring to this *hadith* tradition in his commentary on the Qur'an, Maulana Muhammed Ali has argued against versions that present Isaac as the son to be sacrificed in this story:

> The *hadith* in which Isaac is spoken of as having been sacrificed is according to Ibn Kathir *gharib* [specious], and must be rejected. The Holy Qur'an makes it clear beyond all doubt that it was Ishmael whom Abraham was ordered to sacrifice. (*Holy Qur'an* 1995, 886)

For the purposes of the present analysis, the ongoing polemic between Judeo-Christian and Muslim authorities is not a central concern, though it does provide a degree of background information with respect to the importance of this narrative of sacrifice and faith to Morisco communities living under Christian dominion.

In my analysis of the *Alhadith del xakrifixi'o de Isma'il,* I will be focusing on two specific issues with respect to the *aljamiado-morisco* version of the Qur'anic story: (1) the details of the Qur'anic narrative and its similarities to and differences from the extant *aljamiado-morisco* versions; and (2) information regarding the uses to which members of Morisco communities put their version of the story and the way that these uses (and, inevitably, the text itself) related to the larger issue of temporality and Morisco cultural practice. My goal is to deal with the *aljamiado-morisco* version as a significant recentering of Qur'anic discourse within new settings and to treat in some detail what this (repeated) act of recentering could have meant for the communities that engaged in it.

Sura 37:101–13 is, like most Qur'anic narratives, spare and extraordinarily poetic. It is largely due to the poetic character of the Qur'an's message as a whole that within the Sunni tradition an extensive (and growing) body of *hadith* literature has formed around it. Muhammad Ali makes reference to the inauthentic [*gharib*] *hadith* that presents Isaac as the sacrifice, implicitly drawing attention to the great importance that this commentary tradition had — and continues to have — within Islam. For example, Muhammad Ali also cites the passage in 37:113 that reads: "and we blessed him and Isaac" (*wa barakuna alayhi w 'ala Is'haqa*), pointing out that "Abraham and Isaac are spoken of distinctly to show that by blessing Abraham is here meant blessing the descendants of Ishmael" (*Holy Qur'an* 1995, 887). This interpretation of the passage is not Muhammad Ali's own, but reflects a long chain of Qur'anic readings on this passage that date back to the first Muslim communities and finally to the Prophet himself.

Given the narrative gaps that exist in the Qur'an (as well as the unique linguistic features it employs), it is within the Islamic tradition at once a wholly self-sufficient and divine revelation and a difficult, mysterious text that requires a great deal of reflection and glossing to pierce even its most literal meanings. In spite of its complexity, the Qur'an is also the central text around which a wide range of cultural activity revolves. For this reason, it provokes little wonder that alongside the learned and authoritative *hadith* tradition there has developed a parallel *hadith* tradition that has reworked Qur'anic narratives into popular, even folkloric stories that are recounted by Muslims in a wide range of settings and activities. The *Alhadith del xakrifixi'o de Isma'il* is just such a popular *hadith* (the term also can mean "story" or "conversation" in a more generic sense) that takes the Qur'anic story of Abraham's near-sacrifice of Ishmael and fleshes it out, offering a particular gloss on many of its more difficult passages and reworkings of Judeo-Christian accounts of the life of Abraham in the process.

As in the Qur'anic account, the *aljamiado-morisco* story of the sacrifice of Ishmael begins with Abraham having a terrible dream. The difference is that while Sura 37 mentions the dream, the *aljamiado-morisco* version recounts it, stretching the vision out over a series of four nights. The episode begins:

> After one hundred years the boy [Ishmael] grew and developed a gift for speech. One night in a dream a messenger came to him [Abraham] and

said, "The Lord of all people says to you: 'Oh, Abraham — bring me a sacrifice...of his name...and it will be blessed...'" he said. When God awoke with the morning [Abraham] went and sacrificed a camel, giving it to the poor and wretched so that they might eat. Afterward, Abraham said to his Lord, "Have you received my sacrifice? If not, let me know tonight." When the second night arrived, a messenger came to him and said, "Abraham — bring a sacrifice to me, which will be received from you." When God awoke with the morning, [Abraham] took a cow and slit its throat, distributing the meat to the suffering. And Abraham said, "Lord, you have received [the sacrifice] from me — if not, show me during the third night." And when the third night arrived, the messenger came and said to him, "Abraham — get up and bring me my sacrifice, which I will receive from you in the name of all people from now until the Day of Judgment." When God awoke with the morning, Abraham (peace be upon him) went and took a [ram] and slit its throat and reparted its meat among the poor and miserable, saying, "Lord — have you received this, my sacrifice? If not, show me in the fourth night." When the fourth night arrived, the messenger came and said to him, "Abraham — get up and bring me my sacrifice, which I will receive from you in the name of all people from now until the Day of Judgment." And Abraham said, "My Lord, my Great One — I have already brought a sacrifice of camels, cattle, and sheep. Why do you still ask that I make a sacrifice, Lord?" God came to him and said, "I do not ask of you camels, cattle, or sheep, but rather I want you to slit the throat of your son and the pleasure of your days, Ishmael." (Madrid, BRAH ms. 11/9409 ff. 9^v–10^v)[6]

In this narrative we see the expansion of less than half a verse from the Qur'an into a folio and a half of manuscript text. This sort of expansion, while it does little to change the meaning of the Qur'anic story, greatly alters the tone and performative quality of the episode and encodes a great deal of information about the perceived relations between God and his followers in Morisco communities.

In Sura 37:102, we are presented only with Abraham's revelation of his dream to his son, Ishmael: "But when he became of age to work with him, he said: 'O my son, I have seen in a dream that I should sacrifice you.'..." In the *aljamiado-morisco hadith,* however, the act of "seeing this dream" is stretched over four nights of trial-and-error miscommunication between God and Abraham that ends with a number of well-fed poor and a terrible realization of God's will. The message seems to be that the faithful must not only struggle to understand the will of God, but they must also persevere in their attempts to please Him, no matter how frustrating a process it may be. The message of this portion of the *hadith* — four nights of failure and repetition — seems to be that even Abraham, God's most beloved servant, was made to struggle in order to understand, that he made errors, and that he was forced to endure challenges over time so that he might come to know God's will. And even once God's will was known, it was not always desirable or easy to carry out. For the crypto-Muslims of Castile and Aragon, notions of miscommunication, perseverance, and trial and error with respect to God's will were no doubt important points always to keep in mind.

The next portion of the Qur'anic narrative deals with Abraham and Ishmael both accepting the need to carry out the sacrifice and their arrival at the place of the killing, where Abraham throws his son "down upon his forehead" (37:102–3). The *aljamiado-morisco* narrative uses this moment to insert a touching scene between Ishmael and his mother:

> Abraham said, "Hagar, when God wakes with the morning place my son in the bath and clean him and put his cleanest clothes upon him, as he must accompany me where I am going." When it was morning, Hagar took the boy and put him in the bath and washed his head with *xixbe* leaves and camphor. And Ishmael said to his mother, "Why do you wash me the way they wash the dead, those who pass from this world to the next?" She said, "My son, this is what your father has ordered." He said to her, "Mother, if my father has ordered it, then that is reason enough for it to be done."[7] (Madrid, BRAH ms. 11/9409 f. 11)

This scene not only simultaneously humanizes and dramatizes the imminent sacrifice of Ishmael, but it also provides a textual resource by which women could theorize their place in the miracle to follow. Hagar is a model wife and mother who deeply loves her son and does not question the orders of her husband. Hagar allows readers and the listening public to see another side of the miracle, one that is at once embedded in Islamic ideologies of gender and authority and in the tender relations between a mother and her son. Also, she stoically — even heroically — accepts what she must do, as does Ishmael himself.

Before Abraham and Ishmael reach the place where the latter is to be sacrificed, the devil (*Iblis*) meets them on the road disguised as an old man. He asks Ishmael where his father is taking him. The boy responds that he is going where he is needed. Then Iblis blurts out, "He is going to slit your throat" (Ante te liʸeva a dexgollarte). "Why would he do this?"

asks Ishmael. "Because God has ordered it so," replies Iblis. Ishmael's response to the devil at this point in their conversation is a key element of the narrative as a whole. As he said to his mother while she was bathing him, he calmly states, "If God has ordered it, then may he do it." Ishmael's calm, resolute acceptance of the will of God even at the expense of his own life is an integral feature of his status as a blessed figure within popular Islam. For the Moriscos, Ishmael's devotion both to God and to his father was undoubtedly both exemplary and full of pathos. The story of a brave young boy, loved by both of his parents, sent by God to be sacrificed by his father's hand, could not have failed to evoke a certain amount of emotion from its listeners. That this same brave young boy is the ancestor of all Arabs (and spiritually, of all Muslims) makes the narrative all the more compelling. Also, the direct historic link between Ishmael and the Spanish crypto-Muslims telling his story serves to create a significant link (in the present) between the events of the traditional Islamic past (a past filled with divine tests and faithful servants) and those of an all too uncertain future.

In the *aljamiado-morisco* version of the narrative, Ishmael goes so far as to question his father about his intentions. The devil reappears to the boy in the figure of a bird and repeats to him that his father is getting ready to slit his throat. When Ishmael asks his father about this, Abraham responds: "My son — among the birds there are both tellers of truth and liars." This seems to quiet Ishmael, so then the devil flies into a mountain and begins to rumble: "Oh Son! Today you will be sacrificed on me, and your grave opened on my body. On the Day of Judgment I will be praised above all other mountains because of you." At that, Ishmael turns back to his father and asks him, "Father, if the old man and the bird were lying, the mountain surely isn't — for it neither keeps accounts nor possesses trickery." At this Abraham lets the boy know what awaits him, and why. "My son, give yourself over to the will of God, as I have seen in a dream that I am to slit your throat, so consider what you see." As in the Qur'an, Ishmael responds to his father's declaration calmly, "O my father, do as you are commanded; and you will find me, if Allah please, among the patient. God is great. God is great. God is great. The greatest of the great and many thanks be to God.... (*Allahu akbar, Allahu akbar, Allahu akbar — Kbir kbiran wa alhamdulillah kathiran wa....*)"[8]

The last lines of the preceding passage correspond word-for-word with the Qur'anic original, setting off the narrative *amplificatio* (the four dreams of Abraham, the ritual bathing (*ghusl*) of Ishmael, the meeting with the Devil) from its source text. The alternating textual adhesion to/ departure from the Qur'anic source text is typical of *aljamiado-morisco* narratives; however, it is worth noting that when the Qur'anic text is cited, it is set off in a very noticeable way. For example, after Ishmael accepts his fate as the will of God — expressed in a word-for-word trans- lation of the Qur'anic text — the narrative breaks into a ritual invocation of God in Arabic. In this way, the *aljamiado-morisco* text blends the dis- cursive genre of storytelling with that of ritual prayer, an activity tightly organized within the daily, weekly, monthly, and yearly activities of Mus- lims. As we will see, such a blend occurs (and has meaning) within the context of concrete temporally and socially situated activities carried out by members of Morisco communities. What is interesting about the tex- tual details of this process of discursive blending and juxtaposition — a process that underlies a particular form of intertextuality — is that it involves ideologically specific uses and valorizations of language: the Qur'anic text itself, like the larger narrative, is presented in Romance, while the invocation of God — an index of prayer and ritual observance that always, in the Islamic context, implies embodied practice (such as kneeling, bowing, or simply bowing one's head) — appears in Arabic.[9]

Without much ceremony, the text of the sacrifice of Ishmael picks up after the invocation of God in Arabic with a relatively long passage in which Ishmael expresses his concern about his mother's imminent suffering over the death of her son. Ishmael implores his father to pray to God to give Hagar strength. Then Abraham slides the sacrificial knife out of his shirt sleeve. Seeing the knife, Ishmael says, "Oh Father — death brings much bitterness, but — oh Father! — fix your honored face upon me, and let me find strength in you before my *arruh* [soul] leaves me." Abraham's reply is a dolorous one: "Oh my son! I could not look at you, as my God knows what pain is inside me."

After this exchange, Abraham tries four separate times to slit his son's throat, though the blade is never able to reach the boy's flesh. After the third unsuccessful attempt, the Arabic invocation of God is repeated: *Allahu akbar, Allahu akbar, akbaru kbiran wa alhamdu lillahi kathiran wa subhana Allahu bukratun wa asilan* (God is great, God is great, the greatest of the great and many thanks to God and praise to God at dawn and at sunset). Once again the narrative is juxtaposed with ritual discourse, discourse that situates its telling within Islamic devotional practice and a distinct Islamic temporal frame: "and many thanks be to God and praise to God at dawn and at sunset." In this way the morning and evening prayers, and the embodied practice that accompanies them, are folded into the telling of this story. Also indexed, through the use of Arabic itself, is a whole body of belief and practice that centers around the religious speech of the Castilian and Aragonese crypto-Muslims as they bring centuries-old prayers (in Arabic) and a Qur'anic episode (translated and expanded in Romance) into a text performed in contemporary settings and meant to mediate the performance of communicative practice in the present and future. The past, as it were, steps into the present and future through the use of traditional discourse both in Romance and Arabic. Such discursive "asides," although they may tear readers away from the narrative proper, are fundamental tools for the interpretation, evaluation, and inevitable use of the narrative itself with Morisco communities—the prayer invocations are not digressions or empty religious formulas, but rather indices that anchor the narrative in the cultural practice of Morisco communities struggling to hold on to their culture and their very lives in settings fraught with danger, doubt, and even ignorance about what it means to be Muslim in any full sense.

After trying three times to slit his son's throat, Abraham falls to the ground and asks God for pity. Afterward, he puts the knife to Ishmael's throat a fourth time without any result. At this point, the archangel Gabriel descends from heaven, proclaiming: "Oh Abraham—leave what is in front of you and take that which is just behind you." Abraham turns to find a ram that had previously passed fifty years in paradise (beox un karnero ke abí'a paxido en al-janna çinku^wenta añox). He takes the ram and sacrifices it. Gabriel then tells him, "Oh Abraham — thus is the vision fulfilled. Thus do we reward the doers of good." The line on which this text ends, midway through folio 13^v of BRAH ms. 11/9409, is then filled with small s-shaped designs to fill up the line to the margin. The following line begins with two more ornate figures common in aljamiado-morisco manuscripts, and the following words: tammat bi-hamdi illaahi wa husni 'awn. Then there are three more figures that finish out the line of text, signaling the end of the narrative. I will be discussing this last line of the text (a scribal colophon that translates literally as: "The [hadith] has come to a close with thanks to God and His gracious assistance") in the next section dealing with the characteristics of the manuscript itself, and I will end the present section with a last point regarding the textual interworkings of the Alhadith del xakrifixi'o *de Isma'il,* the Qur'anic original, and its achieved meaning within the context of Morisco communities in Castile and Aragon.

The *aljamiado-morisco* narrative begins by taking certain liberties with the Qur'anic account. While Sura 37:101–2 reads: "So We gave him the good news of a forbearing son. / But when he became of age to work with him...." The *Alhadith del xakrifixi³o de Isma'il* begins in much the same way, speaking of the news that Abraham received about his son: "Fu^we razonado en partida de las nu^wevas ke Ibrahim ('alayhi al-çalam) fu^we albrixado kon Isma'il" (BRAH ms. 11/9409 f. 9^v). Then, however, the *aljamiado-morisco* text assigns a specific age and personal characteristics to Ishmael at the time of his near-sacrifice: "After one hundred years the boy grew and gained clarity in his speech" (Ap^erex de çi^yent añox el mançebo k^ereçi^yó i ^yap^irixó luçençi^ya por xu lengu^wa) (BRAH ms. 11/9409 f. 9^v). It is difficult not to read these details regarding Ishmael (all of which present a significant intertextual gap between the *aljamiado-morisco* text and the Qur'anic original) as a representation of the Moriscos themselves. For the Moriscos too had endured nearly a century as culturally distinct communities of crypto-Muslims since their forced conversion to Christianity in 1502–25, and they were certainly aware that their day — like Ishmael's within the narrative — was coming.

As for Ishmael, it is quite possible that he came to serve the Moriscos both as a spiritual ancestor (as he is for all Muslims) and a sort of foreshadowing of their own crisis, much as the biblical near-sacrifice of Isaac foreshadowed the coming of Jesus as the Messiah within the Christian tradition. As a prefiguring of the human sacrifice initially ordered by God at the hand of Abraham, the story of Ishmael takes on a powerful moral and existential charge for Morisco men and women: like Ishmael, they were to accept God's will patiently and obediently, faithful that in the end the sacrificial knife would not cut through their flesh. This prophetic reading of the Ishmael story also embeds it in the practice of the Moriscos and places it squarely within the activities and interactions by which they reckoned with time. As such, this narrative has the power to lend relatively stable, even transcendent meaning to the uncertain future faced by the Moriscos at the end of the sixteenth century. Jerome Bruner has spoken of the important role that narrative in general has in the shaping of social organization: "one of the most powerful forms of social stability... is the human propensity to share stories of human diversity and to make their interpretations congruent with the divergent moral commitments and institutional obligations that prevail in every culture" (1990, 68). The story of Ishmael — in its capacity as a text that related thematically to the situation faced by the Moriscos — can be seen as a powerful tool for the negotiation of a stable, coherent sense of past, present, and future.

Manuscript Witnesses of the
Alhadith del xakrifixi'o de Isma'il

The manuscript copy of the *Alhadith del xakrifixi'o de Isma'il* of which I have been speaking occupies roughly four and a half folios near the beginning of BRAH ms. 11/9409 (*olim* T-12). The manuscript, once the property of Pascual de Gayangos, contains eighty-six relatively small folios. Within these folios are found no fewer than seventeen separate texts, which, based on Alvaro Galmés de Fuentes's catalogue of the *aljamiado-morisco* manuscripts found in the Biblioteca de la Real Academia de la Historia and my own consultation of the manuscript, can be presented as:

ff. 1–9:	*Hadith de Yuçuf*
ff. 9–13ᵛ:	*Alhadith del xakrifixi'o de Isma'il*
ff. 13ᵛ–18:	*Libro de las luces* (the section on the birth of the Prophet)
ff. 18–19ᵛ:	It was recounted that among the Jews there was one man who went off to the mountains to serve God
ff. 19ᵛ–25:	The moral instruction of Omar to his son
ff. 25–26:	Prayer of a boy for the soul of his mother
ff. 26–29ᵛ:	The lizard that spoke with Muhammad
ff. 29ᵛ–34ᵛ:	Story of the death of Muhammad
ff. 34ᵛ–36:	Story of Bilal ibn Hamama
ff. 36–42:	Dispute with the Christians
ff. 42–45ᵛ:	*Alhadith del baño de Ziryab*
ff. 45ᵛ–49:	A very good story, which deals with some very wise and moral men
ff. 49–58:	Story of Tamim Addar
ff. 58–59ᵛ:	Aljamiado gloss on some Arabic terms used in a work by al-Ghazali, made by the *alfakí* Abu 'Abdullah Muhammad al-Gazi al-Bani Halichi
ff. 59ᵛ–76:	Two sermons in Arabic
ff. 76–77:	Prayer for the end of Ramadan
ff. 77–86:	Text and paraphrased translation of Sura 35 of the Qur'an

The encyclopedic character of this book no doubt made it of great use in a wide range of settings, though the precise selections made of a large number of texts from seemingly disparate genres — from the *Alhadith del baño de Ziryab,* a moral tale set in al-Andalus, to the *Dispute with the Christians,* a polemic against Christianity — suggests a certain order.

Looking at the contents of BRAH, ms. 11/9409 — especially insofar as these relate to the *Alhadith del xakrifixi'o de Isma'il* and in turn to the larger field of cultural practice within Morisco communities in Castile and Aragon — there is, as Hawkins suggests for Madrid, BN ms. 4953, a sort of "philosophy of suffering" developed throughout. However, what I mean here by "suffering" is, as I have stated before, somewhat different from what Hawkins suggests: in BRAH, ms. 11/9409, as in other cases, what we find is a very situated textual theorization of experience (i.e., "suffering") and action that in all cases takes into account the temporal character of both. This reworked "philosophy of suffering and practice" finds explicit expression in the text of the *Alhadith del xakrifixi'o de Isma'il;* however, there are also important data to be taken from the physical characteristics of the manuscript codex in which it is found, as well as in the relations that exist between the texts included in the book.

Madrid, BRAH ms. 11/9409 is a small book (approximately 6.5 x 4 inches), containing eighty-six folios of coarse, sixteenth-century paper bound together within a sheet of parchment of the same period. The book was rediscovered during the nineteenth century in Morés, Aragon, hidden within a flannel bag (Galmés de Fuentes 1998, 83). Upon its rediscovery, the book became the property of Pascual de Gayangos before entering into the collection of the Biblioteca de la Real Academia de la Historia. It contains, as Galmés de Fuentes states in his catalogue of the *aljamiado-morisco* manuscripts held in the Biblioteca de la Real Academia de la Historia, seventeen different texts. These texts, some of which deal explicitly with issues of religious and ritual practice (e.g., *Prayer of a Boy for the Soul of his Mother, Prayer for the End of Ramadan,* and the text and paraphrased translation of Sura 35 of the Qur'an), were copied by a number of different scribes. Importantly, the *Alhadith del xakrifixi'o de Isma'il,* which occupies folios 9–13 of this manuscript, was copied by a different scribe than those who copied the texts that precede and follow it.

Looking at the textual transition between the *Hadith de Yuçuf* and the *Alhadith del xakrifixi'o de Isma'il,* we find a change of scribal hands just before the final lines of the first text. On the verso of folio 8, approximately halfway down the folio, there is an abrupt change of scribal hand, almost in mid-line, and right in the middle of a phrase. The first scribe finishes off on lines six and seven, with a description of the secret palace that the queen's *privada* (maidservant) has built and painted so that Zalifa, the queen, could successfully lure Yuçuf (whom she had raised as a stepson) there and have her way with him: "[the *privada*] had painted on the wall an image of Zalifa and Yuçuf in an intimate and unmeasured embrace" (lo fizo fegurar ke xe abraçaban anbox privado(x)in / mexura). The next scribe finishes out the text, picking up where the first scribe left off: "they seemed alive body and soul because [the painting] was done by a realist master" (ke xemellaban vivox kon xexo i kordura, por / ke era fegurado de maext^uro para natura).

The text of the *Hadith de Yuçuf* finishes up on the next folio, more or less in the middle of this episode, just after the queen's *dueñas* have sliced their hands due to the madness (*lokura*) that the sight of the angelic Yuçuf provoked in them. Justifying her attempted seduction of the boy to them, the queen asks: "What are you crazy women doing? If you lose your minds just from the sight of him, what can you expect of me who has spent years with him?" (¿Ke fechax, locax? De xi por una vixta xola / xodex de xin kordura, ¿ke deberi^ya fer yo del ti^yenpo ke me dura?). The text of the *Hadith de Yuçuf* then comes to an end, the *dueñas* pardoning the queen for her actions and vowing to convince Yuçuf to accept her as a lover: "The *dueñas* said, 'We don't blame you now — in fact we're going to convince him to come to you so that your bodies can be pressed together and intertwined' " (Dixi^yeron las du^weñas ya non te akulpamox — nox xomos lax cherredax ke te ab^alaçmanox max nox guixaremox ke vi^yenga a tux mamox ent^uro xeyadex pegadox entranbox).

This may seem like a strange place for the text to stop, given that it is framed by an initiating invocation of God (*bismillahi arrahmani arrahimi*) on the first folio, and an even more detailed praising of God on folio 9 (*Allahu akbar, Allahu akbar, Allahu akbar, akbar kathiran*). Both Arabic invocations seem to suggest a quasi-ritual setting for the reading of this text, and the fact that the *Hadith de Yuçuf* ends here with an aborted seduction, the imprisonment of Yuçuf, and the *dueñas'* promise to finish the job for the queen makes the overall meaning of this particular text somewhat confusing. I will be discussing the *Ahadith de Yuçuf* in all of its extant manuscripts throughout the next chapter, so this is perhaps not the place to be analyzing the seemingly abrupt (and less than pious) ending of the text in Madrid, BRAH ms. 11/9409. For now, I only wish to point out that the scribe who finishes copying the *Hadith de Yuçuf* on folio 9 is the same one who begins to copy out the *Alhadith del xakrifixi'o de Isma'il* at the bottom of the same folio.

What does this oddly distributed alternation of scribes mean for our efforts to understand the processes by which this manuscript codex was produced? While providing only a partial glimpse of how this book was put together and used (e.g., many of the book's later folios seem to have been copied out at different times and bound together only after their preliminary use as separate texts or parts of other books) the intervention of more than one scribe, cutting across texts and folios (rather than their work being neatly divided by text or signature breaks) seems to suggest a more or less collaborative effort that was focused on copying out a collection of texts as a whole rather than a series of isolated, individual texts that could be bound together or not. At least in the case of Madrid, BRAH ms. 11/9409, Hawkins's larger point that within *aljamiado-morisco* miscellanies "meaning is to be found in the relations between the legends and their emerging logic, and in the parallels between the legends and the current Morisco social situation" (1988, 213) seems to hold true, but with important caveats.

The text of the *Alhadith del xakrifixi'o de Isma'il* begins, as I have argued earlier, with an evocation of the specific ritual celebration within which it was read, the *'Eid al-Adha*. It is copied out in the same hand throughout — the same one that finished copying the *Hadith de Yuçuf* on folios 8–9. Its ending is also significant, in that the scribe indexically situates himself and his own scribal activities within the text through a colophon: "[The *hadith*] has come to a close with thanks to God and His gracious assistance" (*tammat bihamdi illaahi wa husni 'awn*). This sort of colophon, which is hardly common in *aljamiado-morisco* texts, serves to shift the deictic *origo* of the text from the narrated story — temporally framed within a traditional Islamic past — to the socially embedded activities of Morisco scribes and readers. Though there are other discursive elements within the narrative itself that point out toward the cultural and temporal frameworks within which it has been recontextualized (both the *Hadith de Yuçuf* and the *Alhadith del xakrifixi'o de Isma'il* contain Aragonese linguistic traits that further link them — that is, besides their translation into Romance and presentation in Arabic script — to the social world within which the narratives were reproduced and engaged) none are so explicit as the colophon on folio 13ᵛ of Madrid, BRAH ms. 11/9409.

And we may also ask whether this statement of completion is a scribal colophon at all or another textual component of the *Alhadith del xakri-fixiʾo de Ismaʾil*'s performance. As I have just mentioned, colophons are uncommon in *aljamiado-morisco* manuscripts, owing largely to the fact that the written texts of the Moriscos were produced and engaged sur-reptitiously, away from the watchful eyes of Christian authorities. It is perhaps more possible to imagine this short statement as part of the text's performance in social settings. The storyteller — most likely an *alfakí* — steps outside of the narrated frame of the story to signal the end of his reading. This would be in line with much of the back-and-forth between narrative and performative frames that runs throughout the *Alhadith del xakrifixiʾo de Ismaʾil,* a back-and-forth that also brings with it an often dramatic movement between and through temporal frames.

After the statement of completion (by the scribe or the text's reader), the rest of folio 13ᵛ contains the initial six lines of a narrative described by Galmés de Fuentes as "The first verses of a story regarding Fray Leonis" (Los primeros versos de una historia de Fray Leonis) (1998, 83). This story appears to deal with a learned man's quest for truth (*verdat*). After these first six lines, however, the narrative stops abruptly. The reason for this break has to do with the fact that the first signature of the book, which ends between folios 13 and 14, was bound together (in a very haphazard way) with the second one sometime after the redaction of the *Hadith de Yuçuf, Alhadith del xakrifixiʾo de Ismaʾil,* and *Historia de Fray Leonis.* For some reason, or perhaps purely by accident, the rest of the original book (though it itself was but a copy of various other copies) was not included within the newly bound codex. What does this fact mean for our understanding of Madrid, BRAH ms. 11/9409 as a supposedly cohesive collection of manuscript texts? How do we find cohesion and logic in a miscellany pieced together — perhaps without any logic in mind — over time?

To understand the *Alhadith del xakrifixiʾo de Ismaʾil* within its manu-script context (and the social, temporally embedded processes by which the manuscript itself came to be and was engaged), it is necessary to depart somewhat from Hawkins's essentially thematic sense of textual cohesion. Our sense of cohesion — of the forces that hold together in some meaningful ways the texts contained within Madrid, BRAH ms.

11/9409 — must depend rather on what we know about the uses to which Castilian and Aragonese Moriscos could have put the texts under consideration. In specific terms, how were these texts (or this collection of texts) engaged over and within time by the human agents that produced and read them? As the break between folios 13 and 14 shows, this was not a continuous process, but one that entailed the patching together of written discourse from a range of other settings into a new setting designed to facilitate certain modes of use and interpretation.

Perhaps paradoxically, we may reach a deeper understanding of the *Alhadith del xakrifixi'o de Isma'il* as it appears in Madrid, BRAH ms. 11/9409 by looking at another manuscript. This manuscript, Madrid, Junta ms. 25, is described, as I have stated earlier, as a miscellany of prayers in *aljamiado;* however, like Madrid, BRAH ms. 11/9409, it is not without some form. The manuscript first contains two preliminary folios, which contain a brief treatise on Arabic grammar and a guide for determining whether a newborn child enjoys rights of inheritance or not. After these two folios, the first long text of the book (ff. 1–100) consists of a collection of Qur'anic suras (1, 2, 3, 36, 67, and 78–114) with interlinear translations in *aljamiado*. After this long text, the manuscript contains a thirty-folio sermon for the festival of 'Eid al-Adha [*Aljutba de la Paxku^wa de lox adahaex*], which Asín and Ribera describe as a:

> ... collection of moral speeches pronounced on the occasion of the *'Eid al-Adha,* and whose object is to exalt the greatness and excellence of God and his Prophet, and Islam, and to exhort the faithful to carry out precisely their religious obligations.
>
> A number of Qur'anic texts and traditions of the Prophet, as well as a text by ibn Abbas on the sacrifice of Abraham, are intercalated within the text. (1912, 111)[10]

Asín and Ribera, describing this manuscript and its contents just after the turn of the twentieth century, call attention to the performed, mediational role that the texts contained in Madrid, Junta 25 enjoyed within the ritual and devotional practice of the Moriscos, even though they present the story of Abraham's sacrifice of Ishmael as an "intercalation." If we turn to the manuscript itself, the story of Abraham and Ishmael does not seem to be intercalated at all, but rather an integral part of the larger sermon. Looking, for example, at the point where the narrative of Abraham's near-sacrifice of Ishmael begins (f. 124^v), we see that the story is very much a part of the larger text as a whole. The preceding section, which deals with the religious prohibition of a range of actions, such as the defamation of one's neighbors, the committing of adultery, and the drinking of wine, is divided into sections that begin with an invocation of God: "God is great, God is great, the greatest of the great and many thanks be to God and praise to God at dawn and at sunset" (*Allahu akbar, Allahu akbar, akbaru kbiran wa alhamdu lillahi kathiran wa subhana Allahu bukratun wa asilan*). This is the exact same prayer that is embedded within the version of the *Alhadith del xakrifixi'o de Isma'il* found in Madrid, BRAH ms. 11/9409, a prayer that separates, for example, each attempt made by Abraham to cut his son's throat.

The injunctions against adultery and drink end halfway through folio 124^v in Madrid, Junta ms. 25. The transition between these very deliberate points and the narrative of Abraham and Ishmael reads in the following way:

> . . . whoever abstains from wine will be given by God the nectar of Paradise, scented with musk, to drink. * * * Servants of God, God has purified this day, and has made it a Holy Day and a day of meeting for Muslims, and as an obligation in your religion. It is a day in which you give alms, and a day in which all of your good works are multiplied and your sins lessened. On this day you must follow the tradition [*sunna*] and let blood flow and make perfect sacrifices. You must feed the naked and the beggar, as God (t'ala) says that He does not receive the blood [of the sacrifice] but rather your will. And He places your sacrifices under your power in order that you might praise God for the mercy he has shown you and so that the good should be blessed and rejoice. Servants of God, when you return to your houses after having performed your prayers, follow a different path from that which brought you, so that you might provoke the unfaithful to feel remorse. (Madrid, Junta ms. 25 ff. 126^r–127^r)[11]

This sermon focuses on the religious meaning of the day of sacrifice ('*Eid al-Adha*) and the corresponding acts that Muslims must perform. The explicit use of the phrase "this your day" (*vu^{w}ext^{u}ro dí'a akexte*) fixes the sermon within a particular moment in the Islamic year, setting the deictic origo of the performed text within a temporal frame that serves as an intersection between the traditional past (represented directly by the phrase, "On this day you must follow the tradition") and the emergent present. The traditions of Islam, rooted in a past that is at once historical and shaped by divine intervention and will, are brought forward into the present of "this your day," causing human actions — especially insofar as these evoke and follow the requirements of the tradition — to have meaning across temporal frames that are defined solely by Islamic faith.

We find a similar example of this sort of temporal intersection, and the explicit indexing of it, in a well-known episode from the fourteenth-century *Libro de buen amor*. This episode, referred to by Alfonso de Paradinas, the scribe of the Salamanca manuscript of the *Libro de buen amor* as the "Battle between Flesh and Lent" (La pelea que ouo don carnal con la Quaresma), begins in the following way:

> A holy time of God is approaching:
> I left to be in my own land for a time;
> for in seven days Lent would arrive;
> which made the whole world full of fear. (1067)

> (Açercándose viene un tiempo de Dios santo:
> fuime para mi tierra por folgar algund quanto;
> dende a siete días era Quaresma tanto;
> puso por todo el mundo miedo e grand espanto.)

The first-person narrator begins the story by addressing his audience in the immediate present, warning them of the coming of a specific time in the Christian calendar (presumably Lent). The narrator's use of the present progressive (açercándose viene) roots the narrative in the here-and-now of performance, creating a temporal and thematic context for the storytelling event to follow: we are entering a holy time. What follows directly afterward is the preterite verb construction *fuime* (I left). This radical and sudden temporal shift from the description of an ongoing action mutually experienced by the narrator and his or her audience to a completed action in the past (one ostensibly experienced only by the narrator) forges a similar link between the traditional past (evoked by the narrative keyed by *fuime*) and the lived present. Also of extraordinary importance within the opening lines of the "Battle between Flesh and Lent" is an awesome concern for the future: a holy time of God is approaching, one that provokes such concern that the traditional narrative (in which Lent, Ordinary Time, and Shrove Thursday are all personified) begins with the narrator returning to his home to prepare for it.

After Madrid, Junta ms. 25 finishes its presentation of the need of all Muslims to observe *'Eid al-Adha*, it continues by presenting in some detail the manner in which the faithful are to perform their blood sacrifices. Directly afterward, the text begins to mount a theological argument for the celebration of *'Eid al-Adha*, citing the religious practice of the

Prophet Muhammad (the ultimate source of Sunni tradition) and the miraculous calling of Abraham by God. The latter portion, which ends with a citation of Sura 22:26–27, begins in the following way:

> Know, servants of God, that this, your day, is a great and honored festival day. God has made it a sign within your religion, and it is the day on which God honored your law and ennobled your prophet, Muhammad (PBUH). And know that He holds dear months of reverence. In great times God honored [this day] with Islam and he glorified [it] with the calling of Muhammad (PBUH). God heightened its great worth and promised on it His pardon and His mercy. So honor it and praise it. And the *takbirat* on it are three days from from the Prayer of the Sacrifice on the day of the revelation to the ending of the morning prayer on the fourth day. And whoever praises the law of God is blessed by the Lord. . . . How many reach this day that do not know what they have reached and do not take a good part of its blessings? And today is the day of the great pilgrimmage and the greatest part of the blessings it grants; and the Qur'an speaks of its righteousness and calls God as a witness when it says: When We gave the site of the (Sacred) House to Abraham, We said to him: Associate not anything (in worship), O Ibrahim, with Me; and sanctify My House for those who compass it round, or stand up, or bow, or prostrate themselves (therein in prayer). And proclaim the pilgrimage among the people: they will come to you, and I will make it so that they come from every deep valley and from every land. . . . (Madrid, Junta ms. 25 f. 130)[12]

In this short passage the authority of Sunni tradition is bolstered by the divine revelation of the Qur'an, and God is made to speak — through the text of His Qur'an — in support of the importance of the *'Eid al-Adha.* In terms of the temporal frames evoked by this passage, the traditional and historical Islamic past, together with the timeless Word of God, are both embedded in the lived present ("this your day" [*vu^wext^uro di^ya akexte*]) in order to shape the subsequent actions of the listening public, comprised of Castilian and Aragonese Morisco men and women.

Directly after this dense passage regarding the Qur'anic basis for the celebration of *'Eid al-Adha,* the text moves on to embed itself within an overtly narrative frame: "It was recounted by ibn Abbas." What follows is a recontextualization (both within novel textual and performative settings) of ibn Abbas's account of the *Alhadith del xakrifici^yo de Isma'il,* immediately (and seamlessly) preceded by a well-known Islamic folktale regarding the God's naming of the Angel of Death. Ibn Abbas's story begins:

When God (t'ala) decided to take Abraham as his friend, the angels said to him: "Our Lord and Creator, why do you wish to befriend one of the sons of Adam, if they are destroyers of the Earth, corrupters, and spillers of blood without just reason?" And God said to the angels: "I know what you do not." And the Angel of Death said: "My Lord and Creator, and who will succor and receive the soul of that servant who is your friend?" And God answered with these words: "You will receive him, Angel of Death, and you will care for and receive his soul. Go down to him and make him joyous." And the Angel of Death descended in the form of the most beautiful of the sons of Adam in his face, gentleness, aroma, dress, and — the most beautiful of all — in his speech. And Abraham was the most attuned of people, and he smelled the scent of musk in his dwelling and stopped in front of the Angel of Death, asking: "Who has let you in my house without my permission?" The angel said: "The master and builder of the house has let me in." Abraham said to him: 'How? Is there perhaps another owner besides me?' The angel said: "Abraham, He who has sent me has created us both, and is the Lord of this house." And Abraham responded: "You speak the truth, may God bless you." (Madrid, Junta ms. 25 ff. 125ᵛ)[13]

The presence of the Angel of Death introduces a complex element to both the celebration of 'Eid al-Adha in Morisco communities and the meaning of the Alhadith del xakrifixi⁾o de Isma'il. Death brings an acutely human aspect to time as well as to both the traditions and divine revelation of Islam. Also, as a text performed within temporally framed ritual practice, the Aljutba de la Paxkuʷa de lox adahaex necessarily shapes the temporal character of experience, giving form to collective and individual theories of what has, what does, and what can occur. Given these two elements — an explicit concern with and personification of death (as a beautiful, sweet-smelling, well-spoken human) as well as a situated, performed character — the narrative takes part in the larger project of emplotting Morisco being-toward-death. In other words, within the texts that make up the Khutba 'Eid al-Adha in Madrid, Junta ms. 25, we see a philosophy, or perhaps more accurately an ethics, of both suffering and action.

As I have suggested earlier, this longer text within Madrid, Junta ms. 25, which embeds the Alhadith del xakrifixi⁾o de Isma'il within an explicit sermon on the 'Eid al-Adha, provides valuable information regarding the contextualized meaning of the Alhadith del xakrifixi⁾o de Isma'il within Madrid, BRAH ms. 11/9409. For instance, we see that frameworks of performance and a complex network of continuously negotiated temporal frames are what ultimately give the narrative its meaning. Outside of the context of *'Eid al-Adha,* and the text's place within the ritual observance of this festival, the *Alhadith del xakrifixi'o de Isma'il* in fact makes little sense. Looked at in light of its connection to ritual practice and performance, the text's indexical relation to the life world of the Moriscos is every bit as important as its semantico-referential meaning. Far from a static text to be interpreted or responded to, the *Alhadith del xakrifixi'o de Isma'il* is a text to be enacted, embodied (e.g., through prayer and moral action), and lived precisely due to the being-toward-death of the Moriscos. This urgency is at once attributable to traditional Islamic practice (which provides a moral framework for the negotiation of meaning for the "children of Adam"), general human concerns almost universally mediated by narrative, and the specific situation within which the Moriscos found themselves vis-à-vis the rigid policies of the Spanish Crown and their profound detachment from other Muslim communities throughout the Mediterranean.

6

Language Ideologies
and Poetic Form

*One cannot merely define men and women in terms of the webs of signif-
icance they themselves have spun, since ... few do the actual spinning
while the majority ... is simply caught.*
— Bob Scholte, in *Current Anthropology*

One of the most perplexing questions in *aljamiado-morisco* studies is
also one of the most fundamental: why did Moriscos produce texts in
aljamiado in the first place? Given the risks inherent in such an enterprise,
it is easy to see the use of Arabic script for the production of narrative
and devotional works as a practice that could backfire spectacularly,
given the energetic practices of the Inquisition in Castile and Aragon. As
an example of the dangers inherent in the production and possession of
such texts, we may glance briefly at the case of Luis de Córdoba, a jeweler
from San Clemente (Castile) brought before the Inquisition of Cuenca.
Besides having borrowed a copy of the Qur'an in Arabic in order to
have it copied by someone else, Luis was also charged and punished for
possessing an anti-Islamic book (*Sermones del Antialcorán*) whose goal,
paradoxically, was to list out the precepts of the Islamic faith in order
to prove each of them false (García-Arenal 1978, 55–56).

Within the modern tradition of *aljamiado-morisco* studies — a period
that begins with the publication in England of Pascual de Gayangos's
"Language and Literature of the Moriscos" (1839) — two principal theories regarding the use of *aljamiado* among the Moriscos have been
advanced. The first suggests that *aljamiado* was an inherently secretive
written code for the Moriscos, an in-group device designed to keep pry-
ing non-Muslim readers out and generate a sense of community and
history that serves to repel and resist Christian hegemony. Gayangos
himself alludes to this notion, arguing that:

... the total forgetfulness of their national language did not produce among the Moors the effect which might have been apprehended, namely, the entire oblivion of their national customs and religious traditions; on the contrary, the more miserable and wretched their condition became, and the more distant their hopes of future wealth and domination were, the more their priests and other influential people laboured to instruct them in the duties of their religion, in the sense and tenor of their laws, in the substance of their historical records; in one word, in everything that might bring to their recollection their past victories, or inspire them with the hopes of a future regeneration.

This object was at first attained by religious tracts and moral treatises, translated into Spanish, but written with the Arabic letters.... (1839, 80)

While there is little doubt that the use of Arabic script effectively delimited the readership of Morisco texts along tightly defined socioreligious lines, there are three principal problems with the theory suggested above. The first has to do with the already-mentioned point that these texts, in the hands of Christian authorities, would have called attention to themselves in ways that Latin-script texts would not have, as grounds for prosecution no matter what their content.[1] Second, this theory provides no way of explaining the fact that some Islamic texts produced by Morisco scribes were in fact copied out in Latin script. The copies of Içe de Gebir's *Breviario çunni* held in the Biblioteca de la Junta in Madrid (Junta ms. 1) and the Biblioteca de la Real Academia de la Historia (ms. 11/9395 *olim* S-3) are two well-known examples of this phenomenon.

Another problem with the "secret code" theory is that it explicitly views the production and use of *aljamiado-morisco* texts through the lens of their difficult position vis-à-vis the Christian majority. According to this view, Morisco use of Arabic script was in essence a response to Christian hegemony, a way to prevent crypto-Muslim in-group discourse from being accessed by powerful outsiders. As Gerard Wiegers points out, however, an Islamic narrative tradition in Romance manifested itself well before the conquest of Granada and the forced conversions of the beginning of the sixteenth century. Examining manuscript documents from as far back as the twelfth century, Wiegers argues that knowledge of Romance among Andalusi Arabic-speakers was relatively common, and that Muslim storytellers in Romance (*qussas*) existed even during the period just after the fall of the caliphate (1994, 30–40). Citing the *fatwa* of Malikite scholar ibn Rushd al-Djadd (1059–1126 CE), Wiegers relates the case of a man brought before ibn Rushd (who died two years before the more famous ibn Rushd al-Qurtubi, aka Averroes, was born) accused of having cursed the Prophet and the Arabic language and having recited the Sura of Joseph in Romance (1994, 30). The accused — described as a more or less pious man who did not neglect his prayers — denied these charges, though ibn Rushd ordered him to receive corporal punishment if it could in fact be proven that he had made such statements about the Arabic language and had recited the Sura of Joseph in a language other than Arabic. Wiegers's statements regarding this case are significant:

> One might suppose that, if the accusation was false or inaccurate (after all, it will be remembered that only one witness testified that he made this statement), not the actual *sura,* but the story of Yuçuf was recited. We know that both versified and prose versions of the *Hadith Yuçuf* circulated among the Mudejars, and it is very possible that we are actually dealing with a very early version of that very text. In this respect, we cannot exclude the possibility that the accused was a *qass,* a story-teller. (33)

Looked at from the perspective of an established Romance narrative and poetic tradition among Andalusi Muslims, the Andalusi speech community takes on a new, highly polyglot, character. In fact, the *kharjas* — much-studied Romance couplets appearing at the end of many classical Arabic and Hebrew lyrical poems known as *muwashshahat* — similarly can represent a significant form of *aljamiado* textuality that does not serve to contest Christian power, but rather to index the complex workings of a linguistically and culturally diverse speech community. Discussing later written works in *aljamiado* that may in fact serve as the earliest links in an unbroken chain of Romance language/Arabic script textuality that extends up to the Moriscos' expulsion from Spain in 1609–14, López-Morillas makes the claim that "the *aljamiado* phenomenon, so characteristic of the Castilian and Aragonese Muslims, has its roots in the Mudéjar period: the earliest dated manuscript known is of 1424, and some undated ones must go back to the 1300s" (1995, 198). While it must be admitted that historical events after the fall of Granada changed the life-world of Spanish Muslims to such a radical extent that we may accurately speak of some significant breaks in Islamic cultural traditions in the peninsula (as well as relations of power on a large scale), it would be a mistake to see *aljamiado* manuscript texts as *sui generis* textual productions and their use as a direct and immediate Morisco response (after the fact) to the exercise of Hispano-Christian political power during the sixteenth century.

Another influential theory that attempts to explain the production and use of *aljamiado* texts within Castilian and Aragonese Morisco communities has been advanced most clearly by Ottmar Hegyi. Citing generalized language ideologies held by Muslims regarding the Arabic language and its alphabet, Hegyi argues that:

> ... the use of the Arabic alphabet in *aljamiado* languages is the natural result of the prestige of the sacred alphabet which — together with lexical, morphological, and syntactical Arabisms — gives non-Arabic Muslim writings an openly Islamic look. It functions as a cultureme, an exterior sign that signals its pertinence to the *umma*, the Muslim community. (1981, 16–17)[2]

L. P. Harvey remains to some extent neutral on the reasons that underlie the use of Arabic script in Morisco writing. He explains in his work on Morisco social and political history:

> It may come as a surprise to some otherwise well-informed about Spain and about Spanish Islam to learn that there was a not inconsiderable literature in Hispanic dialects (mainly in varieties of Castilian and Aragonese) which circulated among the Moriscos. This was a literature for crypto-Muslims, and so was itself secret. To the best of my knowledge there is no evidence that any Christian Spaniard, however well informed, was ever aware of its existence. Even the Inquisition, which certainly impounded some manuscripts, seems to have been content to classify them as Qurans, and to have left matters there. The language, basically Romance, was often much influenced by Arabic, not only because it incorporated many more elements of Arabic vocabulary than did standard Spanish, but also because, at the levels of morphology and syntax, Semitic models made themselves felt. This literature in Spanish using Arabic characters is known to modern scholars as *literatura aljamiada,* or simply as *aljamía.* (1993, 213)

Harvey is more concerned in this essay with describing in some detail the historical issues surrounding the forced conversion and expulsion of the Moriscos, and for this reason he does not explain the factors that underlie the influence that Arabic had over Morisco scribes and readers.[3] Nonetheless, he does sketch out a picture of the Moriscos' linguistic repertoire and textuality that maintains a significantly close — though not necessarily conscious or aimed-at — relation with Arabic at a number of levels.

Significantly for the present study, Antonio Domínguez Ortiz emphasizes the temporal aspects of Morisco textuality, underlining a desire to maintain links with established linguistic and literary traditions from the Islamic past:

> It is a detail worth keeping in mind that on occasion the written word was able to persist with more vitality than spoken language, a phenomenon that gave rise to the curiosity of *aljamiado literature*. A more detailed study would also have to examine the efforts of a learned minority to save from destruction Arabic manuscripts — which represented for them a link to a very long tradition. After the Royal Decree of June 20, 1511, which ordered the surrender of all Arabic books, it was dangerous to keep them, at least those that dealt with the Islamic faith; however, some accidental findings made in old Morisco homes prove that there was no shortage of people willing to run the risk of hiding what was for them a precious cultural treasure. (1962, 51–52)[4]

The "precious cultural treasure" to which Domínguez Ortiz refers is at once the textual content of books in Arabic and the perceived power of the Arabic language itself to index values and beliefs that transcended time and history. The conservation and use of the Arabic alphabet, even when Arabic itself had all but disappeared from the linguistic repertoire of most Iberian Muslims, is then framed as a component of the larger cultural project of conserving some significant link to the "long tradition" — an evolving temporal frame that begins with the Archangel Gabriel's revelation of the Word of God to Muhammad in Arabic — of Islamic discourse and textuality.

Looked at from this perspective, the use of *aljamiado* by Castilian and Aragonese Moriscos has an extraordinarily important cross-temporal as well as cross-cultural function. It is a mistake, in other words, to view the use of Arabic script in the production of Romance texts simply as a means of connecting the Moriscos to the larger Islamic *umma* situated around the Mediterranean during the sixteenth and seventeenth centuries. This synchronic view of *aljamiado-morisco* textuality ignores the powerful manner in which the use of Arabic script situated Morisco scribes and readers within a thousand-year tradition of God's relationship with Muslims. It also ignores the tremendous promises for the future that came with such a relationship, such as the rewards that would come to the faithful on the Day of Judgment. What I wish to emphasize here is that the use of *aljamiado* by Castilian and Aragonese Moriscos functioned primarily as a way by which the Moriscos could simultaneously connect themselves to traditional Islamic discourse from a past framed, through narrative and its implementation in practice, as *their own* and bring that past to bear on a present and future that they saw as uncertain and even confusing.[5] In this respect, there is an important temporal element to the use of Arabic script in Morisco written discourse — both from the perspective of the continuation of a literary practice of writing in Romance that had begun at least a century earlier (and built on the foundation of a much longer oral tradition of Romance narrative) and the ability of the Arabic alphabet itself to index the very tradition that Morisco scribes were consciously attempting to preserve and shape to their own needs.

We should be cautious about our conclusions, however, when we speak about the production and use of *aljamiado-morisco* texts. For while a significant feature of Morisco written texts, the use of Arabic script — or the production of books, for that matter — is not a universal feature of all Morisco discourse and engagement of texts. As Domínguez Ortiz maintains, the copying and recopying of books in *aljamiado* is essentially the practice of a learned minority. In other words, for the majority of Moriscos — at least in the rural areas of Castile and Aragon where the largest number of extant books originate — writing in Arabic script was not an issue of primary concern, given the fact that most people did not do it. This is not to say that there was not an active book trade within and among Morisco communities in Aragon and Castile. There is in fact a good deal of documentary proof, some of which I have presented in earlier chapters, that many Moriscos owned books in *aljamiado* and Arabic. However, what is not certain is the extent to which (nor the manner in which) these books were actively read and/or recopied by their owners. Fournel-Guérin argues, for example, that for most Moriscos, these books held a primarily totemic value (1979, 245). Such totemic use of books is significant, and Arabic script — which even a person without alphabetic literacy could recognize as such — certainly played an important role in determining the value of these books in this respect. It is widely known, for example, that while most Christians during the Middle Ages were alphabetically illiterate and knew little if any Latin, the presentation of biblical verse (mostly along with illuminations) during the Latin Mass was an integral part of this celebration. Looked at in this broader way, the uses to which even "illiterate" members of communities put books and other forms of written texts serve as potent means of shaping cultural practice and even textual meaning.

One of the most important conclusions of the present book has been that the meaning of *aljamiado-morisco* texts — as well as the meaning of Morisco textuality more generally — is a socially embedded one most commonly linked to ritual practice and the performative activities that characterize such practice. In line with this focus, we may ask what the text-mediated activities were in which private individuals and families in Morisco communities would have engaged? It is certainly possible that some readers participated in private study or the instruction of their children. However, in the majority of cases these activities seem to have been handled by the local or itinerant *alfakí,* a learned or at least semi-learned Muslim man charged with the ordering of Muslim life in most Morisco communities. As we saw in the previous chapters in our discussions of 'Eid al-Adha and the celebration of the Prophet's birth, the role of the *alfakí* in the regimentation of ritual practice, as well as in the carrying out of educational activities in group settings, could be quite extensive and hands-on.

In essence, when we speak of the linguistic practices and habitus of Castilian and Aragonese Moriscos — at least insofar as these are rooted in our analysis of *aljamiado-morisco* manuscripts — we are inevitably forced to deal at some level with the locally, and often surreptitiously, sanctioned activities of Morisco *alfakíes.* Given the central role of these men in the development and operation of Morisco book culture, when we speak of the "Morisco use of Arabic script" we are to a large extent speaking of the socially embedded (and therefore ideologically situated) practices of this particular subset of crypto-Muslim society: paid semi-professionals whose very livelihood depended to some extent upon the preservation — and perhaps more importantly the regimentation — of Islamic knowledge within sixteenth- and early seventeenth-century Aragon and Castile. These men in fact served, as we shall see, as powerful agents in the continuous process of shaping *aljamiado-morisco* textual practices and language ideologies.

Questions related to Morisco language ideologies and the tremendous influence of *alfakíes* in their negotiation and reproduction — through the copying of books, their public reading in ritual settings, and the carrying out of socializing activities such as religious and literacy instruction — are at the very heart of any fine-grained analysis of one of the best known *aljamiado-morisco* narratives, the verse *Hadith de Yuçuf*

(=*Poema de Yusuf*). This text, which, like the *Alhadith del xakrifixi'o de Isma'il,* is a recontextualization of a Qur'anic narrative (Sura 12), is significant to scholars of Spanish literature due to its having been composed in *cuaderna vía,* a poetic form popularized by clerical Christian poets in the early thirteenth century. An analysis of the *Poema de Yuçuf* in light of its use of *cuaderna vía* is the main focus of the present chapter. My argument is that the use of an archaic, essentially Christian poetic form has to do with localized language ideologies within Morisco communities that placed specific values on poetic form as a powerful index of textual authority. The use of *cuaderna vía* by Morisco scribes and/or local *alfakíes* intersects with the expression of language ideologies related to ideas of literary tradition and religious discourse as a means of encoding textual and social authority by a semi-professional subgroup within Morisco society.

Language Ideologies and Literary Analysis

Before speaking about the language ideologies at work in the *Poema de Yuçuf* and their significance for questions regarding Morisco linguistic repertoire and cultural practices, it is useful to present, albeit briefly, what I mean by the term "language ideologies." A domain of study developed in the 1990s within the field of linguistic anthropology, language ideologies have found their most thorough elaboration in two recent collections of essays: *Language Ideologies: Practice and Theory* (1998) and *Regimes of Language* (2000). The first collection, edited by Bambi B. Schieffelin, Kathryn A. Woolard, and Paul V. Kroskrity, maps out language ideologies (alternatively referred to as "linguistic ideologies" and "ideologies of language") as a field of analysis within anthropology, highlighting the research link that language ideologies form between "social forms and forms of talk" (Woolard 1998, 3). In her introduction to the volume, Woolard presents an in-depth discussion of what the term "ideology" itself has to add to the framing of this mode of inquiry, citing the use (itself situated) of "ideology" from the Napoleonic period in France through more widely held Marxist conceptions of the term such as those developed by Louis Althusser and Frederic Jameson. While stopping short of reducing "language ideologies" to any fixed, univocal definition, Woolard does offer a more or less concrete vision of what is entailed in such analysis:

> To be sure, almost any human act of signification in some respect serves to organize social relations. But this does not necessarily mean that enlarging the focus of the ideology concept beyond signification in service of power necessarily enlarges the term to the point of uselessness. Although it does not distinguish one form of signification from another (almost all signification having an ideological aspect), the concept can still very usefully hold one *facet* of signification to light, what [Karl] Mannheim called the "social and activist" roots of thinking and signification. (1998, 9)

These "facets of signification" are manifold and change from context to context, though they can include such phenomena as the metapragmatic indexicality that underlies all verbal interaction (Silverstein 1993), ideas and practices revolving around linguistic register (e.g., use of *usted* or *tú* in Spanish), language maintenance and standardization efforts at the local and national level, orthographic regimentation, and choices regarding textual representation and reproduction. If we look at the use of Arabic script by Morisco scribes, a picture begins to emerge regarding how such practice both reflects and structures cultural ideologies that are inseparable from socially embedded language use.

Research in language ideologies essentially provides a means of speaking with some specificity about the ways in which language use intersects with social practice and the asymmetrical power relations that permeate such practice over time. While early twentieth-century Boasian ethnographic study paid little attention to the secondary explanations of native collaborators, the field of language ideologies places these native explanations, justifications, and judgments at the center of analysis, allowing researchers to attend to the operation of cultural systems of "ideas about social and linguistic relationships, together with their loading of moral and political interests" (Irvine 1989, 255).

Judith Irvine's focus on the "moral and political interests" of specific groups indexed through the implementation of language ideologies is further developed in *Regimes of Language,* a collection of essays edited by Paul V. Kroskrity that focus somewhat explicitly on the regimes of institutionalized power that sustain language ideologies, and vice versa. In this volume's introduction, Paul Kroskrity argues that language ideologies essentially "represent the perception of language and discourse that is constructed in the interest of a specific social or cultural group" (Kroskrity 2000, 8). He adds:

> [L]anguage ideologies are profitably conceived as multiple because of
> the multiplicity of meaningful social divisions (class, gender, clan, elites,
> generations, and so on) within sociocultural groups that have the po-
> tential to produce divergent perspectives expressed as indices of group
> membership. Language ideologies are thus grounded in social experi-
> ence which is never uniformly distributed throughout polities of any
> scale. (2000, 12)

The distributed and manifold nature of language ideologies — mirroring,
in essence, the distributed and manifold nature of social identities themselves — manifests itself quite clearly in the *aljamiado-morisco* narratives
studied in the present book. Community *alfakíes* as well as other locally
sanctioned scribes and readers do not only serve as activists against the
linguistic, cultural, and religious hegemony (which at times spilled over
into direct, violent confrontation) of Christian Spain. They also serve as
gatekeepers within their own communities, employing language, and the
ideologies that underlie its signifying power at various levels, to regiment
meaning and knowledge at the local level. In other words, what appears
as cultural resistance on the part of the Moriscos from the Christian (or
historical) perspective can also be approached as more locally targeted
modes of institutionally situated structuration that work to shape the
cultural habitus of the members of Morisco communities in Castile and
Aragon. Even within Morisco communities, there is evidence of asymmetrical relations of power (between, for example, men and women);
and the written texts of these communities — produced, reproduced, and
performed to a large extent by sanctioned "experts" — play an integral
role in the workings of these power relations.

Before moving on to discuss the importance of language ideologies
for an analysis of temporality and poetic form (specifically in the case
of the *Poema de Yuçuf*), it is useful to focus upon the manner in which
ideologies of language can yield useful results in literary analysis. To
accomplish this, we turn now to a short but well-known episode from
Spanish literature that offers a complex representation (in part linguistic)
of the Moriscos just after their expulsion. The episode is found in chapter
54 of the second volume of Miguel de Cervantes's *Don Quijote*. In this
passage, Sancho Panza meets up with his one-time Morisco neighbor,
Ricote. The point of interest for our purposes is found just before the
two begin to converse, when the narrator implicitly offers an opinion
regarding the language of the Moriscos, one that intersects with ideas
related to their social identity within the larger context of early modern

Spain. He presents Ricote, dressed as a Frenchman and traveling in Spain with some German pilgrims, as one who speaks to Sancho "without stumbling over his Morisco language" (sin tropezar nada en su lengua morisca). Rather, Ricote speaks to Sancho in what the narrator describes as "pure Castilian" (la pura castellana). The narrator's explicit mention of linguistic purity and the "stumbling" (the verb *tropezar* also carries the meaning of "to err") that underlies the use of Morisco speech outside of the context of crypto-Muslim communities serves to evoke social relations of power that inevitably favor his own elite speech community. Ideas of language standardization (leaving aside more highly charged ideas of purity) are inherently tied to situated ideologies of language, as are characterizations of others' speech that index physical clumsiness and lack of restraint.

From a socio-political point of view, Ricote is to be trusted in this episode, in part because of his ability to "tame his wild tongue" (Anzaldúa 1987) and make use of the pure, sanctioned code. As René Quérillacq (1992) argues, it becomes clear through this and other episodes (e.g., Ricote's tearful reunion with his daughter, Ana Félix) that Cervantes is actually critical of the Moriscos' expulsion, a massive process that was for the most part finalized by the year in which the second volume of the *Quijote* appeared; however, the tools that Cervantes employs to criticize this process do little to undermine dominant ideas of the Moriscos as an inferior group. In fact, the crux of Cervantes's argument in *Don Quijote* seems to be that the Moriscos as a whole could have been successfully made to assimilate themselves into Castilian society — a process whose culmination is indexed by the "pure Castilian" speech of Ricote and his collegiality with the Old Christian, Sancho. This connection between "standard speech" as an index of one's ability to function within a given community is directly addressed by Michael Silverstein in an essay on linguistic relativity and modern nationalism:

> Manifested and enforced through such writing- and reading-dependent institutions as government, schooling, and so on, standardization is a modern and inclusive societal project in the classic Praguean sense. One's familiarity with and ability to navigate within these various institutions becomes indexically tied to one's language use. Even outside them, one "voices" one's very identity in terms of the registers — for example, degree of standardization — that one controls and can deploy. Every speaker has a repertoire of registers that become, when used,

second-order indexes of class and related social positionings in modern social formations of inequality.

In this way a language community acquires what we would term a hegemonic standard relative to which variation is experienced as a pyramidical or conical space of divergence: standard-register usage is at the top-and-center, and each coherent cluster of variance is experienced as mere "dialect." The standard that informs the language community's norm thus becomes the very emblem of the existence of that community, with a characteristic social distribution of strength and mode of allegiance that can be studied with some precision. Those with the greatest allegiance to this emblem of community-hood tend to imagine the existence of the perfect standard-using member of the language community as a democratically and universally available position of inhabitance of the language community to which everyone can, and even should, aspire. (2000, 121–22)

As Silverstein describes it, social identities and dispositions are powerfully indexed by one's use of standardized or nonstandardized forms of speech. The *lengua morisca* referred to by Cervantes — together with his narrator's encoded assessment of its value in conversational settings (signaled by the verb *tropezar*) — clearly falls near the bottom of the pyramid described by Silverstein; and given the low place that it occupies within the larger Spanish language community (a community in fact characterized by a fair amount of diversity during the early seventeenth century), the use of *lengua morisca* indexes a whole suite of negative dispositions and markers of stance with respect to the larger language community and the burgeoning Spanish nation-state. Consequently, Ricote's ability to speak *pura castellana* without "stumbling over" his low-status, even subversive "dialect" can index his cohesion with the larger Spanish language community, as well as his favorable disposition toward the institutions of power that legitimate the standardized form of the Spanish language. Interestingly, these issues revolving around language ideologies and state power — which underscore a solid if complex link between micro- and macro-level social interaction and structure — find expression in a literary narrative that purports to deal with a low-ranking Spanish nobleman's deluded chivalric sojourn through the Castilian countryside.

As is evident from our brief glance at even a very short passage of text, language ideologies, as indexes of power relations that intersect with language use, suggest a potentially rich field of inquiry within literary analysis. What I would like to develop in what remains of this chapter is a sense not only of the language ideologies encoded in the *Poema de Yuçuf* through its implementation of *cuaderna vía,* but also how these ideologies of language operate to evoke and maintain temporal frameworks that similarly intersect with locally regimented systems of power in Castilian and Aragonese Morisco communities.

The *Poema de Yuçuf*
in Its Manuscript and Narrative Context

The *Poema de Yuçuf* is extant in two manuscripts. The first and most extensive of these is Madrid, BN ms. Res. 247, a well-preserved manuscript containing fifty folios (142 x 212 mm), which is copied out in a very neat Maghrebi hand and organized in four-verse stanzas. The first edition of this manuscript was published in 1849 by George Ticknor, who included it as an appendix in his *History of Spanish Literature.* Thirty-four years later, Heinrich Morf published a reproduction of the *Poema de Yuçuf* (1883), from which Michael Schmitz made a Latin-character transcription in 1899. Aside from William Weisiger Johnson's 1972 edition, which combines Madrid, BN ms. Res. 247 with the other extant copy, Madrid, BRAH ms. 11/9409 (*olim* T-12), there have been no other editions of this text.

The other extant copy of the *Poema de Yuçuf* occupies the first nine folios (140 x 200 mm) of an encyclopedic book found in the Biblioteca de la Real Academia de la Historia that was the focus of our analysis in the previous chapter. The text of this version of the *Poema de Yuçuf* is significant for the work's textual history (from a philological perspective) in that it contains nine quatrains at the beginning that are not present in Madrid, BN ms. Res. 247. In all other respects, the text of Madrid, BRAH ms. 11/9409 is much rougher than the other version, written in varying small, cramped hands and copied out as if it were a prose work. Also, the text of Madrid, BRAH ms. 11/9409 ends after quatrain 95 (with quatrain 33 missing and a *lacuna* between quatrains 82 and 92), while Madrid, BN ms. Res. 247 — which itself breaks off before the narrative's end — contains 312.

The shorter manuscript version of the *Poema de Yuçuf* found in the Biblioteca de la Real Academia de la Historia in Madrid was first edited in 1846, appearing as an appendix to the third edition of Ticknor's *History of Spanish Literature.* Several decades later, Ramón Menéndez

Pidal produced a critical edition of the text, which appeared in the *Revista de Archivos, Bibliotecas y Museos* (7 [1902]: 91–129; 276–309; 347–62). Menéndez Pidal's edition was subsequently reproduced, with photographic reproductions of the manuscript's folios, by the University of Granada in 1952. Since that time, there has been no critical edition of this manuscript, aside from Weisiger Johnson's 1974 edition of both extant manuscripts of the *Poema de Yuçuf*.

The *Poema de Yuçuf* is a Hispano-Romance version (i.e., Castilian with significant Aragonese inflections) of Sura 12 of the Qur'an. It recounts the story of Joseph, the son of Jacob, who is tricked and abandoned by his half brothers before eventually becoming the king of Egypt's treasurer, in fulfillment of a vision that Joseph has at the narrative's beginning. This vision is revealed in Sura 12:4: "When Joseph said to his father: O my father! I saw eleven stars and the sun and the moon — I saw them making obeisance to me." The eleven stars are none other than Joseph's brothers, while the sun and moon seem to indicate his parents, as evidenced in his exclamation at the end of the episode:

> And he raised his parents upon the throne, and they fell prostrate for his sake. And he said: O my father, this is the significance of my vision of old — my Lord has made it true. And He was indeed kind to me, when He brought me forth from the prison, and brought you from the desert after the devil had sown dissensions between me and my brethren. Surely my Lord is benignant to whom He pleases. Truly He is the Knowing, the Wise. (12:100)

The *aljamiado* version of this story adds a number of novel elements to its Qur'anic source, most notably the Egyptian queen's attempted seduction of the young Joseph discussed in the previous chapter. Another important difference between these two versions of the Joseph story is the manner in which they begin.

The Qur'anic version begins with an invocation of God, three Arabic letters of mysterious meaning, and a metadiscursive reference back to the revealed text itself:

> In the name of Allah, the Beneficent, the Merciful.

> 12.1: Alif Lam Ra. These are the verses of the Book that makes (things) manifest.

> 12.2: Surely We have revealed it — an Arabic Qur'an — that you may understand.

This reference back to the Qur'an itself as a divinely revealed text in Arabic is significant, as through this revelation Arabic is elevated not only as a liturgical language, but also the language that the Archangel Gabriel spoke to Muhammad, the language within which the divine word of God is encoded. The story of Joseph, which directly follows this meta-reference to the language of the text itself, is an integral part of this divine revelation, as underscored by the third verse of the Sura: "We narrate to you the best of narratives, by Our revealing to you this Qur'an, though before this you were certainly one of those who did not know" (12:3). There is a link within the Qur'an then, through the juxtaposition in verses 2 and 3 of Arabic as the language of revelation and the story of Joseph as part of what is revealed to Muhammad, between the divinely configured authority and meaning of the Joseph story and its presentation in Arabic.

What happens to this authority and meaning when the narrative is translated into Hispano-Romance? We can consider this question by looking closely at the manner in which the Morisco *Poema de Yuçuf* begins. Like the Qur'anic version, the *aljamiado-morisco* narrative begins with the title of the work itself, an invocation of God and description of His powers, and finally a keying of the narrative by a first-person storyteller:

> The Story of Joseph.
> (peace be upon him).
> In the name of God, the Compassionate, the Merciful.
> Praise to God; He is the most high and true.
> Honored and perfect Lord of justice, frank
> And powerful, and certain bestower of order. Great is
> His power; the entire world is within it;
> Nothing that is born in the world nor in the sea is hidden to Him,
> Neither in the black nor the white earth.
> I am letting you know — listen, my friends — that which
> Occurred in the ~~glorious~~ past to Jacob and
> To Joseph and to his ten brothers.... (Madrid, BRAH 11/9409 f. 1ʳ)

> (Hadith de Yuçuf
> ['Alayhi al-çalam]
> Bismillahi arrahmani arrahimi
> Loᵂamiᵞento ad Allah; él alto ᵞex y verdadero
> Onrrado y qonp'lido, xeñor dereyturero, fᵃranko
> Y poderoxo ordenador xertero. Gᵃran ᵞex

> El xu poder todo el mundo abarqa; non xe le enqubre
> Koxa ke en el mundo naçqa xiqui^yere en la mar
> Ni en toda la komarna ni ^yen la ti^yerra pⁱri^yeta ni ^yen la b^alanka
> Fagovox a xaber oyadex mix amadox lo ke konte-
> [çi^yo] en lox altox ti^yenpox paxadox a Chaqó i
> a Yuçuf i ^ya xux di^yex ermanox....)

This first-person storyteller is not the archangel Gabriel, and most of the divine veneer of the narrative has been rubbed off through its translation out of Arabic. However, there is a different form of authority that is worked out through the introduction of this narrative, one that finds its foundation in distinctly Morisco cultural frameworks of time.

That the *Poema de Yuçuf* begins with an invocation of God and two stanzas that detail His power to right wrongs and fix injustices (e.g., *xeñor dereyturero*) provides a strong link for the force that this narrative could possess within Morisco communities consistently set upon by Christian authorities.[6] As in the case of the *Alhadith del xakrifixi^yo de Isma'il*, the *Poema de Yuçuf* forges a strong link not only between the discourse of the Qur'an and storytelling activities within Morisco communities, but also between the historical time of the recounted events — a time in which God performed miracles for those who were faithful to Him — and the lived "now" inhabited by members of Morisco communities. The valorization of this historical frame, which is both particularly Muslim and encoded within Hispano-Romance rather than Arabic, is evidenced by the crossed-out word at the end of the cited passage from (Madrid, BRAH 11/9409 f. 1ʳ): "That which occurred in the glorious past" (Lo ke konteçi^yo en lox altox ti^yenpox paxadox). The scribe's first, perhaps absent-minded impulse to copy out *altox tie^ynpox paxadox* reveals a discursive formula that may have been common in Morisco religious discourse. It was most likely not found in the copy of the *Poema de Yuçuf* that he used as the source for his copy. However, that he inserted it suggests a significant elevation of the Islamic past for Morisco scribes and readers — a commonplace to be sure, but a significant one given the manner in which Morisco texts regularly negotiate the cultural value and meaning of the human dimension of time. But several questions remain for Morisco scribes and readers: how to link the Hispano-Romance story of Joseph, as well as the storytelling activities of Castilian and Aragonese Moriscos, to that "glorious" past? How to form a discursive bridge between the *altox ti^yenpox paxadox,* in which those faithful to God had their visions realized, and the present? How to encode the weight of a Qur'anic narrative within a Hispano-Romance story of jealousy, lust, rivalry, and liberation?

Perhaps before attempting to answer these questions it is a good idea to address the smaller though no less thorny question of who would be invested with the authority to forge such a bridge in the first place. I have spoken already about the importance of local and itinerant *alfakíes* in the shaping of Morisco textuality, through their instructional, ritual, and scribal activities. In the case of the *Poema de Yuçuf* and its relation to the textual activities of *alfakíes,* it is important to keep in mind that although the *aljamiado* poem was most likely first redacted before the conquest of Granada and the forced conversions of 1502–25 (Menéndez Pidal 1952; Johnson 1974), it was copied more than once during the sixteenth century and also repeatedly read as a part of the carrying-out of situated activities such as ritual practice.

Given the *Poema de Yuçuf*'s use within Castilian and Aragonese Morisco communities during the sixteenth century, what is significant about the use of the *cuaderna vía* poetic form within the two extant versions of the poem? To answer this question, we should begin by discussing what exactly the *cuaderna vía* poetic form was within its late medieval literary and social context.

Cuaderna Vía and Christian Literature in Medieval Spain

The earliest known use of the term *cuaderna vía* is found in the second stanza of the *Libro de Alexandre,* a roughly ten-thousand-stanza work in Castilian from the early thirteenth century. The poem, based on a number of other texts in Latin and French (among these the *Alexandreis* of Gautier de Châtillon and the *Roman d'Alexandre*), deals with the life, conquests, and death of Alexander the Great. In the second stanza of the *Libro de Alexandre,* we find the following metadiscursive reference to the form of the text itself, along with a strongly ideological statement regarding the epistemological and aesthetic value of this form:

> I bring a poetry of great beauty, one not of minstrelsy,
> A poetry without flaw, as it is of the clergy;
> To speak at length in the rhyme of *cuaderna vía*
> with a regular meter — this requires great mastery.

(Mester traigo fermoso, non es de joglaría,
mester es sin pecado, ca es de clerezía;
fablar curso rimado por la cuaderna vía,
a sílabas contadas, ca es grant maestría.)

The sense of *poetry* in these lines (my rough translation of the Old Castilian *mester*) implies not only poetic product, but also practice. *Mester* can
be understood to signify a sort of poetic school, though it is clear that the
mester de clerezía, which characterized itself by the use of the *cuaderna
vía* poetic form, was never an associated poetic school as such, but more
of a style and mode of poetry linked to learned, largely clerical, Castilian poets from the early thirteenth to the late fourteenth centuries. At
its root a manifesto of moral and artistic prestige, the second stanza of
the *Libro de Alexandre* seeks to legitimate the authority of this poetic
"school" over the much less regimented practices and discourse of popular poetry characterized by the so-called *mester de joglaría* against which
it defines itself.

What is important to keep in mind with regard to the term *mester*
in the second stanza of the *Libro de Alexandre* is the explicit sense of
poetry as practice: *"Mester traigo fermoso."* This short phrase does not
speak so much of poetic form (and the beauty that is associated with it)
as of the activities of poets themselves. By speaking in terms of *mesteres,*
the second stanza of the *Libro de Alexandre* explicitly announces the
advent of a novel mode of poetic practice while simultaneously indexing
the social institutions (however ad hoc and fluid these may at times be)
that support it.

What does this notion of poetic practice, linked to social institutions
of power (*clerezía*) have to do with the *cuaderna vía* poetic form itself?
Besides being a simultaneous vehicle for and index of the ideologies and
social relations that legitimate the *mester de clerezía* as both a mode
and style of poetic production — with strong roots in French and Latin
poetry as well as the cultural contact facilitated by the pilgrimage trail between Paris and Santiago de Compostela (Dutton 1973; Rico 1985) —
cuaderna vía serves to marginalize other, less learned forms of poetic
practice: *non es de joglaría*. Regularity of verse form replaces "irregularity," which is relegated to a subordinate, even defective status within
the newly fashioned learned form. Like the standardization of specific
languages, the standardization and subsequent legitimation of a particular verse form (as "regular," "learned," "written," and "clerical" as

opposed to "irregular," "popular," "oral," and *"juglaresca"*) implies complex relations of power that intersect with the specific "regimes of language" that obtain in a given community.

Moving now to a discussion of form, *cuaderna vía* itself consists of a series of (consonantally) monorhymed quatrains whose verses are divided into two seven-syllable hemistichs. The form is a variation of the French *alexandrine,* which has survived in modern Castilian poetry (e.g., Pablo Neruda's "Me gustas cuando callas"), although by the beginning of the fourteenth century the *mester de clerezía* begins to undergo an evolution that sees changes with respect to the number of syllables in each verse, due in part to the persistent influence of more popular forms of Castilian versification. What is a nearly universal characteristic of the poetic output of the *mester de clerezía,* however, is the regularity of verse length (whether they contain twelve, fourteen, or sixteen syllables) from poem to poem — a feature that separates this poetry from that of other modes of poetic expression in medieval Castile.

The principal works of the *mester de clerezía* are for the most part openly religious and didactic in character. These include Gonzalo de Berceo's *Vida de Santo Domingo de Silos, Vida de San Millán de la Cogolla, Vida de Santa Oria,* and *Milagros de Nuestra Señora.* Also included in this group of poems are the *Loores de Nuestra Señora, Duelo de la Virgen el día de la pasión de su hijo, El martirio de San Lorenzo, El xakrifixi°o de la misa,* and *Los signos que aparecerán antes del juicio.* Of more epico-novelistic character are the *Libro de Apolonio, Poema de Fernán González,* and the aforementioned *Libro de Alexandre.* Another later work that makes use of *cuaderna vía,* but within an even more complex ideological and poetic context, is the *Libro de buen amor,* a simultaneously learned and popular work first redacted sometime during the middle of the fourteenth century.

Cuaderna Vía and Morisco Language Ideologies

Having established that the principal formal trait of *mester de clerezía* poetry is the regularity of its verse (presented in direct opposition to other, "irregular" verse forms), it is necessary to mention from the outset here that the verse form of the *Poema de Yuçuf* does not share this feature. This sort of variation can be explained in part by the fact that the *Poema de Yuçuf* is a work undoubtedly translated from an Arabic original that was never intended to be part of the decidedly Christian *mester de clerezía*. Also important is the fact that the text has its origins in a much later period of poetic production — most likely during the later fourteenth or early fifteenth centuries (Saavedra 1878; Menéndez Pidal 1952) — than that in which the primary works of *cuaderna vía* poetry are first redacted. Finally, we should mention the significance of the Aragonese morphological and lexical traits that run through the *Poema de Yuçuf*. A work marginalized at once by its Islamic theme, its redaction in Arabic script, and its use of a low-prestige peninsular Romance "dialect," the *Poema de Yuçuf* seems to be working against the very principles of regularity and socio-moral authority that characterize the *mester de clerezía* and, more broadly, the use of *cuaderna vía*. For even if we look at the creative use to which Juan Ruiz puts *cuaderna vía* in the *Libro de buen amor,* what remains in this fourteenth century work is the regularity of his verse and the consistent implementation of a high-prestige form of Castilian (that from Toledo). Perhaps morally ambiguous with respect to the theme of its discourse, the *Libro de buen amor* is nonetheless linguistically and poetically straightforward about its relation to forms of symbolic power that abide in fourteenth-century Castile.

With respect to the *Poema de Yuçuf,* the use of *cuaderna vía* necessarily indexes something other than what it points to in works of the *mester de clerezía*. Although first redacted during the late Mudéjar period (late fourteenth- to early fifteenth centuries), which may have preserved elements of *mester de clerezía* practice as a sort of parallel or even subversive tradition vis-à-vis its Christian counterpart, the *Poema de Yuçuf* was also recopied and engaged during the sixteenth and early seventeenth centuries in much the same way that the *Hadith del sacrificio de Isma'il* was. And what principally concerns us here is how the *use* of *cuaderna vía* — which refers as much to its engagement by readers and scribes as to its initial recontextualization from Arabic into Hispano-Romance long before the conquest of Granada — mediated the negotiation of cultural practice and social organization with Morisco communities during the sixteenth and seventeenth centuries.

Such a line of questioning leads us once again to consider the role of the *alfakí* in the textual and social life of Morisco communities. The *Poema de Yuçuf* simultaneously indexes a form of authoritative poetic discourse in Hispano-Romance (i.e., *cuaderna vía*) as well as a traditional narrative tradition linked thematically as well as formally (i.e., through Arabic grammatical features and discursive formulae) to Islam.

This mixture of elements, when contextualized within storytelling events and other situated activities centered around the text of the *Poema de Yuçuf,* serves to help fashion — within a shifting present and with consequences for social organization and practice in the future — a peculiarly "Morisco past" that can provisionally be framed as a hybrid form of temporality that consists of both Islamic and Christian elements. Such a social project would have been to a large degree carried out and given shape by *alfakíes,* especially in rural Aragon and Castile (such as Morés, where Madrid, BRAH ms. 11/9409 was found), where alphabetic literacy and knowledge of Islam were relatively low.

What I am suggesting here is that the use (that is, the *continued use* if we are speaking within the context of sixteenth-century Morisco communities) of *cuaderna vía* reflects the language ideologies of a particular group of Moriscos, namely, the *alfakíes* who copied out and read these texts as part of devotional and educational activities. What such language use helps to construct, beyond a singularly Morisco form of textual and discursive authority that builds equally upon traditional Islamic narrative and high-prestige Castilian poetic (though not linguistic) form, is a means of valorizing local theories of the past. These local theories of the past, neither fully Islamic nor Hispano-Christian, operate principally as a means of carving out a cultural niche for the Moriscos as Muslims dwelling in a nation-state openly hostile to them.

But these theories of the past also work to shape the present and the future. They serve to regiment human experience and action within more or less tightly described moral frameworks that are at all points shaped by notions of where individuals and the community at large have been, are, and will be in the future. The power of conversational narratives of the past to "step into the future" has been studied by Ochs, who argues that "stories of personal experience regularly step out of the temporal domain of the past into the temporal domain of the future to make *story-coherent* predications of possible events to take place after the present moment" (1994, 107). Taking this notion of narrative as social practice and organization further, Ochs has shown how conversational narrative in interactive settings helps to shape the "scientific" knowledge of physicists (1996). In line with Ochs's research, it is my contention that the traditional Islamic narratives of the Moriscos — insofar as these narratives are repeatedly recopied and performed in situated activities — likewise serve to generate culturally specific frames for knowledge, authority, and practice.

Looking with finer detail at this process of generation (although in the absence of the sort of live, naturally occurring data available to Ochs and other discourse analysts), it is necessary to emphasize that the *Poema de Yuçuf*, like other traditional Islamic narratives, operates within dynamic and shifting fields of power not only between Morisco communities and the dominant Hispano-Christian state, but also within Morisco communities themselves. This is to say that there is a strong ideological component to the process of generation described above that intersects with issues that at first glance seem purely formal and grammatical. As Kroskrity has observed, the operation of language ideologies inevitably advances the interests of a "specific social or cultural group" over another, though such operation need not pit one social group against those seen to be outside of their own language community. In the case of the formal and linguistic characteristics of the *Poema de Yuçuf*, it is my contention that specific language ideologies at work within the text do not necessarily create a relation of opposition between Moriscos and Christians (both understood to be a discursively homogenous whole), but rather serve as symbolic tools employed by Castilian and Aragonese *alfakíes* to regiment the cultural practice of their neighbors and legitimate their position as purveyors of Islamic knowledge within these communities.

In this sense, the continued use of *cuaderna vía*, which is minimized in Madrid, BRAH ms. 11/9409 through its prose form, though powerfully highlighted in Madrid, BN ms. Res. 247 through a layout that divides the text into quatrains, plays much the same role in Morisco communities as it does during an earlier period in Christian Iberia. Metrical regularity replaces irregularity as a desirable and authoritative discursive feature, a process of poetic standardization that evokes (and mirrors) similar social processes of religious and social standardization along the lines of Sunni tradition. The narration of the Islamic past through the *Poema de Yuçuf*, which at the referential level tells of a faithful servant of God who eventually receives his reward in spite of a period of not inconsequential suffering, works at the indexical level of reference to advance the religious and discursive agenda (as well as the social status) of a religiously learned minority elite.

While the earliest redaction of the *Poema de Yuçuf* in *cuaderna vía* likely speaks to social relations of power in fifteenth-century Mudéjar communities whose situation and culture were quite different from those of their Morisco descendants, it can be said that in general terms the poem works to shape discourse and practice in the present, even as it explicitly presents a powerful valorization of a traditional, Islamic past. In the case of the Moriscos' repeated recopying and performance of this text in socially embedded settings of verbal interaction, we may imagine that such an engagement of the past evoked a dialogic relation between this past and emergent forms of present and future that inevitably served to shape social organization in the present while legitimating the discourse and practices of those who continued to give that past narrative as well as performative shape and meaning.

Conclusions

When we study *aljamiado-morisco* literature from the perspective of the human agents that engaged it, temporal frameworks, such as specific times in the Islamic calendar or hours of the day and the devotional practices that correspond to them, can take center stage. This feature is of course not limited to *aljamiado-morisco* literature; however, it is such a salient feature of the handwritten texts of the Moriscos of Castile and Aragon that I have chosen to focus upon it throughout the present book.

Turning briefly to more general questions involving textuality and time, we may present some of the specific questions that drive such research. How do members of human communities make use of written narrative texts to order and make sense of their lives? What role do these texts play in the social processes by which members of these communities collaboratively construct moral frameworks for practice? These questions have increasingly moved to the center of research efforts in academic disciplines concerned with language use in social settings. In fields such as applied linguistics, cultural psychology, literary studies, linguistic anthropology, and folklore studies (disciplines also acutely aware of the complexities of oral narratives and performance) there has been a steadily growing appreciation of the dynamic and complex interrelations always in force between written narratives and the social settings in which they are produced and engaged.[1]

A fundamental aspect of the interrelations between written narrative and social context is the important role of time and temporality in their operation. Time, famously described by Augustine of Hippo as something one "knows" well enough provided one is not asked to explain it (*Confessions* XI: 14), is at the very center of the social workings of all forms of narrative. It is also, as a long tradition of phenomenological theory in the humanities and social sciences has persistently argued, at the very center of our lived existence.[2] Because of the complex and dynamic intersections that exist between time, human experience, and narrative, I have framed the present study so that I might focus upon the precise points where these intersections occur. My larger goal in focusing upon these intersections is to shed light on the mechanisms by which Castilian and Aragonese crypto-Muslims fashioned and made use of written narratives in order to act in and make sense of the world around them.

Narrative and the Human Dimension of Time

In order not to fall into the same dilemma poetically described by Augustine ("Quid est ergo tempus? Si nemo ex me quaerat, scio; si quaerenti explicare velim, nescio"), I should explain what it is that I mean when I use the word "time" in this book. In very specific terms, I have been speaking of what Gary Saul Morson has termed the "human dimension of time," a much-narrowed frame of inquiry having little to do with larger "questions arising out of contemporary physics or of technical interest to philosophers" (1994, 4). Instead, a consideration of the "human dimension of time," much like William James's psychology of temporality and experience (1890) or more explicitly anthropological approaches to time and cultural practice, stems directly from a concern with the inherently social and contingent "relation of temporalities to how people live and think about their lives" (Morson 1994, 4). In following Morson, I am likewise not directly concerning myself with issues related to quantum physics or purely philosophical considerations of determinism and free will. Rather, I am interested in time as the common thread that runs through human experience and the narrative theorization of it. These ideas have also been elaborated by Anthony Paul Kerby, who begins his study of time, narrative, and identity in the following way:

> If we wish to grasp the nature of our specifically human existence, an existence that has a certain self-identity and consciousness of that identity, it is appropriate to begin our investigation with the question of temporality, for if one thing is to be admitted, it is that our lives are temporally determined both by the beginning and the end that our physical being exhibits and by the history that threads between, and even beyond these two poles. (1991, 15)

As metaphorical fabrics woven and rewoven through the human inter-action to which they continuously give form, time and narrative are both, to paraphrase Morson, "of the essence" (1994, 1).

Proceeding with these general ideas regarding the relation between narrative and time, we may agree that there is nothing particularly controversial about the notion that narratives encode and reflect specific temporal frames that relate to genre, modes of lectoral performance, and historical context. For example, the "Once upon a time..." of fairy tales, as well as the more specific "En un lugar de la Mancha, de cuyo nombre no quiero acordarme, no ha mucho tiempo..." that begins Miguel de Cervantes's *Don Quijote* both frame the telling of their respective stories within a limited range of possible temporalities that intersect with existing lectoral expectations regarding genre and textual meaning — even as they can help to shape new ones. These ideas regarding temporality and textual meaning are integral features of many influential paradigms of literary analysis, ranging from traditional philological approaches to more recent poststructuralist frameworks. I have discussed some of these approaches throughout the course of this book. However for the moment it is possible to rest with the rela-tively broad idea that time, in its various forms and frames, is encoded within narrative and plays an important role in the shaping of textual meaning.

There is also another side to the relation between time and narrative. For while culturally structured temporal frames are certainly encoded within narrative, much of what human agents do through the produc-tion, telling, and engagement of narrative — whether we are speaking of explicitly fictional narratives or not — is co-construct and implement no-tions of time and experience at both the individual and collective level. In other words, narratives not only encode and reflect temporality — they also help to shape it. This mediational, temporally constitutive function of narrative is especially salient, as Elinor Ochs has argued (1994), in oral narratives of personal experience, though written narratives also serve as effective tools for the social construction of time and, by extension, reality. Historical narratives provide a good example of the effectiveness of written narratives for the negotiation of diverse, often competing tem-poral frameworks, as these narratives are, after all, explicitly concerned with the fashioning of reality through a particular mode of storytelling (White 1987). The case of fictional narratives (including narratives con-sidered to be "literary" in the modern, Western sense of the term) is somewhat more complex. Not primarily concerned with the fashioning of reality through the theorization (in narrative) of "what really occurred," fictional narratives instead rely upon other means — such as the more or less genre-specific temporal frames mentioned above — to shape, reproduce, and problematize existing notions of time while suggesting new temporal frameworks against and within which people might make sense of their lives. Narratives, whether fictional, personal, historical, folkloric, or just blatantly propagandistic (even some mix of all of the above, as in the case of medieval epics such as the *Poema de mio Cid*) are powerful tools by which we give form and meaning to our individual and collective experiences and actions. These experiences and actions are, like our very existence, temporal in nature — they occur within time. But they, as well as time itself, take on specific, culturally embedded form when they are contextualized and engaged within narrative. As Paul Ricoeur has put it, "[the] common feature of human experience, that which is marked, organized, and clarified by the act of storytelling in all of its forms is its temporal character" (1991, 2).

Ricoeur's ideas on time and narrative, as well as David Carr's more narrowly philosophical consideration of time, narrative, and human experience (published in 1986 — only a year after the third and final volume of Ricoeur's *Temps et récit* appeared in France), depend upon an established tradition of phenomenological thought in the humanities and social sciences. According to this tradition, especially as it has developed in the wake of Martin Heidegger's seminal *Being and Time*, time constitutes the very warp and weft of what it means to be in any authentic sense. Indeed, Heidegger's statement that "being is in each instance comprehensible only in regard to time" (1996, 19) has served as a touchstone for an immense corpus of subsequent research in philosophy and beyond. And while it is beyond the scope of the present book to analyze this tradition (or even its most influential avatars) in any real detail, I have been concerned throughout the present book with unpacking phenomenological approaches to time and human experience insofar as these relate directly to the narrative texts about which I have been directly concerned.

In having focused in my analyses upon the "uncertain future" faced by the Moriscos, I have not wished to portray them as a helpless, hapless, or lachrymose group of scribes, readers, and social actors. Rather, I follow Martin Heidegger in asserting that such angst about an uncertain future that must ultimately end — all too certainly — in our death is the ultimate expression of our very human existence. This does not imply weakness or fear, but a very authentic (to use Heidegger's term) reckoning with our potentiality-as-being. To "care" about our mortality is what provides the very horizon of what we can be, according to Heidegger, and it is this direct engagement with human care that characterizes much of the traditional Islamic narratives of the Moriscos.

Acknowledgments

This book has benefited from the help and support of a great number of people. I was initially inspired to write a book on *aljamiado-morisco* narrative while a postdoctoral research assistant for Kathryn A. Woolard, and without her early input this project might never have seen the light of day. Also instrumental in the early development of this book were the faculty and students associated with UCLA's Center for Language, Interaction, and Culture during my time in Westwood from 1999 to 2001. The CLIC community, especially Alessandro Duranti, Charles Goodwin, Marjorie Harness Goodwin, Paul Kroskrity, and Elinor Ochs, was always an invaluable source of ideas, strategies, and inventive solutions to seemingly impossible problems.

I have been fortunate to work with colleagues and friends in medieval Iberian studies who were able to contribute excellent ideas and insights to this project. Special thanks go to Samuel Armistead, Josiah Blackmore, John Dagenais, Michael Gerli, and George Greenia.

This book also benefited from the generous support and assistance of several institutional sources. I would like to thank the UCLA Center for Medieval and Renaissance Studies for awarding me a travel grant in 2001 to do necessary archival work in Spain. I also thank Todd Gleeson, dean of the College of Arts and Sciences at the University of Colorado at Boulder, for supporting this project with a Dean's Fund for Excellence Grant in 2002.

An enormous debt of gratitude is due the people working in libraries and archives in Spain and France (from the executive directors to the *porteros*), who always went out of their way to make manuscript materials available when I needed them. Marie-Geneviéve Guesdon of the Bibliothèque Nationale de France and the staff at the Biblioteca de la Real Academia de la Historia, the Biblioteca Nacional, the Real Biblioteca, and the Biblioteca de la Junta para la Ampliación de los Estudios (all in Madrid) provided invaluable resources and help during my research work in Europe.

Special thanks go to Mohammed Sawaie for his help with the transcription and proper translation of Arabic materials. Thanks also to Luis F. Berbabé Pons, Consuelo López-Morillas, Alberto Montaner Frutos, and Juan Carlos Villaverde Amieva for their interest in my work as well as their ongoing efforts to shed light on the literature of the Moriscos. If this book has managed a contribution to *aljamiado-morisco* studies, it is largely because I was able to stand on very high shoulders to begin with.

I have benefited from the tremendous efforts and interest shown to this project by Richard Morrison and the editorial staff of the University of Minnesota Press. Their hard work, and the careful reading of the manuscript by two outside readers, has helped to make this book a much more readable and coherent piece of scholarship. I have endeavored to incorporate their many suggestions and insights into the final version; of course, any errors that may remain are completely my own.

I thank all of the friends and family who helped me in different ways. I've already thanked Joe Blackmore as a colleague, but I need to thank him again as a friend — if not for his encouragement and advice, this book would have amounted only to a large pile of notes. To my wife, Laura, I can only begin to express my gratitude for her patience and support. To my parents and grandparents I owe the largest debt, for helping me to see the beauty in a day of hard work and to enjoy what I have when I've worked for it. Special thanks go to my aunt and *madrinha*, Barbara Peichoto, for always pointing to worlds beyond the one I could see and touch.

It is necessary also to thank my friends and colleagues in the Department of Spanish and Portuguese at the University of Colorado at Boulder. I couldn't ask for a better community of readers, and it's been both a pleasure and an honor to write this book while working with them. Much of what is contained in these pages came from discussions with graduate students in a seminar on Morisco literature that I taught at the University of Colorado during the spring of 2002, and I would like to acknowledge that intellectual debt and express my thanks to those students for working hard and questioning nearly everything.

Finally, I would like to thank, though four centuries too late, the Morisco scribes and readers whose written work forms the center of my analysis. I hope that in these pages my enormous respect for their efforts has become abundantly clear.

Notes

Introduction

1. With respect to terminology, in this book I use the term "crypto-Muslim," which points to the secretive practice of the Islamic faith that characterized much Morisco practice, interchangeably with the more popular term "Morisco." I am aware that many people characterized as "Moriscos" throughout the sixteenth and seventeenth centuries were not necessarily crypto-Muslims; a good number of historical analyses make the very important point that a small percentage of Spanish Muslims willingly converted to the Christian faith before and after the conquest of Granada and began new lives as Christians. It is also true that many Moriscos, especially those residing in Castile, were so far removed from the Muslim faith and cultural milieu that it is difficult to refer to them as anything but heterodox Christians when they speak of the Prophet Muhammad as a "good man" while in a tavern (Cardaillac 1979, 33) or refer to the miraculous birth of Jesus in terms that loosely mirror Islamic popular versions of this story. However, when we begin to speak about the steady production, recopying, and use of traditional Islamic narratives within ritual and other communal practices, it seems relatively clear that we are speaking about Moriscos (or, as they were also called, *cristianos nuevos de moros* [New Christians once Moors]) who were also eminently committed to the practice of Islam despite their new official status as Christians.

2. Xiᵞervox de Allah — Allah a purifikado vuʷextᵘro diᵞa akexte i la puʷexto Paxkuʷa i ᵞapelagamiᵞento a lox muçlimex i shar'a a vuʷextᵘro al-din i ᵞex diᵞa del pᶜrexentadero de la zaka i de vuʷextᵘrax obrax muntipˡikadero i de lox poxadox de vuʷextᵘrox pekadox amahadero....

3. For more on this text, see Harvey 1981.

4. "Las manifestaciones moriscas que se quieren reprimir no pertenecen en modo alguno al ámbito religioso, sino a la esfera de las costumbres locales. Son manifestaciones externas que en nada tocan al hecho de la fe, sino al de la respetada herencia recibida de los antepasados."

5. For more on the roots of the War of the Alpujarras (1568–1570), see Domínguez Ortiz and Vincent 1978, 30–33.

6. "Estos moriscos granadinos, que viajan con un bagaje cultural distinto, son vistos como extraños — en ocasiones peligrosamente extraños — por los

moriscos que llevan generaciones habitando un mismo lugar de forma pacífica
y muy posiblemente ellos mismos eran conscientes de su particular 'otreidad.' "

1. Toward an Activity-Centered Approach to Aljamiado-Morisco Narrative

1. El rrekontami^yento del traxponami^yento del annabi Muhammad çala Allahu 'alayhi w'çalam i de xu agu^welo 'Abdu al-Muttalib. Dixo: akella ora xakó
'Abdu al-Muttalib xu expada i dixo: xákalo o hazme a xaber del moço; xi no,
te mataré o yo me mataré. I ku^wando vidó Amina akello dixo: Kátalo allí allá
te a bi^yen kon él. Dixo: ¿Dónde extá? Dixo: En exa caxa extá envu^welto en un
paño de lana b^alanka. Dixo 'Abdu al-Muttalib: I fu^weme a la kaxa i quixo entrar
a él i vino de dent^uro de la kaxa un ombre ke no lo vid máx expantible kél
i una expada en xu mano i di^yo un apellido ke me hizo t^eremolar todox mix
mi^yembrox i mi coraçón dexmayar i díxome: ¿A dó vax? I díxele yo: A ver mi
hijo. Dixo: No lo pu^wedex ver tú ni nenguno de todax lax gentex agora. Díxole:
Yo debo ve^yerlo máx ke ninguno de lax gentex kes mi hijo. Díxome: Abxentado
xerá de todax lax naçionex dakí a ke xe kumpla la vexitaçión de lox almalakex
ke lox almalakex de lox çi^yelox vexitan agora xubi^yentex i deçendi^yentex i no
xe akabará la vexitaçión dakí a t^erex di^yas. I ku^wando vido 'Abdu al-Muttalib
akello tornóxe med^eroxo expantado de lo ke vido i ^yoyó i dixo: Exto ex un g^aran
milagro. (Madrid, BRAH ms. 11/9414 *olim* T18 ff. 103^v–104).

2. The full passage reads: "Pero esta obra es fecha so emienda de aquellos
que la quisieren emendar e çertas deuenlo fazer los que quisieren e la sopieren
emendar siquier porque dize la escriptura que sotilmente la cosa fecha emienda
más de loar es que el que primeramente la falló; E otrosí mucho deue plazer
a quien la cosa comiença a fazer que la emienden todos quantos la quisieren
emendar e sopieren ca quanto más es la cosa emendada tanto más es loada."

3. The abbreviations *S* and *T* stand for the Salamanca and Toledo manu-
script copies of the *Libro de buen amor* respectively. The former is held in the
Biblioteca Universitaria in Salamanca (ms. 2663) and the latter in the Biblioteca
Nacional in Madrid (ms. V^a 6–1). A third manuscript, referred to as "Gayoso"
(*G*), is held by the Biblioteca de la Real Academia Española (ms. 19 *olim* ms.
Est. 2 Er. 5a). There are also loose fragments of portions of the *Libro de buen
amor*. The best well-known of these is a partial Portuguese translation of the
text found in Porto (Biblioteca Pública Municipal ms. 785).

4. For more on the notion of socialization with respect to linguistic practices
and culture, see Ochs (2001) and Schieffelin and Ochs (1986).

5. *Biçmillahi irrahmani irrahimi*. Kapítulo de Muhammad. La estori^ya i
rrekontami^yento de Ayub '*lm* de sus rreprobaçiones i de su paçiençia. Rekontónos
'Abdu Allahi bnu 'Abdu al-Wahab, por Juman bnu Kazir, por Çaad bnu Jamir,
por 'Abdu Allah ibnu al-'Abaç, akóntentese Allah de todos ellos, ke ellos dixieron del rrekontami^yento de Ayub sobre él sea la salvaçion, así komo lo oímos

al-annabi Muhammad, *s'm,* k'él dixo ke Ayub, sobre él sea la salvaçión era siervo de Allah agradeciente, purifikado, onrrado en poder de Allah, *ta'ala* y-era fazedor de *asadaqa* a los pobres i neçesitados y-a los k-estaban en el serviçio de Allah, el alto. (Vespertino Rodríguez 1983, 272).

6. For more on Hymes's notion of narrative keys in storytelling performance, see Bauman (1986, 143–75) and Kroskrity (1993, 143–75).

7. The Qur'an mentions Job in four separate Suras, and only briefly:

The Women (Sura 4:163)
Surely We have revealed to thee as We revealed to Noah and the prophets after him, and We revealed to Abraham, Ishmael, Isaac, Jacob and the tribes, and Jesus, Job, Jonah, Aaron, and Solomon, and We gave to David a scripture.

The Cattle (Sura 6:84–85)
And this was Our argument which We gave to Abraham against his people: We exalt in degrees whom We please. Surely thy Lord is wise and knowing.

And We gave him Isaac and Jacob. Each did We guide; and Noah did We guide before, and of his descendants, David and Solomon and Job and Joseph and Moses and Aaron....

The Prophets (Sura 21:83–84)
And [remember] Job, when he cried to his Lord, "Distress has afflicted me! And Thou art the Most Merciful of those who show mercy."

So We responded to him and removed the distress that he had, and We gave him his people and the like of them with them: a mercy from Us and a reminder to the worshippers.

Saad (Sura 38:41–44)
And remember Our Servant Job. When he cried to his Lord: "The Devil has afflicted me with toil and torment!"

"Urge with thy foot; here is a cool washing-place and a drink."

And We gave him his people, and the like of them with them: a mercy from Us and a reminder for men of understanding.

"And take in thy hand few worldly goods and earn goodness therewith and incline not to falsehood." Surely We found him patient; most excellent the servant! Surely he turned (to Us)!

2. Written Narrative and the Human Dimension of Time

1. For a highly developed criticism of Goody and Ong, see Street (1993, 1984) and Scribner and Cole (1981).

2. For more on the notion of literacy socialization and its workings within a particular speech community, see Heath (1983); and Duranti and Ochs (1997).

3. These ideas, of course, presuppose a philosophy of language rooted in interaction. Moving beyond the inherent division in structuralist (specifically Saussurian) linguistic frameworks between the system of language (*langue*) and its actual use (*parole*), such a socially bounded notion of language sees the system of language and its use (*competence/performance* in the Chomskyan model) as mutually constructive and thoroughly intertwined.

4. "Las versiones orales y las performances más complejas no nos son asequibles, por definición, pero nada más hacedero que comprobar la versatilidad de las copias. Nada tampoco más comprensible: cada copia no podía sino reflejar el impulso que le había dado origen."

5. "el texto implicaba y movilizaba un contexto no escrito y acarreaba alguna actividad."

6. For more on this notion of residue, see Ong (1982); and Dagenais (1991).

7. According to Bauman, the term *kraftaskáld* is most literally translated into English as "power poet," though it is also common to see it translated as "magical poet" (1992, 128).

3. Contexts of Rediscovery, Contexts of Use

1. "Una verdadera América por descubrir."

2. Manuela Manzares Cirre describes Estébanez's interest in *aljamiado-morisco* texts as a "constant theme" in his regular correspondence with Gayangos (1971, 115).

3. "...daría mucha materia al escritor de costumbres y el novelista, que tendría tema de gran novedad, pudiendo apartarse del camino trillado por la imitación francesa."

4. "...nadie seguramente ha mirado con tan especial amor, como Estébanez, esta literatura aljamiada. Parecía en él manía a veces, bien que inofensiva, como los suelen ser las literarias."

5. "Américo Castro y sus beatos epígonos, entre los españoles, han construido la ficción de unos conversos (marranos o moriscos, todos juntos: todo vale) que se infiltran en los medios culturales de la época y los inficionan con su propia *identidad* — ¿se percatarán siquiera de que éste es un concepto recientísimo? — inoculándoles la preocupación por el vivir desviviéndose, la crítica al sistema de valores dominante, el temor a la Inquisición, la conciencia casticista, la búsqueda de la fama..., que sólo pueden explicarse, según ellos, por la procedencia *semítica* de los autores; despachan 'la literatura del Siglo de oro en el marco de una *sociedad conflictiva* — ¿cuál no lo es? — de enfrentamiento de castas; y en toda la literatura subyacería el ejuste de cuentas entre cristianos viejos (el Romancero, la novela de caballería, la comedia lopesca, Quevedo pertenecían a este bando) contra cristianos nuevos. Los orígenes conversos (de judíos) de

Santa Teresa o Alemán (ambos buenos católicos) sirven para estupendas generalizaciones, olvidando que los primeros interesados en mostrarse como fieles servidores y adictos a la cultura y la ideología dominantes eran esos mismos cristianos nuevos."

6. "Diríjese nuestro trabajo, en primer término, á procurar el inmediato y mayor aprovechamiento de los alumnos que estudian lengua árabe, para que vencida pronto la dificultad de la lectura, puedan salvar con agrado y rapidez las que sucesivamente se les ofrezcan, acostumbrándose además, desde el primer día, al giro propio de la frase árabe, de que se resienten casi todas las traducciones que hicieron nuestros moriscos."

7. "Estamos hoy día, ciertamente, muy lejos de la valoración romántica de la literatura aljamiado-morisca. Cuando en la primera mitad del siglo XIX se descubren y ponen en juego algunas obras de los moriscos, la mentalidad del siglo XIX encarece el interés de tales escritos en términos que hoy día no podemos compartir en su totalidad."

8. For an account of Lope de Vega's treatment of the Moriscos in his *comedias,* see Thomas Case (1981, 1982, 1992).

9. "Naturalmente, en ningún momento, podemos hoy día considerar los escritos aljamiado-moriscos como fuente de inspiración de nuevas creaciones literarias, y, en parte, por ello la literatura aljamiada, después de recibimiento eufórico del siglo XIX, cayó en el olvido. Sólo de vez en cuando algún especialista le prestaba momentánea atención, pero, con frecuencia, nuestros textos eran valorados nada más desde el punto de vista puramente lingüístico o como base de divagaciones exóticas."

10. Cf., for example, García-Arenal (1978, 55–56), and Tulio Halperin Donghi (1955–57).

11. " . . . los chicuelos de Almonacid de la Sierra, en medio de infantil algazara, hacían fogatas en las eras con montones de papeles y libros árabes y aljamiados, que unos albañiles encontraron guardados cuidadosamente, y colocados uno a uno en saquetes de lienzo, bajo un piso de madera, al practicar el derribo de éste y del inferior que era de yeso. Por fortuna . . . intervino a tiempo el R. P. Fierro de las Escuelas Pías de [Zaragoza], que accidentalmente residía en Almonacid."

12. For a catalogue of these manuscripts, see Ribera and Asín Palacios (1912) as well as *Colección de manuscritos árabes* (1998).

13. " . . . hubo casa cuyo hogar fue alimentado en largas noches de invierno, y calentados sus pucheros por espacio de algunos meses, con los pergaminos, papeles y libros forrados de cuero y madera que se descubrieron en parcial derribo de una casa."

14. The Castilian word *Pascua* refers to the Christian holiday of Easter; however, in the context of crypto-Muslim communities in early modern Spain the word took on a broader meaning, equivalent to "religious holiday." In BRAH ms. 11/9415, a Morisco *alfakí* lists out the *paxku^wax del año: Paxku^wax del*

Atuçiya (holiday of the ninth day of Muharram; the first nine days of Muharram, the first month of the Muslim calendar); Paxku^wa de al-Nabi (holiday of the Prophet; the twelfth day of the Muslim month of Rabi'a al-Awwal); Paxku^wa de Ramadan (holiday of the month of Ramadan; the first of the new moon in Ramadan); Paxku^wax de Korderox (holiday of the lambs; the tenth day of the Muslim month of Dhi-al-Hijja).

15. Saavedra's original transcription of this manuscript's contents reads as follows:

(1) Azora XCIX del alcorán.

(2) Aquesta es l'alfadila del día de axora. f. 2.

(3) Aquesta es l'alfadila del día de alchomúa. f. 5ᵛ.

(4) A siete de marzo fué la vintisetena noche del mes de romadan. f. 10ᵛ.

(5) L'alhadiz del anabí, cuando puyó a los cielos. f. 12.

(6) Estos son los dichos de Bias, los cuales son los siguientes, y para ser bien entendidos, piense el leytor que cada sabio habla con él. f. 61.

> Mírate todos los días
> Que vivieres al espejo;
> Toma de mí este consejo.
> Si juzgas qu'estas hermoso
> Sin hallar en tí çoçobras,
> Pareçcan á ti tus obras.
> Si vieres tu gesto feo
> Trabaja como la lumbre
> Con nobleza de costumbres.

(7) Acabáronse los dichos de escribir el çaguero de marzo del año de mil quinientos y sesenta y tres años. f. 80ᵛ.

(8) Capítulo de cómo se ha de tratar con cualquier persona de edad que está á la muerte, sea onbre ó muger el que está doliente. f. 82.

(9) Año de mil y quinientos y sesenta y seis, á diez días de setiembre, tomé el huerto de Lope Jimel, izo la carta Pellares el d'alberite y en sus notas está y allí lo hallarán toda vía que fuese menester. f. 83ᵛ.

(10) Alhotba primera de Pascua. f. 91.

(11) Memoria del regimiento de cómo se face el açala. f. 93.

(12) Alhotba segunda de Pascua. f. 110.

(13) Dixo Allah en su alcorán, ize probó á Ibrahim. f. 114.

(14) Capítulo de quien alexa ó abrá lexado l'açala por torpeza, despúes se rrepentería. f. 120.

(15) Capítulo de lo que debe fazer el muslim ó la muslima cuando se le muere padre ó madre. f. 132.

(16) La petición que onbre debe fazer ad Allah. f. 136.

(17) Remembrança de los días aquellos que puso Allah en ellos nozimiento sobre los de Beni-Israil. f. 138.

(18) De los escogidos días de la luna. f. 139.

(19) Fué rrecontado por Atrima ibno Abén. f. 140.

(20) Estos son los meses del año, con las alfadilas. f. 158.

(21) Predicar muy onrado para el mes de Xaben. f. 171.

16. "La tesis tradicional, según la cual los moriscos formaban una minoría iletrada, con cultura residual más oral que escrita, no puede ya sustentarse a la vista de los numerosos estudios realizados en los últimos cincuenta años, sobre todo los referidos a bibliotecas y aportaciones literarias, tanto en árabe como en castellano aljamiado."

17. Cf. for example, the following interlinear note found on folio 198 of Miguel de Zeyne's *memorial:* "Nació mi hijo Muhammad de Zeyne a doze de setienbre año de mil y quinientos y sesenta y cuatro al ca[le]ndario de los cristianos erejes" (My son Muhammad de Zeyne was born on the twelfth of September of 1564 according to the calendar of the heretical Christians) (Saavedra 1878, 117).

4. The Prophet Is Born, Muslims Are Made

1. Consuelo López-Morillas, in her study and partial edition of the *Libro de las luces* (1994), makes this claim while pointing out that a comparative study of the *Sirat Rasulullah* and the *Kitab al-anwar* is greatly complicated by the lack of any critical edition of the latter. She does not mention the existence of any manuscript copies of the *Kitab al-anwar;* however, she seems to conclude that the *Libro de las luces* is a more or less faithful translation of the Arabic original.

2. According to López-Morillas, al-Bakri's text is known by two different titles: *Intiqal anwar mawlid al-Mustafa l-muhtar wa-mugizatuhu wa-magazih* (The transmission of the lights of the birth of the Chosen Prophet and his miracles and expeditions) and *Al-anwar wa-miftah al-surur wa-l-afkar fi mawlid al-nabi al-muhtar* (The lights, the key to happiness, and the consideration of the birth of the preferred prophet) (1994, 26).

3. I dizi^{y}an lax nubex: Noxotrox abemox máx razón de k^{i}ri^{y}arlo ke nox andamox en el aire ent^{e}re çi^{y}elo i ti^{y}erra; levarlo emox por todo el mundo i a toda xu anazeha ke konoçemox lox bu^{w}enox árbolex de bu^{w}enax f^{u}ruitax i komerá dellax i bu^{w}enas fu^{w}entex i beberá dellax; darlemox dél awa agraçi^{y}ada de xu al-arx. Dixi^{y}eron lox almalakex: noxotrox abemox máx razón de k^{i}ri^{y}arlo i máx onra i ^{y}enxalçami^{y}ento i onrado de nu^{w}exo señor. Dixi^{y}eron las avex: noxotras abemox máx razón de k^{i}ri^{y}arlo ke lo levremox xobre nuexax alax a todox viçi^{y}ox

del mundo. Oyeron un kᵃlamador ke dixo: Dexadvox dexo, ke ya tiʸene Allah ordenado ke a de xeʸer kⁱriʸado por mano de Halima hija de Abi Duwayb al-Ça'adiyya. I dixo: El annabi s'm xaliʸó de kaxamiʸento kaxto xin adulteriʸo dexde Adam 'alayhi al-çalam no me tokó adulteriʸo de lox jahilex i naçiʸó el annabi 'alayhi al-çalam diʸa de lunex a doze diʸax de Rabi'a al-Awwal depuʷéx de la venida de la konpañiʸa del al-fil i el fᵃraguʷamiʸento de la kaxa de Maka kinze añox. I de ke xe akabó la vexitaçiʸón de los almalakex depuʷéx de tᵉrex diʸax xoltáronxe lax gentex a ir a veʸerlo i fuʷe el pⁱrimero ke lo vido su aguʷelo 'Abdu al-Muttalib i vídolo altax xux manox tendidax enta el çiʸelo i mirando alto i la kaxa llena de kᵃlaredad de xu luz i axí komo lo vido xu awelo xonrióxe en xu kara i de ke vido exto 'Abdu al-Muttalib dixo a Amina: De buʷena ventura erex xobre todax lax mujerex ke exte tu hijo ex de gᵃrande hecho.

The formula "PBUH" is a common abbreviation for the English translation of *çala Allahu 'alayhi w'çalam,* which reads "Peace Be Upon Him."

4. The influence of the Moriscos upon the Christian imagination saw its full expression only after the expulsion of the Moriscos in 1609–14.

5. The term "engagement" takes into full account the notions of *adaptation* and *application* discussed by Dagenais in his arguments regarding the "ethics of reading in manuscript culture" (1994).

6. Of course, in cultural settings where knocking on a door is either not done or simply seen as rude (e.g., in many parts of rural Spain), such an act can bring wholly unintended results or be completely ignored. Such contextual issues problematize attempts to universalize issues of language use, as in the case of speech-act theory. For a detailed analysis of the limitations of speech-act theory in cross-cultural discursive analysis, see Rosaldo (1982).

7. "... eran lax fijox [sic] de Abdu al-Muttalib de muʷitax madrex i Abi Talib i Abdullah eran de una madre i kⁱriʸó Abu Talib a Muhammad (çala Allahu alayhi w'çalam) i dixo ke xu padre: Ya fijo Abi Talib toma a mi fijo Muhammad (çala Allahu alayhi w'çalam) kon biʸen i kon al-çalam i kon al-baraka i buʷenaventura ke xi vivex aun verex en él maravillax; ya fijo kuʷando faráx viʸenda no komax della tú ni konpaña dekí manke xi ʸaxiʸente Muhammad i ponga xu mano en ella ke tú veráx xu al-baraka i maravilla. Dixo él: yo faré xi quera Allah. Dixo el padre: Porké ya xabex ke lax kⁱriʸaturax de mi kaxa xon muʷitax i lax vegadax fago poka viʸanda i de ke pone en ella xu mano Muhammad (çala Allahu alayhi w'çalam) amuʷitiguaxe vivanda i querexe en ella bendiçiʸon i kon pake para todox...."

8. Oyeron un kᵃlamador ke dixo: Dexadvox dexo, ke ya tiʸene Allah ordenado ke a de xeʸer kⁱriʸado por mano de Halima hija de Abi Duwayb al-Ça'adiya. I dixo: El annabi s'm xaliʸó de kaxamiʸento kaxto xin adulteriʸo dexde Edam ('alayhi al-çalam) no me tokó adulteriʸo de lox jehilex i naçiʸó el annabi ('alayhi al-çalam) diʸa de lunex a doze diʸas de Rabi'a al-Awwal depuʷéx de la venida de la konpaña del al-fil i ʸel fᵃraguʷamiʸento de la kaxa de Maka kinze añox...

9. The five extant manuscripts of the *Libro de las luces* render this passage in the following ways:

1. Madrid, Biblioteca Nacional ms. 4955 f. 118ʳ.

...I oyeron un kᵃlamador ke dixo dexa lox / dexo ke ya ti^{y}ene Allah ki^{y}en lo kⁱri^{y}e dixi^{y}er / on i ki^{y}en xerá / dixo Halima fija de Abi Duwayb al-Ça'adiya i dixo annabi ('sm) / xali^{y}ó de kaxami^{y}ento kaxto xin adulteri^{y}o de lox / torpex i naçi^{y}ó annabi ('sm) di^{y}a de lunex a doze di^{y}as de Rabi^{y}a al-Awwal....

2. Madrid, Real Biblioteca ms. II/3225 f. 137ʳ⁻ᵛ.

...Oyeron un kᵃlamador ke / dixo lexadvox se^{y}er ke ya ti^{y}ene Allah / ki^{y}en lo kⁱri^{y}e dixi^{y}ero i ki^{y}en dixo Halima fija / de Abi Duwayb al-Ça'adiya i dixo annabi ('sm)
{f. 137ᵛ}
xali^{y}ó de kaxami^{y}ento xin adulteri^{y}o dexde Edam / 'alayhi al-çalam no me tokó adulteri^{y}o de lox / torpex i naçi^{y}ó annabi....

3. Madrid, Biblioteca de la Real Academia de la Historia ms. 11/9410 (olim T-13) f. 264ᵛ.

...Un kᵃlamador ke dixo dexadvox de / (?) do exa dixtuta ke ya ti^{y}ene Allah / ke a de se^{y}er kⁱri^{y}ado por mano de Halima / fija de / Abi Duwayb al-Ça'adiya i naçi^{y}ó annabi 'alayhi al-ça / lam en di^{y}a al-ithna^{y}n a / doze di^{y}as del alba de Rabi^{y}a al-Awwal....

4. Madrid, Biblioteca de la Real Academia de la Historia ms. 11/9413 (olim T-17) ff. 106ᵛ–107ʳ.

...Un kᵃlamador ke dixo lexadvox se^{y}er ke ti^{y}ene / Allah ordenado ke a de se^{y}er kⁱri^{y}ado por mano de Halima / fija de Abi Duwayb al-Ça'adiya i dixo annabi Muhammad
{107ʳ}
('asm) xali^{y}ó de xu kaxami^{y}ento kaxto / xin adulteri^{y}o de lox / jehilex i naçi^{y}ó Muhammad nuʷextᵘro / annabi ('sm) en di^{y}a de lunex a doze di^{y}as / de Rabi^{y}a al-Awwal....

5. Madrid, Biblioteca de la Real Academia de la Historia ms. 11/9414 (olim T-18) ff. 103ʳ.

...I oyeron un kᵃlamador ke dixo dexad vox dexo / ke ya ti^{y}ene Allah ordenado ke a de se^{y}er kⁱri^{y}ado por mano / de Halima fija de Abi Duwayb al-Ça'adiya i dixo annabi ('asm) / xali^{y}ó de kaxami^{y}ento kaxto xin adulteri^{y}o dexde / Edam ('alayhi al-çalam) no me tokó adulteri^{y}o de lox jehilex i naçi^{y}ó / annabi ('alayhi al-çalam) di^{y}a de lunex a doze di^{y}as / de Rabi^{y}a al-Awwal....

10. "A côté du Coran dont les préceptes accompagnent le fidèle dans sa vie quotidienne, on trouve parmi les livres saisis par l'Inquisition des biographies de Mahomet, des textes polémiques visant à dénigrer la religion chrétienne, des recueils de prière ainsi que des prophéties musulmanes.... Plusieurs nouveaux convertis aragonais sont aussi condamnés pour avoir lu un livre intitulé *De las luces* traitant de la religion musulmane."

11. In fact, two times during the second half of the sixteenth century, *Mawlid al-Nabi* fell within three days of Christmas, the Christian celebration of the birth of Jesus (12 Rabi'a al-Awwal 967 AH / Tuesday, December 22, 1559 CE and 12 Rabi'a Awwal 1000 AH / Saturday, December 28, 1591 CE).

12. Cf. also Tedlock and Mannheim (1995)

13. For more on this idea of distributed knowledge, see Hutchins (1995), Duranti (1997), and Goodwin and Goodwin (1996).

14. "...pero nada más hacedero que comprobar la versatilidad de las copias. Nada tampoco más comprensible: cada copia no podía sino reflejar el impulso que le había dado origen."

5. A Morisco Philosophy of Suffering and Action

1. ff. 1–41: Contestaciones de Muhammad por el Qur'an, a cuestiones de teología, liturgia, ciencias naturales; ff. 41–58: Letanía; ff. 58–60: Trata de la revelación de la oración a Muhammad por el ángel Gabriel; ff. 66–71: Explicación en rima de una jaculatoria escrita como amuleto; ff. 75–87: Leyes sobre herencias....

2. Significantly, Hawkins uses as the basis of his analyses Ottmar Hegyi's 1981 edition of Madrid, BN ms. 4953 (*Cinco leyendas*) rather than the manuscript itself.

3. I dixo el-annabi: Díxome Jibril ('lm) ke xi un desk°reyente la bebiʸexe kitariʸa Allah de xu koraçón mala k°reʸençiʸa, i lançariʸa en él la k°reʸençiʸa i kiʸen terná en xu koraçón malkerençiʸa o anxiʸa o olvido o envidiʸa o maliçiʸa i la beberá tirarle a Allah de xu koraçón i xanarle a Allah dello.... (153ʳ)

4. For more on the topic of Christian preaching in the Middle Ages, specifically the idea of amplification or "thematic preaching," see Baldwin (1959, 232–54), Kennedy (1999, 221–25), and Murphy (1974, 269–355).

5. On the identity of the son to be sacrificed, both in the biblical and Qur'anic traditions, Maulana Muhammad Ali has written, in his commentary on this portion of Sura 37: "That the child spoken of here was Ishmael and not Isaac is made clear by v. 112, which states that it was after this incident that Abraham received the news of the birth of Isaac. This, no doubt, contradicts the Bible statement, but the fact that Ishmael's descendants kept a memorial of this sacrifice in the annual pilgrimage to Makkah shows clearly that Ishmael, not Isaac, was the son whom Abraham was commanded to sacrifice. Moreover, the Bible contradicts itself when it speaks of Isaac as 'thine only son' (Gen

22:2). Only Ishmael can be spoken of as 'only son' before the birth of Isaac" (1995, 886).

6. Ap^{e}rex de çi^{y}ent añox el mançebo k^{e}reçi^{y}o i ^{y}ap^{i}rixó luçençi^{y}a por xu lengu^{w}a axí komo él era una nu^{w}eyt ent^{e}re xu^{w}eño vínole un k^{i}ridant i díxole: Dize a tú el xeñor de lax gentex: Ya Ibrahim — açerka a mí al-qurban … de xu nomb^{a}rami^{y}ento … i xerá bendezido … Dixo (el rrekontador): Kuwando amaneçi^{y}ó Allah kon la mañana fu^{w}e un kamello i ^{y}akorólo i di^{y}ole a komer a pobrex i ^{y}a mixarablex. Dep^{w}uéx dixo Ibrahim a xu xeñor: ¿Ax rreçebido mi al-qurban? Xi no amu^{w}éxt^{a}ramelo a demoxt^{a}rar exta nu^{w}eyt. Ku^{w}ando fu^{w}e i la nu^{w}eyt xegunda vínole un vini^{y}ente i díxole: Ya Ibrahim — açerka al-qurban a mí xerá rreçebido de tú. Ku^{w}ando ameneçi^{y}ó Allah kon la mañana p^{i}rixó una vaka i degollóla i parti^{y}ó xu karne a pobrex i ^{y}a meçkinox i dixo Ibrahim: Xeñor xe las rreçebido de mí; xi no mu^{w}éxtramelo en la nu^{w}eyt terçera. I ku^{w}ando fu^{w}e la nu^{w}eyt terçera vínole el k^{i}ridant i dixo: Ya Ibrahim — levántate i ^{y}açerka a mí al-qurban rreçebirlo a de tú i miterlo a nob^{a}rami^{y}ento en lax gentex dakí ^{y}al di^{y}a del judiçi^{y}o. Ku^{w}ando ameneçi^{y}o Allah kon la mañana fu^{w}e Ibrahim ('alayhi al-çalam) i p^{i}rixó un … i degollólo i parti^{y}ó xu karne a pobrex i ^{y}a mixarablex i dixo: Ya Xeñor — ¿ax rreçebido mi al-qurban exte? Xi no muwéxt^{a}ramelo en la nu^{w}eyt ku^{w}arta. Ku^{w}ando fu^{w}e a la nu^{w}eyt ku^{w}arta vino el k^{i}ridant i dixo: Ya Ibrahim — levántate i ^{y}açerka a mí al-qurban rreçebirlo^{w}é de tú i meteré lonb^{a}rami^{y}ento en lax gentex dakí ^{y}a di^{y}a del judiçi^{y}o. I dixo Ibrahim: Mi xeñor, mi mayor — ya e çerkado al-qurban kemellos i baqí^{y}o i ganado; ¿kon ke mandax ke yo faga al-qurban ya xeñor? Envi^{y}óle a él Allah i díxole: No te demando kamellox ni baqi^{y}o ni ganado max ki^{y}ero ke degu^{w}ellex a tu fillo i p^{a}lazer de tux gu^{w}ellox Isma'il.

Due to the deterioration of the bottom third of the manuscript, some sections of these lines are illegible. For a longer transcription, cf. Vespertino Rodríguez (1983).

7. Dixo Ibrahim: Ya Hajara ~~al mançe~~ ku^{w}ando amaneçe Allah kon la mañana meta a mi fillo Isma'il en el baño al-linpi^{y}ami^{y}ento y vi^{y}extalo xux ropax lax máx linpi^{y}ax kél irá kon mí dó yo ki^{y}ero ir. Ku^{w}ando fu^{w}e la mañana p^{i}rixo Hajar el mançebo i mixólo al baño i lavó xu kabeça kon fu^{w}ellax de xixbe i kanfor. Dixo Isma'il a xu madre: ¿Por ké me lavax kon al-abañeri^{y}o de lox mu^{w}ertox akellox ke xe van dexta al-dunya a la otra? Dixo: Ya fillo, axí me ex mandado de tu padre. Díxole: Ya madre, xi mi padre te lo a mandado razón faréz de fer.

The version of this passage in Madrid, Biblioteca de la Junta ms. 25 reads as follows: "Ya Hajara, ku^{w}ando xea en la mañana de madurgada insha'Allah ke dent^{e}rex a mi fijo Içma'il al baño i baña xu kabeça i lávala lavami^{y}ento bu^{w}eno i linpi^{y}o i víxtile rrobax linpi^{y}ax i nu^{w}evax i irá kon mí adónde ki^{y}ero ir a fazer al-qurban. Dixo (el rrekontador): Pu^{w}ex ku^{w}ando amaneçi^{y}ó Allah kon la bu^{w}ena de la mañana tomó Hajara, madre de Isma'il i dent^{u}rólo al baño i púxoxe a lavar xu kabeça kon al-çidri i ^{y}al-kanfor i dixo xu fijo tan amado Isma'il a xu madre: Exto ke veo ke lavax mi kabeça kon al-çidri i ^{y}al-kanfor ex el lavar de lox mu^wertox akellox ke lox arrean kon él de la kaxa del mundo a la kaxa del otro mundo. Dixo a él xu madre: Ya fijo kon exto me a mandado tu padre Ibrahim. I dixo a ella: Xi ex ke mi padre te lo a mandado pu^wex debdo ex sobre tú en ke obedeçkax xu mandami^yento" (f. 137^{r-v}).

The term *xixbe,* which appears in Madrid, BRAH ms. 11/9409, presents certain difficulties. As the preceding transcription shows, the text of the episode found in Madrid, Biblioteca de la Junta ms. 25 uses a completely different term (*al-çidri*) to describe the substance added, with camphor, to the water used to bathe the body of a dead person in the Islamic ritual known as *ghusl.* According to Federico Corriente's *Dictionary of Andalusi Arabic* (1997), the term *al-çidri* corresponds to "Christ's thorn" (*Paliurus aculeatus*), a spiny shrub indigenous to the Middle East. It seems unlikely that the scribe of Madrid, BRAH ms. 11/9409 miscopied *al-çidri* from another manuscript, rendering it *xixbe*; to do so would mean he somehow mistook a medial *dal* together with a medial *ra* (در) for a medial *shin* together with a medial *ba* (شب). What is most likely is that *xixbe* is derived from the Latin *zizyphus,* which is the genus of various plants, including the *Zizyphus Spina-Christi* (another name for Christ's Thorn), *Zizyphus vulgaris* (also known as *Zizyphus jujuba*), and *Zizyphus lotus* (lote fruit). While Corriente's translation of *al-çidri* singles out Christ's Thorn, it has long been common to mix leaves from *Zizyphus vulgaris* (jujube) and camphor with water to form a cleansing agent in the performance of *ghusl.* To complicate matters some, Longás writes in a footnote to this passage that *al-çidri* corresponds to "a certain species of lotus used in the Orient as a soap" (1998, 205). Whatever the specific plant that is intended in both texts might be, it seems certain that *xixbe* refers to the genus of the plants listed above.

8. The manuscript text becomes illegible here.

9. Regarding the embodied aspects of prayer, Longás (1998)cites two manuscripts, Madrid, BN ms. 5305 (ff. 11–14) and Madrid, Junta ms. 4 (f. 120), both of which describe in some detail the many and precise "movements and postures of the body during prayer" (55).

10. ...colección de pláticas morales pronunciadas con motivo de la fiesta así llamada y cuyo objeto es ensalzar las grandezas y excelencias de Dios y su Profeta y de la religión musulmana, y exhortar á los fieles al exacto cumplimiento de sus deberes religiosos. Intercálanse multitud de textos alcoránicos y tradiciones del Profeta, y una de Abenabás sobre el sacrificio de Abraham.

11. ...I ki^yen lo dexará a bebrarlo a Alla kon bebraje del al-janna xillado kon al-miçki.... Xi^yervox de Allah — Allah a purifikado vu^wext^uro di^ya akexte i la pu^wexto Paxku^wa i ^yapelagami^yento a lox muçlimex i shar'a a vu^wext^uro al-din i ^yex di^ya del p^erexentadero de la zaka i de vu^wext^urax obrax muntip^likadero i de lox poxadox de vu^wext^urox pekadox amahadero pu^wex seguid en el la çunna i ^yadebdeçed en el la enkomi^yenda konvertir xang^are corri^yente i konpⁱlir xakrefiçi^yox perfectox i dar a komer al dexnudo i ^yal demandante ke Allah ta'ala

dize no reçibe Allah xux karnex xux xang^erex max enpero reçibe la voluntad de voxotrox i ^yaxe lax a sujekto a voxotrox para ke lo ex ad Allah xobre lo ke ox a gui^yado i para ke sean albⁱriçi^yadox lox bu^wenox i ke xe alegren; xi^yervox de Allah pu^wex ku^wando ox volveréix de vu^wext^uro fazadero de la çala [*oración*] a vu^wext^urax caxax pu^wex tornaox por otro kamino menox del kamino akel ke fu^wisteix por el por fazer pexar a lox dexk^ere^yentex.... (Madrid, Junta ms. 25 ff. 124^v=-125^v)

12. Xabed xi^yervox de Allah ke vu^wext^uro di^ya akexte ex g^arande i ^yex paxku^wa onrrada ya lo puxo Allah xeñal de lox señale de vu^wext^uro al-din i ^yex el di^ya akel ke onrró Allah vu^wext^ara rregla i ^yexpeçi^yal kon xu al-fadila a vu^wext^uro al-nabi Muhammad (çala Allah alayhi w' çalam) i xabed ke él ex rreverente de mexex rreverentex en di^yax g^arandex onró Allah kon el al-Islam i ^yenxalçó kon él nonb^arami^yento de Muhammad (alayhi al-çalam) eng^arandeçi^yó Allah xu g^aran valor i p^orometi^yó en él xu perdonança i xu piedad pu^wex onrradlo i ^yeng^arandeçedlo i lax al-takbirax en el xon t^erex di^yax dexde el açala de aduhar del di^ya del akoran faxta a el akabar de la çala de açubhi el di^ya ku^watreno i ki^yen eng^arandeçerá el derecho de Allah pu^wex ex mejor a él en poder de xu xeñor: Pu^wex rrepintençi^ya a lox defaltantex i ^yapartami^yento a lox inorantex o ku^wantox alkançan exte di^ya ke no xaben la kantidad de lo ke alkançan i dexan en él parte de bu^wenaventura ke no xaben la kantidad ke dexan i ^yex el di^ya del al-haj mayor i la parte qonpⁱlida de bu^wenaventura i habla el al-Qur'an dexo xu al-fadila i llama Allah a xu textimonança i dize tan alto ex i ku^wando deçendimox a Ibrahim el lugar de kaxa dixímoxle no dexk^ereax ni pongax aparçero kon mí ya Ibrahim eninguna koxa i ^yalinpi^ya mi kaxa para lox rrodeantex i ^ya lox al-rrakmantex i ^yaçachdantex i llama a lax gentex al al-haj i vend^arán a tú lox onb^erex i yo meteré en voluntad ke vengan de todo valle fondo i de todax partex....

13. Ku^wando kixo Allah (tabaraka wa ta'ala tan bendito ex xu nonb^ere él ex nu^wext^uro xeñor i p^erkurador) tomar a Ibrahim por amigo i ^yordenó en xu fecho orden fermoxo dixeron lox almalakex: Ya nu^wext^uro xeñor i nu^wext^uro p^erekurador — ¿para ke ki^yerex tomar amigo de lox fijox de Edam i ^yellos xon agolladorex de la ti^yerra i konrronpedorex i xon derramadorex de xang^eres a de xin rrazon? Dixo Allah a lox almalakex: Yo xe lo ke voxotrox no xabeyx. Dixo Malaku al-Maute: Mi xeñor i mi p^erekurador i ki^yen enpararrá ni xe aterebirá rreçebir el arru^wah de akel xi^yervo xi^yendo tu amigo? I rrebeló Allah a él i díxole: Tú lo rreçebiráx ya Malaku al-Mauti i tú enpararráx rreçebir xu al-ru^wah; ya Malaku al-Mauti — deçi^yendi a él i ^yalbiriçi^yalo. Dixo i deçendi^yó a él Malaku al-Mauti en la max fermoxa de lax figurax de lox fijox de Edam en kara i ^yen gentileza i ^yen bu^wena olor i ^yal máx dulçe dellox en habla i ^yel max linpi^yo dellox en rropax i ^yera Ibrahim ('alayhi al-çalam) el máx avixado de lax gentex i goli^yó olor de al-miçki en xu apoxento faxta ke xe paró kon el Malaku al-Mauti i ... díxole: ¿Ki^yen te a dent^arado en mi kaxa de xin mi liçençi^ya? I díxole Malaku al-Mauti: A me dent^arado el xeñor de la kaxa i ^yel ke lo kⁱri^yó. Dixo a él Ibrahim: ¿Pu^wex komo? ¿A mi kaxa ay otro du^weño xin xé yo? Díxole Malaku al-Mauti:

Xí ya Ibrahim akel ke me a jaleqado a mí i te a jaleqado a tú ex el xeñor della. Dixo: Verdad dizex a piʸadete Allah ... (ff. 130–131).

6. Language Ideologies and the Human Dimension of Time

1. It is unknown to what extent officers of the Holy Office knew how to distinguish between books written in Arabic and those written in *aljamiado*, although Hegyi addresses this issue, claiming that state and Inquisition officials would have had Arabic experts in their employ (1978, 147–48).

2. En cuanto al empleo del alfabeto árabe en las lenguas aljamiadas, éste es el resultado natural del prestigio del alfabeto sagrado que — junto con arabismos léxicos, morfológicos y sintácticos — reviste a la aljamía de un ropaje islámico. Se trata de un culturema, un signo exterior que señala la pertinencia a la *umma*, la comunidad islámica.

3. Mercedes Sánchez Alvarez also deals with the social issues that underlie Moriscos' use of Arabic script, citing Hegyi and adding that it could serve as "an effective tool for religious practice, as it was accessible to the majority of community members, who instructed their children once they had arrived at an age that permitted them to assume the risk of practicing Islam in secret" (1981, 447). Sánchez Alvarez's focus on practice intersects with the concerns of the present book. However, the accessibility of Arabic script for the "majority of community members" remains doubtful, even if we imagine the instructive practices of *alfakíes* and learned parents to be widespread. For more on the issue of Qur'anic literacy in non Arabic-speaking communities, see Scribner and Cole (1981).

4. Es un detalle digno de tenerse en cuenta que en ocasiones la letra escrita persistiera con más vigor que el lenguaje hablado, fenómeno que dio lugar a la curiosa *literatura aljamiada*. Un estudio más amplio también habría de examinar los esfuerzos hechos por la minoría culta por salvar de la destrucción los códices arábigos, que representaban para ellos el enlace con una antiquísima tradición. Después de la Real Cédula de 20 de junio de 1511 que les ordenaba la entrega de todos los libros arábigos, era peligroso guardarlos, por lo menos aquellos que tuvieran relación con la secta mahometana; sin embargo, algunos hallazgos hechos casualmente en viejas viviendas moriscas prueban que no faltaron los que se arriesgaron a ocultar en escondites lo que para ellos era un precioso tesoro cultural.

5. As I mentioned in chapter 2 Richard Bauman has described this process as "traditionalization," which he defines as "an act of symbolic construction, drawing the links of continuity by which [a storyteller] may tie [his or her] story to past discourses as part of [the] recounting of it" (1992, 136). This process, which constructs a dialogic link between the telling of the story, previous and alternate tellings of the story, and the text itself, is an integral part, according to Bauman, of "the process of endowing the story with situated meaning" (1992, 136).

6. There is also a prose version of the Qur'anic Joseph story in *aljamiado* (contained in Madrid, BN ms. 5292 ff. 1–15), though it is acephalous. According to Ursula Klenk, who edited this text in 1972, roughly one or two folios are missing from the beginning of the text (1).

Conclusions

1. See, for example, Silverstein and Urban (1996); Goodwin and M. H. Goodwin (1996); Heath (1983); and Carruthers (1990).

2. Martin Heidegger's *Being and Time* remains the most important and far-reaching of phenomenological considerations of time and existence, although Edmund Husserl's *On the Phenomenology of the Consciousness of Internal Time* and Maurice Merleau-Ponty's *Phenomenology of Perception* are also fundamental. In the social sciences, Christopher Tilley's analysis of physical space and ritual, *A Phenomenology of Landscape Places, Paths, and Monuments,* and Alessandro Duranti's *From Grammar to Politics: Linguistic Anthropology in a Western Samoan Village* are of particular value.

Bibliography

Manuscripts

Madrid, Biblioteca de la Junta Para La Ampliación de Estudios ms. 1.
Madrid, Biblioteca de la Junta Para La Ampliación de Estudios ms. 4.
Madrid, Biblioteca de la Junta Para La Ampliación de Estudios ms. 25.
Madrid, Biblioteca de la Real Academia de la Historia ms. 11/9395.
Madrid, Biblioteca de la Real Academia de la Historia ms. 11/9409.
Madrid, Biblioteca de la Real Academia de la Historia ms. 11/9410.
Madrid, Biblioteca de la Real Academia de la Historia ms. 11/9413.
Madrid, Biblioteca de la Real Academia de la Historia ms. 11/9414.
Madrid, Biblioteca de la Real Academia de la Historia ms. 11/9415.
Madrid, Biblioteca de la Real Academia de la Historia ms. 19.
Madrid, Biblioteca Nacional ms. 11.309.
Madrid, Biblioteca Nacional ms. 4953.
Madrid, Biblioteca Nacional ms. 4955.
Madrid, Biblioteca Nacional ms. 5292.
Madrid, Biblioteca Nacional ms. 5305.
Madrid, Biblioteca Nacional ms. Res. 247.
Madrid, Biblioteca Nacional ms. Vitrina 6–1.
Madrid, Real Biblioteca ms. II/3225.
Porto, Biblioteca Pública Municipal ms. 785.
Salamanca, Biblioteca Universitaria ms. 2663.
Toledo, Biblioteca de Castilla-La Mancha ms. 395.

Print Sources

The Bible: New Revised Standard Version (Catholic Edition). 1999. Oxford: Oxford University Press.
Holy Qur'an: Arabic Text, English Translation, and Commentary. 1995. Translated with Commentary by Maulana Muhammad Ali. Lahore: Ahmadiyyah Anjuman Isha'at Islam.

Abu-Lughod, Lila. 1986 *Veiled Sentiments: Honor and Poetry in a Bedouin Society*. Berkeley and Los Angeles: University of California Press.

Ali, Muhammad Yunis. 1999. *Medieval Islamic Pragmatics: Sunni Legal Theorists' Models of Textual Communication.* London: Curzon.

al-Suyuti, Imam Jalaluddin. 2004. *Celebreating [sic] Eid-e-Milad-un-Nabi* [Internet]. Islamic Academy, cited January 14, 2005. Available from www.islamicacademy.org/html/Articles/English/Milad.htm.

Anderson, Benedict. 1983. *Imagined Communities.* New York: Verso.

Anzaldúa, Gloria. 1987. *Borderlands: La Frontera = the New Mestiza.* San Francisco: Aunt Lute.

Augustine. 1999. *Confessions.* Translated by William Watts. Cambridge, Mass.: Harvard University Press.

Bakhtin, Mikhail M. 1981. *The Dialogic Imagination: Four Essays.* Austin: University of Texas Press.

———. 1986. *Speech Genres and Other Late Essays.* Translated by Caryl Emerson. Edited by Caryl Emerson and Michael Holquist. Austin: University of Texas Press.

Baldwin, Charles Sears. 1959. *Medieval Rhetoric and Poetic (to 1400): Interpreted from Representative Works.* Gloucester, Mass.: Peter Smith.

Baquedano-López, Patricia. 1997. "Creating Social Identities in *Doctrina* Narratives." *Issues in Applied Linguistics* 8, no. 1: 27–45.

Barletta, Vincent. 1999." 'Por ende deuemos Creer': Knowledge and Social Practice in the *Libro del cauallero de Dios.*" *La corónica* 27, no. 3: 13–34.

———. 2001. "Context and Manuscript Discourse in Late Medieval Castile." *La corónica* 30, no. 1: 3–35.

———. 2004. "Agency and Intertexts: Natural Philosphy as Christian Ethics in the *Libro del cavallero de Dios.*" *Hispanic Review* 72, no. 2: 239–59.

Barthes, Roland. 1970. *L'empire des signes.* Geneva: Skira.

Basso, Keith H. 1990. *Western Apache Language and Culture: Essays in Linguistic Anthropology.* Tucson: University of Arizona Press.

Bauman, Richard. 1986. *Story, Performance, and Event: Contextual Studies of Oral Narrative.* Cambridge: Cambridge University Press.

———. 1992. "Contextualization, Tradition, and the Dialogue of Genres: Icelandic Legends of the Kraftaskáld." In *Rethinking Context: Language as an Interactive Phenomenon,* edited by Alessandro Duranti and Charles Goodwin, 77–99. Cambridge: Cambridge University Press.

———. 1996. "Transformations of the Word in the Production of Mexican Festival Drama." In *Natural Histories of Discourse,* edited by Michael Silverstein and Greg Urban, 301–28. Chicago: University of Chicago Press.

Bauman, Richard, and Charles L. Briggs. 1990. "Poetics and Performance as Critical Perspectives on Language and Social Life." *Annual Review of Anthropology* 19: 59–88.

Ben Jemia, Mohamed Nejib. 1984. "Le bilinguisme morisque à travers la littérature aljamiada." In *Actes du II Symposium International du CIEM: Religion, identité et sources documentaires sur les morisques andalous,* edited by Abdeljelil Temimi, 45–52. Tunis: Institut Supérieur de Documentation.

———. 1986. "Lengua morisca y aljamía calco." In *Les actes de la première table ronde du CIEM: Sur la littérature aljamiado-morisque: Hybridisme linguistique et univers discursif,* edited by Abdeljelil Temimi, 12–26. Tunis: Centre de Recherches en Bibliothéconomie et Sciences de l'Information.

———. 1987. *La langue des derniers musulmans de l'Espagne.* Tunis: Publications de l'Université, Faculté des Lettres et Sciences Humaines.

Bernabé Pons, Luis F. 1998. "Una visión propicia del mundo: España y los moriscos de Granada." In *Averroes dialogado y otros momentos literarios y sociales de la interacción cristiano-musulmana en España e Italia,* edited by André Stoll, 89–137. Kassel: Reichenberger.

Besnier, Niko. 1995. *Literacy, Emotion, and Authority: Reading and Writing on a Polynesian Atoll.* Cambridge: Cambridge University Press.

———. 1999. "Literacy." *Journal of Linguistic Anthropology* 9, nos. 1–2: 141–43.

Bhabha, Homi K. 1994. *The Location of Culture.* London: Routledge.

Biblioteca Nacional (Spain), Pascual de Gayangos, and Pedro Roca. 1904. *Catálogo de los manuscritos que pertenecieron a D. Pascual de Gayangos existentes hoy en la Biblioteca Nacional.* Madrid: Revista de Archivos Bibliotecas y Museos.

Blackmore, Josiah, and Gregory S. Hutcheson. 1999. *Queer Iberia: Sexualities, Cultures, and Crossings from the Middle Ages to the Renaissance.* Durham, N.C.: Duke University Press.

Bourdieu, Pierre. 1977. *Outline of a Theory of Practice.* Translated by Richard Nice. Cambridge: Cambridge University Press.

———. 1990. *The Logic of Practice.* Translated by Richard Nice. Stanford, Calif.: Stanford University Press.

———. 1991. *Language and Symbolic Power.* Translated by Gino Raymond and Matthew Adamson. Cambridge, Mass.: Harvard University Press.

Bourdieu, Pierre, Jean Claude Passeron, and Monique de Saint Martin. 1994. *Academic Discourse: Linguistic Misunderstanding and Professorial Power.* Translated by Richard Teese. Stanford, Calif.: Stanford University Press.

Bourdieu, Pierre, and Loïc J. D. Wacquant. 1992. *An Invitation to Reflexive Sociology.* Translated by Matthew Adamson. Chicago: University of Chicago Press.

Boyarin, Jonathan. 1993. *The Ethnography of Reading.* Berkeley and Los Angeles: University of California Press.

Briggs, Charles L. 1988. *Competence in Performance: The Creativity of Tradition in Mexicano Verbal Art.* Philadelphia: University of Pennsylvania Press.

Briggs, Charles L., and Richard Bauman. 1992. "Genre, Intertextuality, and Social Power." *Journal of Linguistic Anthropology* 2, no. 2: 131–72.

Bruner, Jerome S. 1986. *Actual Minds, Possible Worlds.* Cambridge, Mass.: Harvard University Press.

———. 1990. *Acts of Meaning.* Cambridge, Mass.: Harvard University Press.

Cánovas del Castillo, Antonio. 1878. *Literatura aljamiada: Discurso de contestación al presentado por E. Saavedra.* Madrid: Real Academia Española.

Capps, Lisa, and Elinor Ochs. 1995. *Constructing Panic: The Discourse of Agoraphobia.* Cambridge, Mass.: Harvard University Press.

Cardaillac, Louis. 1979. *Moriscos y cristianos: Un enfrentamiento polémico (1492–1640).* Madrid: Fondo de Cultura Económica.

Carr, David. 1986. *Time, Narrative, and History Studies in Phenomenology and Existential Philosophy.* Bloomington: Indiana University Press.

Carrasco Urgoiti, María Soledad. 1969. *El problema morisco en Aragón al comienzo del reinado de Felipe II: Estudio y apéndices documentales.* Chapel Hill, N.C.: Department of Romance Languages, University of North Carolina Press.

Carruthers, Mary. 1990. *The Book of Memory: A Study of Memory in Medieval Culture.* Cambridge: Cambridge University Press.

———. 1998. *The Craft of Thought: Meditation, Rhetoric, and the Making of Images, 400–1200.* Cambridge: Cambridge University Press.

Case, Thomas E. 1981. "El morisco gracioso en el teatro de Lope de Vega y los orígenes del teatro español." In *Lope de Vega y los orígenes del teatro español,* edited by Manuel Criado de Val, 785–90. Madrid: EDI-6.

———. 1982. "The Significance of Morisco Speech in Lope's Plays." *Hispania* 65, no. 4: 594–600.

———. 1992. "Lope and the Moriscos." *Bulletin of the Comediantes* 44, no. 2: 195–216.

Caton, Steven C. 1990. *"Peaks of Yemen I Summon!": Poetry as Cultural Practice in a North Yemeni Tribe.* Berkeley and Los Angeles: University of California Press.

Cerquiglini, Bernard. 1989. *Éloge de la variante: Histoire critique de la philologie.* Paris: Seuil.

Certeau, Michel de. 1973. *L'Absent de l'histoire.* Tours: Mame.

———. 1984. *The Practice of Everyday Life.* Berkeley and Los Angeles: University of California Press.

Chabas, Roque. 1890. "El juicio final: Trozo de un sermón morisco." *El Archivo* 4: 116–17.

Chartier, Roger. 1994. *The Order of Books: Readers, Authors and Libraries in Europe between the Fourteenth and Eighteenth Centuries.* Translated by Lydia G. Cochrane. Cambridge: Polity.

Chejne, Anwar G. 1974. *Muslim Spain, Its History and Culture.* Minneapolis: University of Minnesota Press.

———. 1983. *Islam and the West: The Moriscos.* Albany: State University of New York Press.

Colección de manuscritos árabes y aljamiados de la Biblioteca del Instituto de Filología del CSIC. Versión CD-ROM. Madrid: Centro Superior de Estudios Científicos, 1998.

Clanchy, Michael. 1979. *From Memory to Written Record 1066–1307.* London: Arnold.

Clifford, James, and George E. Marcus. 1986. *Writing Culture: The Poetics and Politics of Ethnography.* Berkeley and Los Angeles: University of California Press.

Codera Zaydin, Francisco. 1884. "Almacén de un librero morisco descubierto en almonacid de la Sierra." *Boletín de la Real Academia de la Historia* 5: 269–76.

Cole, Michael. 1996. *Cultural Psychology: A Once and Future Discipline.* Cambridge, Mass.: Harvard University Press.

Corriente, Federico. 1997. *A Dictionary of Andalusi Arabic.* Leiden and New York: Brill.

Dagenais, John. 1991. "That Bothersome Residue: Toward a Theory of the Physical Text." In *Vox Intexta: Orality and Textuality in the Middle Ages,* edited by Alger Nicolaus Doane and Carol Braun Pasternack, 246–62. Madison: University of Wisconsin Press.

———. 1994. *The Ethics of Reading in Manuscript Culture: Glossing the "Libro de Buen Amor."* Princeton, N.J.: Princeton University Press.

Daniel, E. Valentine, and Jeffrey M. Peck. 1996. *Culture/Contexture: Explorations in Anthropology and Literary Studies.* Berkeley and Los Angeles: University of California Press.

Díaz García, Amador. 1981. *Devocionario morisco en árabe dialectal hispánico.* Granada: Universidad de Granada.

Digges, Diana, and Joanne Rappaport. 1993. "Literacy, Orality and Ritual Practice in Highland Colombia." In *Ethnography of Reading,* edited by Jonathan Boyarin, 139–55. Berkeley and Los Angeles: University of California Press.

Domínguez Ortiz, Antonio. 1962. "Notas para una sociología de los moriscos españoles." *Miscelánea de estudios árabes y hebráicos*: 39–54.

Domínguez Ortiz, Antonio, and Bernard Vincent. 1978. *Historia de los moriscos: Vida y tragedia de una minoría.* Madrid: Revista de Occidente.

Drewal, Margaret Thompson. 1992. *Yoruba Ritual: Performers, Play, Agency.* Bloomington: Indiana University Press.

Duranti, Alessandro. 1994. *From Grammar to Politics: Linguistic Anthropology in a Western Samoan Village.* Berkeley and Los Angeles: University of California Press.

———. 1997. *Linguistic Anthropology.* Cambridge: Cambridge University Press.

Duranti, Alessandro, and Elinor Ochs. 1997. "Syncretic Literacy in a Samoan American Family." In *Discourse, Tools, and Reasoning: Essays on Situated Cognition,* edited by edited by Lauren Resnick, Roger Säljö, Clotilde Pontecorvo, and Barbara Burge, 169–202. Berlin and New York: Springer.

Dutton, Brian. 1973. "French Influences in the Spanish *Mester de Clerecía.*" In *Medieval Studies in Honor of Robert White Linker,* edited by Brian Dutton et al., 73–93. Valencia: Castalia.

Fanjul, Serafín. 2002. *al-Andalus contra España: La forja del mito.* Madrid: Siglo Veintiuno.

Fish, Stanley. 1980. *Is There a Text in This Class?: The Authority of Interpretive Communities.* Cambridge, Mass.: Harvard University Press.

Fletcher, Richard. 1992. *Moorish Spain.* Berkeley and Los Angeles: University of California Press.

Fournel-Guérin, Jacqueline. 1979. "Le livre et la civilisation écrite dans la communauté morisque aragonaise (1540–1620)." In *Mélanges de la Casa de Velázquez,* 241–59. Paris: Boccard.

Fraser, J. T. 1966. *The Voices of Time.* New York: Braziller.

Freeman, Mark. 1998. "Mythical Time, Historical Time, and the Narrative Fabric of the Self." *Narrative Inquiry* 8, no. 1: 27–50.

Gal, Susan. 1990. "Between Speech and Silence: Problematics of Research on Language and Gender." In *Gender at the Crossroads of Knowledge: Feminist Anthropology in the Postmodern Era,* edited by M. DiLeonardo, 175–203. Berkeley and Los Angeles: University of California Press.

Galmés de Fuentes, Alvaro. 1978. "El interés literario en los escritos aljamiado-moriscos." In *Actas del Coloquio Internacional sobre Literatura Aljamiada y Morisca: Departamento de Filología Románica de la Facultad de Filosofía y Letras de la Universidad de Oviedo (10 al 16 de julio de 1972),* edited by Alvaro Galmés de Fuentes, 189–209. Madrid: Gredos.

———. 1981. "Lengua y estilo en la literatura aljamiado-morisca." *Nueva Revista de Filología Hispánica* 30: 420–44.

———. 1983. "La literatura aljamiado-morisca como fuente para el conocimiento del léxico aragonés." In *Serta Philológica F. Lázaro Carreter,* 175–92. Madrid: Cátedra.

———. 1986. "La lengua española de la literatura aljamiado-morisca como expresión de una minoría religiosa." *Revista Española de Lingüística* 16, no. 1: 21–38.

———. 1989. "Mudejares, moriscos, textos aljamiados." *Aljamía* 1: 1–29.

———. 1994. *Glosario de voces aljamiado-moriscas.* Oviedo: Universidad de Oviedo.

———. 1996. "La lengua de los moriscos." In *Manual de Dialectología Hispánica: El Español de España,* edited by Manuel Alvar, 111–18. Barcelona: Ariel.

———. 1998. *Los manuscritos aljamiado-moriscos de la Biblioteca de la Real Academia de la Historia.* Madrid: Real Academia de la Historia.

Galmés de Fuentes, Alvaro, ed. 1965. "Interés en el orden lingüístico de la literatura española aljamiado-morisca." In *Actes du Xe Congres International de Linguistique et Philologie Romanes,* edited by Georges Straka, 527–46. Paris: Klinckseick.

———, ed. 1978. *Actas del Coloquio Internacional sobre Literatura Aljamiada y Morisca: Departamento de Filología Románica de la Facultad de Filosofía y Letras de la Universidad de Oviedo (10 al 16 de julio de 1972).* Madrid: Gredos.

García-Arenal, Mercedes. 1978. *Inquisición y moriscos: Los procesos del tribunal de Cuenca.* Madrid: Siglo Veintiuno.

Garrad, Kenneth. 1954. "The Original Memoir of D. Francisco Núñez Muley." *Atlante* 2: 198–226.

Garro, Linda C., and Cheryl Mattingly. 2000. "Narrative as Construct and Construction." In *Narrative and the Cultural Construction of Illness and Healing,* edited by Cheryl Mattingly and Linda C. Garro, 1–49. Berkeley and Los Angeles: University of California Press.

Gayangos, Pascual de. 1839. "Language and Literature of the Moriscos." *British and Foreign Review* 8: 63–95.

———. 1853. "Glosario de las palabras aljamiadas y otras que se hallan en dos trabajos y en algunos libros de moriscos." *Memorial Histórico Español* 5: 423–49.

———. 1853. "Tratados de legislación musulmana: (1) Leyes de Moros del Siglo XIV; (2) Suma de los principales mandamientos y devedamientos de la ley de çunna por don Içe de Gebir, alfaquí mayor y mufti de la aljama de Segovia, año de 1462." *Memorial Histórico Español* 5: 11–421.

Geertz, Clifford. 1973. *The Interpretation of Cultures.* New York: Basic.

Giddens, Anthony. 1984. *The Constitution of Society: Outline of the Theory of Structuration.* Cambridge: Polity.

Gil y Gil, Pablo. 1890. "Las coplas del alhichante de Puey Monzon." *El Archivo* 4: 171–81.

Gil y Gil, Pablo, Julián Ribera, and Mariano Sánchez. 1888. *Colección de textos aljamiados.* Zaragoza: Comas.

Gilman, Stephen. 1972. *The Spain of Fernando de Rojas: The Intellectual and Social Landscape of La "Celestina."* Princeton, N.J.: Princeton University Press.

———. 1989. *The Novel according to Cervantes.* Berkeley and Los Angeles: University of California Press.

Goffman, Erving. 1959. *The Presentation of Self in Everyday Life.* New York: Anchor.

Goodwin, Charles. 1997. "The Blackness of Black: Color Categories as Situated Practice." In *Discourse, Tools, and Reasoning: Essays on Situated Cognition,* edited by Lauren Resnick, Roger Säljö, Clotilde Pontecorvo, and Barbara Burge, 111–40. Berlin and New York: Springer.

Goodwin, Charles, and Alessandro Duranti. 1992. "Rethinking Context: An Introduction." In *Rethinking Context: Language as an Interactive Phenomenon,* edited by Alessandro Duranti and Charles Goodwin, 1–42. Cambridge: Cambridge University Press.

Goodwin, Charles, and Marjorie Harness Goodwin. 1996. "Seeing as a Situated Activity: Formulating Planes." In *Cognition and Communication at Work,* edited by Yrjö Engeström and David Middleton, 61–95. Cambridge: Cambridge University Press.

———. 2000. "Emotion within Situated Activity." In *Communication: An Arena of Development,* edited by Ina C. Uzgiris, Nancy Budwig, and James V. Wertsch, 33–54. Mahwah, N.J.: Erlbaum.

Goodwin, Marjorie Harness. 1990. *He-Said-She-Said: Talk as Social Organization among Black Children.* Bloomington: Indiana University Press.

Goody, Jack. 1986. *The Logic of Writing and the Organization of Society: Studies in Literacy, Family, Culture and the State.* Cambridge: Cambridge University Press.

———. 1987. *The Interface between the Oral and the Written.* Cambridge: Cambridge University Press.

Goody, Jack, and Ian Watt. 1968. "The Consequences of Literacy." In *Literacy in Traditional Societies,* edited by Jack Goody, 27–68. Cambridge: Cambridge University Press.

Graff, Harvey J., ed. 1981. *Literacy and Social Development in the West: A Reader.* Cambridge: Cambridge University Press.

Guichard, Pierre. 1993. "The Social History of Muslim Spain." In *The Legacy of Muslim Spain,* edited by Salma Khadra Jayyusi, 679–708. Leiden: Brill.

Guillaume, Alfred. 1955. *The Life of Muhammad: A Translation of Ishaq's Sirat Rasulallah.* Lahore: Oxford University Press.

Guillén Robles, Francisco. 1885. *Leyendas moriscas sacadas de varios manuscritos existentes en las Bibliotecas Nacional, Real y de don P. de Gayangos.* 3 vols. Madrid: Tello.

———. 1888. *Leyendas de José hijo de Jacob y de Alejandro Magno. Sacadas de dos manuscritos moriscos de la Biblioteca Nacional de Madrid.* Zaragoza: Imprenta del Hospicio Provincial.

———. 1889. *Catálogo de los manuscritos árabes existentes en la Biblioteca Nacional de Madrid.* Madrid: Biblioteca Nacional.

Gumperz, John. 1982. *Language and Social Identity.* Cambridge: Cambridge University Press.

Halperin Donghi, Tulio. 1955–57. "Un conflicto nacional: Moriscos y cristianos viejos en Valencia." *Cuadernos de Historia de España* 23–24 (1955): 5–115; 25–26 (1957): 83–250.

Hanks, William. 1990. *Referential Practice: Language and Lived Space among the Maya.* Chicago: University of Chicago Press.

———. 1996. *Language and Communicative Practices.* Boulder, Colo.: Westview.

———. 2000. "Discourse Genres in a Theory of Practice." In *Intertexts: Writings on Language, Utterance, and Context,* 133–64. Lanham, Md.: Rowman & Littlefield.

Harvey, L. P. 1958. "The Literary Culture of the Moriscos (1492–1609)." Ph.D. diss., Oxford University.

———. 1978. "El Mancebo de Arévalo y la tradición cultural de los moriscos." In *Actas del Coloquio Internacional sobre Literatura Aljamiada y Morisca: Departamento de Filología Románica de la Facultad de Filosofía y Letras de la Universidad de Oviedo (10 al 16 de julio de 1972),* edited by Alvaro Galmés de Fuentes, 20–41. Madrid: Gredos.

———. 1981. "La leyenda morisca de Ibrahim." *Nueva Revista de Filología Hispánica* 30, no. 1: 1–20.

———. 1993. "The Political, Social, and Cultural History of the Moriscos." In *The Legacy of Muslim Spain,* edited by Salma Khadra Jayyusi, 201–34. Leiden: Brill.

Havelock, Eric A. 1982. *The Literate Revolution in Greece and Its Cultural Consequences.* Princeton, N.J.: Princeton University Press.

Hawkins, John P. 1988. "A Morisco Philosophy of Suffering: An Anthropological Analysis of an Aljamiado Text." *Maghreb Review* 13, nos. 3–4: 199–217.

Heath, Shirley Brice. 1980. "The Functions and Uses of Literacy." *Journal of Communication* 30, no. 1: 123–34.

———. 1982. "What No Bedtime Story Means: Narrative Skills at Home and School." *Language in Society* 11: 49–76.

———. 1983. *Ways with Words: Language, Life, and Work in Communities and Classrooms.* Cambridge: Cambridge University Press.

Hegyi, Ottmar. 1978. "El uso del alfabeto árabe por minorías musulmanas y otros aspectos de la literatura aljamiada, resultantes de circunstancias históricas y sociales análogas." In *Actas del Coloquio Internacional sobre Literatura Aljamiada y Morisca: Departamento de Filología Románica de la Facultad de Filosofía y Letras de la Universidad de Oviedo (10 al 16 de julio de 1972),* edited by Alvaro Galmés de Fuentes, 147–64. Madrid: Gredos.

———. 1981. *Cinco leyendas y otros relatos moriscos (Ms. 4953 de la Bibl. Nac. Madrid).* Madrid: Gredos.

Heidegger, Martin. 1982. *The Basic Problems of Phenomenology.* Studies in Phenomenology and Existential Philosophy. Bloomington: Indiana University Press.

———. 1996. *Being and Time.* Translated by Joan Stambaugh. Albany: State University of New York Press.

Hesse, Herman. 1999. *Siddhartha.* Translated by Joachim Neugroschel. Oxford: Penguin.

Husserl, Edmund. 1991. *On the Phenomenology of the Consciousness of Internal Time.* Translated by John Barnett Brough. Boston: Kluwer.

Hutchins, Edwin. 1995. *Cognition in the Wild.* Cambridge, Mass.: MIT Press.

Hymes, Dell. 1972. "Models of the Interaction of Language and Social Life." In *Directions in Sociolinguistics: The Ethnography of Communication,* edited by John J. Gumperz and Dell Hymes. New York: Holt, Rinehart and Winston.

———. 1974. *Foundations in Sociolinguistics: An Ethnographic Approach.* Philadelphia: University of Pennsylvania Press.

———. 1975 "Folklore's Nature and the Sun's Myth." *Journal of American Folklore* 88: 345–69.

Irvine, Judith. 1989. "When Talk Isn't Cheap: Language and Political Economy." *American Ethnologist* 16: 248–67.

———. 1996. "Shadow Conversations: The Indeterminacy of Participant Roles." In *Natural Histories of Discourse,* edited by Michael Silverstein and Greg Urban, 131–59. Chicago: University of Chicago Press.

James, William. 1890. *The Principles of Psychology.* New York: Holt.

Johnson, Carroll B. 1978. *Inside Guzmán de Alfarache.* Berkeley and Los Angeles: University of California Press.

———. 2000. *Cervantes and the Material World*. Urbana: University of Illinois Press.

Johnson, William Weisiger. 1974. *The Poema de José: A Transcription and Comparison of the Extant Manuscripts*. University, Miss.: Romance Monographs.

Keesing, Roger M. 1987. "Anthropology as Interpretive quest." *Current Anthropology* 28, no. 2: 161–76.

Kennedy, George Alexander. 1999. *Classical Rhetoric and Its Christian and Secular Tradition from Ancient to Modern Times*. 2nd ed. Chapel Hill: University of North Carolina Press.

Kerby, Anthony Paul. 1991. *Narrative and the Self: Studies in Continental Thought*. Bloomington: Indiana University Press.

Kermode, Frank. 2000. *The Sense of an Ending: Studies in the Theory of Fiction*. Oxford: Oxford University Press.

Klenk, Ursula, ed. 1972. *La leyenda de Yuçuf: Ein aljamiado-text*. Tübingen: Niemeyer.

Kroskrity, Paul V. 1993. *Language, History, and Identity: Ethnolinguistic Studies of the Arizona Tewa*. Tucson: University of Arizona Press.

———. 2000. "Regimenting Languages: Language Ideological Perspectives." In *Regimes of Language: Ideologies, Polities, and Identities*, edited by Paul V. Kroskrity, 1–34. Santa Fe, N.Mex.: School of American Research Press, and Oxford: J. Currey.

———, ed. 2000. *Regimes of Language: Ideologies, Polities, and Identities*. Santa Fe, N.Mex.: School of American Research Press, and Oxford: J. Currey.

Kulick, Don, and Christopher Stroud. 1993. "Conceptions and Uses of Literacy in a Papua New Guinean Village." In *Cross-Cultural Approaches to Literacy*, edited by Brian V. Street, 30–61. Cambridge: Cambridge University Press.

Labov, William. 1972. *Language in the Inner City: Studies in the Black English Vernacular*. Philadelphia: University of Pennsylvania Press.

Lakoff, George, and Mark Johnson. 1980. *Metaphors We Live By*. Chicago: University of Chicago Press.

Lea, Henry Charles. 1901. *The Moriscos of Spain: Their Conversion and Expulsion*. London: Quaritch.

Leitch, Vincent. 1991. "(De)Coding (Generic) Discourse." *Genre* 24: 83–98.

Longás, Pedro. 1998. *La vida religiosa de los moriscos*. 2nd edition. Granada: Universidad de Granada.

López Baralt, Luce. 1980. "Crónica de la destrucción de un mundo: La literatura aljamiado-morisca." *Bulletin Hispanique* 82, nos. 1–2: 16–58.

————. 1981. "Estudio sobre la religiosidad popular en la literatura aljamiado-morisco del Siglo XVI: *La Mora de Ubeda El Mançebo de Arévalo y San Juan de la Cruz.*" *Revista de Dialectología y Tradiciones Populares* 36: 17–51.

————. 1985. "Historia de un hombre que prefirió la muerte al adulterio: Leyenda morisca del manuscrito S-2 BRAH." *Revista de Estudios Hispánicos* 12: 93–102.

————. 1987. "La angustia secreta del exilio: El testimonio de un morisco de Túnez." *Hispanic Review* 55, no. 1: 41–57.

————. 1988. "Un morisco astrólogo, experto en mujeres (Ms. Junta XXVI)." *Nueva Revista de Filología Hispánica* 36, no. 1: 261–76.

————. 1990. "La estética del cuerpo entre los moriscos del Siglo XVI o de cómo la minoría perseguida pierde su rostro." In *Actes Du IV Symposium International d'Etudes Morisques Sur: Metiers, Vie Religieuse et Problematiques d'Histoire Morisque,* edited by Abdeljelil Temimi, 359–60. Zaghouan, Tunisia: CEROMDI.

————. 1992. "El extraño caso de un morisco maurófilo." In *Actas del X Congreso de la Asociación de Hispanistas,* edited by Antonio Vilanova and Josep María Bricall, 255–66. Barcelona: Promociones y Publicaciones Universitarias.

————. 1995. "Un místico de Fez, experto en amores: El modelo principal del *Kama Sutra* español." In *Erotismo en las letras hispánicas: Aspectos, modos y fronteras,* edited by Luce López-Baralt and Francisco Márquez Villanueva, 219–57. Mexico City: Colegio de México.

————. 2000. "The Moriscos." In *The Literature of al-Andalus,* edited by María Rosa Menocal, Raymond P. Scheindlin, and Michael Sells, 472–87. Cambridge: Cambridge University Press.

López-Morillas, Consuelo. 1975. "Aljamiado 'akosegir' and Its Old Provençal Counterparts: Studies in the Romance Transmission of Latin Con-S-." *Romance Philology* 28: 445–61.

————. 1978. "Etimologías escogidas del Corán aljamiado (Ms. 4938 de la Biblioteca Nacional)." In *Actas del Coloquio Internacional sobre Literatura Aljamiada y Morisca,* edited by Alvaro Galmés de Fuentes and Emilio García Gómez, 365–72. Madrid: Gredos.

————. 1981. "La oración como diálogo en un comentario morisco sobre la Fatih." *Nueva Revista de Filología Hispánica* 30, no. 1: 168–73.

————. 1982. *The Qur'an in Sixteenth-Century Spain: Six Morisco Versions of Sura 79.* London: Tamesis.

————. 1984. "Copistas y escribanos moriscos." In *Actes du II Symposium International du CIEM: Religion, Identité et Sources Documentaires sur les*

Morisques Andalous, edited by Abdeljelil Temimi, 71–78. Tunis: Institut Superieur de Documentation.

———. 1986. "Más sobre los escribanos moriscos." In *Actes de la première table ronde du CIEM: Sur la litterature aljamiado-morisque: Hybridisme linguistique et univers discursif,* edited by Abdeljelil Temimi, 105–7. Tunis: Centre de Recherches en Bibliotheconomie et Sciences de l'Information.

———. 1990. "Los comentarios exegéticos del manuscrito J18: Corán 43:65." In *Actes du IV Symposium International d'Etudes Morisques Sur: Metiers, Vie Religieuse et Problematiques d'Histoire Morisque,* edited by Abdeljelil Temimi, 362–63. Zaghouan, Túnez: CEROMDI.

———. 1994. *Textos aljamiados sobre la vida de Mahoma: El profeta de los moriscos.* Madrid: Consejo Superior de Investigaciones Científicas.

———. 1995. "Language and Identity in Late Spanish Islam." *Hispanic Review* 63, no. 2: 193–210.

———. 1998. "Los manuscritos aljamiados." *Al-Qantara* 19, no. 2: 425–44.

———. 2000. "The Moriscos and Christian Doctrine." In *Christians, Muslims, and Jews in Medieval and Early Modern Spain: Interaction and Cultural Change,* edited by Mark D. Meyerson and Edward D. English, 290–305. Notre Dame, Ind.: University of Notre Dame Press.

Lucy, John A. 1993. *Reflexive Language: Reported Speech and Metapragmatics.* Cambridge: Cambridge University Press.

Manzares Cirre, Manuela. 1971. *Arabistas del siglo XIX.* Madrid: Instituto Hispano-Arabe de Cultura.

Márquez Villanueva, Francisco. 1973. *Fuentes literarias cervantinas.* Madrid: Gredos.

———. 1975. *Personajes y temas del "Quijote."* Madrid: Taurus.

———. 1977. *Relecciones de literatura medieval.* Sevilla: Universidad de Sevilla.

———. 1991. *El problema morisco: Desde otras laderas.* Madrid: Libertarias.

Menéndez Pidal, Ramón. 1902. "*Poema de Yúçuf,* materiales para su estudio." *Revista de Archivos, Bibliotecas y Museos* 7: 91–129; 276–309; 47–62.

———. 1952. "*Poema de Yúçuf,* Materiales para su estudio." Granada: Universidad de Granada.

Merleau-Ponty, Maurice. 1996. *Phenomenology of Perception.* London: Routledge.

Messick, Brinkley Morris. 1993. *The Calligraphic State: Textual Domination and History in a Muslim Society.* Berkeley and Los Angeles: University of California Press.

Montaner Frutos, Alberto. 1988a. "Aproximación a una tipología de la literatura aljamiado-morisco aragonesa." In *Destierros aragoneses. I: Judíos y moriscos,* 313–26. Zaragoza: Instituto Fernando el Católico.

———. 1988b. "El depósito de Almonacid y la producción de la literatura aljamiado (En torno al ms. Miscelaneo XIII)." *Archivo de Filología Aragonesa* 41: 119–52.

———. 1989. "Tradición, oralidad y escritura en la literatura aljamiado-morisca." *Stvdia Zamorensia* 10: 171–81.

———. 1993. "El auge de la literatura aljamiada en Aragón." In *II Curso sobre lengua y literatura aljamiada en Aragón (Siglos de Oro),* edited by José María Enguita. Zaragoza: Instituto Fernando el Católico.

Morf, Heinrich, ed. 1883. *El Poema de José.* Leipzig: Universität Bern and Universität Zürich.

Morson, Gary Saul. 1994. *Narrative and Freedom: The Shadows of Time.* New Haven, Conn.: Yale University Press.

Murphy, James Jerome. 1974. *Rhetoric in the Middle Ages: A History of Rhetorical Theory from Saint Augustine to the Renaissance.* Berkeley and Los Angeles: University of California Press.

Nirenberg, David. 1996. *Communities of Violence: Persecution of Minorities in the Middle Ages.* Princeton: Princeton University Press.

Nykl, A. R. 1929. *A Compendium of Aljamiado Literature.* Paris: Protat.

Ochs, Elinor. 1994. "Stories That Step into the Future." In *Perspectives on Register: Situating Language Variation in Sociolinguistics,* edited by Douglas Biber and Ed Finegan, 106–35. Oxford: Oxford University Press.

———. 1999. "Socialization." *Journal of Linguistic Anthropology* 9, nos. 1–2: 230–33.

———. 2001. "Language Socialization." In *Key Terms in Language and Culture,* edited by Alessandro Duranti, 227–30. Malden, Mass.: Blackwell.

Ochs, Elinor, and Lisa Capps. 2001. *Living Narrative: Creating Lives in Everyday Storytelling.* Cambridge, Mass.: Harvard University Press.

Ochs, Elinor, Patrick Gonzales, and Sally Jacoby. 1996. " 'When I Come Down I'm in a Domain State': Talk, Gesture, and Graphic Representation in the Interpretive Activity of Physicists." In *Interaction and Grammar,* edited by Emanuel A. Schegloff, Elinor Ochs, and Sandra A. Thompson., 328–69. Cambridge: Cambridge University Press.

Ong, Walter J. 1982. *Orality and Literacy: The Technologizing of the Word.* London: Methuen.

Orduna, Germán. 2001. "La textualidad oral del discurso narrativo en España e Hispanoamérica (Ss. XIV–XVII)." In *Estudios sobre la variación textual: Prosa castellana de los siglos XIII a XVI,* edited by Germán Orduna, Hugo O. Bizzarri, et al., 1–24. Buenos Aires: Secrit.

Pano y Ruata, Mariano. 1897. *Las coplas del peregrino de Puey Monçon, viaje a la Meca en el siglo XVI.* Zaragoza: Comas.

Paredes, Américo. 1958. *"With His Pistol in His Hand," A Border Ballad and Its Hero.* Austin: University of Texas Press.

———. 1976. *A Texas-Mexican Cancionero: Folksongs of the Lower Border.* Urbana: University of Illinois Press.

———. 1993. *Folklore and Culture on the Texas-Mexican Border.* Austin: Center for Mexican American Studies, University of Texas at Austin.

Perceval, José María. 1997. *Todos son uno: Arquetipos, xenofobia y racismo: La imagen del morisco en la monarquía española durante los siglos XVI y XVII.* Almería: Instituto de Estudios Almerienses.

Pinto, Julio C. M. 1988. *The Reading of Time: A Semantico-Semiotic Approach.* Berlin: Mouton de Gruyter.

Quérillacq, René. 1992. "Los Moriscos de Cervantes." *Anales Cervantinos* 30: 77–98.

Rappaport, Joanne. 1998. "The Reconfiguration of Civic and Sacred Space: Architecture, Image, and Writing in the Colonial Northern Andes." *Latin American Literary Review* 26: 174–200.

Rappaport, Joanne, and Tom Cummins. 1998. "Between Images and Writing: The Ritual of the King's *Quillca.*" *Colonial Latin American Review* 7, no. 1: 7–27.

Reynolds, Suzanne. 1996. *Medieval Reading: Grammar, Rhetoric, and the Classical Text.* Cambridge: Cambridge University Press.

Ribera, Julián, and Miguel Asín Palacios. 1912. *Manuscritos árabes y aljamiados de la Biblioteca de la Junta.* Madrid: Consejo Superior de Estudios Científicos.

Rico, Francisco. 1985. "La clerecía del mester." *Hispanic Review* 53: 1–23; 127–50.

———. 1996. "Entre el códice y el libro." In *Libro del Caballero Zifar: Códice de París,* edited by Francisco Rico, 246–58. Barcelona: Moleiro.

Ricoeur, Paul. 1988. *Time and Narrative.* 3 vols. Chicago: University of Chicago Press.

———. 1991. *From Text to Action.* Evanston, Ill.: Northwestern University Press.

Roca, Pedro. 1904. *Catálogo de los manuscritos que pertenecieron a D. Pascual de Gayangos existentes en la Biblioteca Nacional.* Madrid: Tipografía de la Revista de Archivos, Bibliotecas y Museos.

Rosaldo, Michelle Z. 1982. "The Things We Do with Words: Ilingot Speech Acts and Speech Act Theory in Philosophy." *Language in Society* 11: 203–37.

Rosaldo, Renato. 1986. "From the Door of His Tent: The Fieldworker and the Inquisitor." In *Writing Culture: The Poetics and Politics of Ethnography,* edited by James Clifford and George E. Marcus, 77–97. Berkeley and Los Angeles: University of California Press.

Saavedra Moragas, Eduardo. 1878. *Discursos leídos ante la Real Academia Española en la recepcion pública*. Madrid: Impresores y Libreros.

———. 1889. "Indice general de la literatura aljamiada." *Memorias de la Real Academia Española* 6: 140–328.

Sánchez-Albornoz, Claudio. 1946. *La España musulmana: Según los autores islamitas y cristianos medievales*. 2 vols. Buenos Aires: El Ateneo.

———. 1956. *España, un enigma histórico*. Buenos Aires: Sudamericana.

Sánchez Alvarez, Mercedes. 1981. "La lengua de los manuscritos aljamiado-moriscos como testimonio de la doble marginación de una minoría islámica." *Nueva Revista de Filología Hispánica* 30, no. 2: 441–52.

Sánchez Pérez, Francisco. 1990. *La liturgia del espacio: Casarabonela, un pueblo aljamiado*. Madrid: Nerea.

Sapir, Edward. 1949. *Language: An Introduction to the Study of Speech*. New York: Harcourt.

Schieffelin, Bambi B., and Elinor Ochs. 1986. *Language Socialization across Cultures*. Cambridge: Cambridge University Press.

Schmitz, Michael. 1899. *Über Das altspanische "Poema de José."* Erlangen: Junge.

Scholte, Bob. 1984. "Comments on P. Shankman, 'The Thick and the Thin: On the Interpretive Theoretical Paradigm of Clifford Geertz.'" *Current Anthropology* 25: 261–70.

Scribner, Sylvia, and Michael Cole. 1981. *The Psychology of Literacy*. Cambridge, Mass.: Harvard University Press.

Silverstein, Michael. 1993. "Metapragmatic Discourse and Metapragmatic Function." In *Reflexive Language: Reported Speech and Metapragmatics*, edited by John A. Lucy, 33–58. Cambridge: Cambridge University Press.

———. 1996. "The Secret Life of Texts." In *Natural Histories of Discourse*, edited by Michael Silverstein and Greg Urban, 81–105. Chicago: University of Chicago Press.

———. 1998. "The Uses and Utility of Ideology: A Commentary." In *Language Ideologies: Practice and Theory*, edited by Bambi B. Schieffelin, Katherine A. Woolard, and Paul V. Kroskrity, 123–45. Oxford: Oxford University Press.

———. 2000. "Whorfianism and the Linguistic Imagination of Nationality." In *Regimes of Language: Ideologies, Polities, and Identities*, edited by Paul Kroskrity, 85–138. Santa Fe, N.Mex.: School of American Research Press.

Silverstein, Michael, and Greg Urban, eds. 1996. *Natural Histories of Discourse*. Chicago: University of Chicago Press.

Stanley, H. E. J. 1868. "The Poetry of Muhammad Rabadan." *Journal of the Royal Asiatic Society of Great Britain and Ireland* 3: 81–104, 379–413; 4 (70): 138–77; 5 (71): 119–40, 303–37; 6 (73):165–212.

Stock, Brian. 1983. *The Implications of Literacy.* Princeton, N.J.: Princeton University Press.

Strathern, Marilyn. 1987. "Comments on Roger M. Keesing's 'Anthropology as Intrepretive Quest.'" *Current Anthropology* 28, no. 2: 173–74.

Street, Brian V., ed. 1993. *Cross-Cultural Approaches to Literacy.* Cambridge: Cambridge University Press.

———, ed. 1984. *Literacy in Theory and Practice.* Cambridge: Cambridge University Press.

———, 1995. *Social Literacies: Critical Approaches to Literacy in Development.* London: Longman.

Tedlock, Dennis, and Bruce Mannheim, eds. 1995. *The Dialogic Emergence of Culture.* Urbana, Ill.: University of Illinois Press.

Temimi, Abdeljelil, ed. 1986. *Les actes de la Première Table Ronde du CIEM: Sur la Littérature Aljamiado-Morisque: Hybridisme Linguistique et Univers Discursif.* Tunis: Centre de Recherches en Bibliothéconomie et Sciences de l'Information.

Teza, E. 1891. "Di un compendio del Corano in espagnolo con lettere arabiche (manoscritto fiorentino)." *Rendiconti della Reale Accademia dei Lincei* 3: 81–88.

Thompson, John B. 1990. *Ideology and Modern Culture: Critical Social Theory in the Era of Mass Communications.* Cambridge: Polity.

Ticknor, George. 1849. *History of Spanish Literature.* 3 vols. New York: Harper.

Tilley, Christopher. 1994. *A Phenomenology of Landscape: Places, Paths, and Monuments.* Oxford: Berg.

Turner, Mark. 1996. *The Literary Mind.* Oxford: Oxford University Press.

Vespertino Rodríguez, Antonio, ed. 1983. *Leyendas aljamiadas y moriscas sobre personajes bíblicos.* Madrid: Gredos.

Vilar, Juan B. 1996. "Una biblioteca morisca requisada en 1592 en la villa de Monóvar." *Sharq al-Andalus* 13: 169–80.

Vincent, Bernard. 1999. "Ser morisco en España en el siglo XVI." In *El saber en al-Andalus: Textos y estudios,* edited by Julia María Carabaza Bravo and Aly Tawfik Mohamed Essawy, 301–07. Sevilla: Universidad de Sevilla.

Voloshinov, V. N. 1986. *Marxism and the Philosophy of Language.* Translated by Ladislav Matejka and I. R. Titunik. Cambridge, Mass.: Harvard University Press.

Vygotsky, L. S. 1978. *Mind in Society: The Development of Higher Psychological Processes*. Edited by Michael Cole, Vera John-Steiner, Sylvia Scribner, and Ellen Souberman. Cambridge, Mass.: Harvard University Press.

———. 1987. *The Collected Works of L. S. Vygotsky*. Vol. 1. Edited by Robert W. Rieber and Aaron Carton. New York: Plenum.

Weiss, Julian. 1990. *The Poet's Art: Literary Theory in Castile c. 1400–60*. Oxford: Society for the Study of Mediæval Languages and Literature.

Wertsch, James V. 1981. "Introduction." In *The Concept of Activity in Soviet Psychology*, edited by James V. Wertsch. Armonk, N.Y.: Sharpe.

———. 1998. *Mind as Action*. Oxford: Oxford University Press.

White, Hayden V. 1987. *The Content of the Form: Narrative Discourse and Historical Representation*. Baltimore: Johns Hopkins University Press.

Whorf, Benjamin Lee. 1956. *Language, Thought, and Reality: Selected Writings*. Cambridge, Mass.: MIT Press.

Wiegers, Gerard Albert. 1994. *Islamic Literature in Spanish and Aljamiado: Yça of Segovia, His Antecedents and Successors*. Leiden: Brill.

Wittgenstein, Ludwig. 1999 [1958]. *Philosophical Investigations*. Translated by G. E. M. Anscombe. Malden, Mass.: Blackwell.

Woolard, Kathryn A. 1998. "Language Ideologies as a Field of Inquiry." In *Language Ideologies: Practice and Theory*, edited by Bambi B. Schieffelin, Kathryn A. Woolard, and Paul V. Kroskrity, 3–50. Oxford: Oxford University Press.

———, Paul V. Kroskrity, and Bambi B. Schieffelin, eds. 1998. *Language Ideologies: Practice and Theory*. Oxford: Oxford University Press.

Index

Vincent Barletta is assistant professor of medieval Iberian literature at the University of Colorado at Boulder.